States' Rights and the Union

AMERICAN POLITICAL THOUGHT

Edited by
Wilson Carey McWilliams
and Lance Banning

STATES' RIGHTS
AND THE UNION

Imperium in Imperio, 1776–1876

Forrest McDonald

University Press of Kansas

Published by the University Press of Kansas (Lawrence, Kansas 66049), which was organized by the Kansas Board of Regents and is operated and funded by Emporia State University, Fort Hays State University, Kansas State University, Pittsburg State University, the University of Kansas, and Wichita State University

Library of Congress Cataloging-in-Publication Data

McDonald, Forrest.
States' rights and the union : imperium in imperio, 1776–1876 / Forrest McDonald.
p.   cm. — (American political thought)
Includes bibliographical references and index.
ISBN 0-7006-1040-5 (cloth : alk. paper)
ISBN 0-7006-1227-0 (pbk: alk. paper)
1. States' rights—History.   2. Federal government—United States.   3. United States—Politics and government—18th century.   4. United States—Politics and government—19th century.   I. Title.   II. Series.
JK311 .M37 2000
320.8'0973'09034—dc21   00-039242

British Library Cataloguing in Publication Data is available.

Printed in the United States of America

10   9   8   7   6   5   4

The paper used in this publication meets the minimum requirement of the American National Standard for Permanence of Paper for Printed Library Materials Z39.48-1984.

CONTENTS

PREFACE

Of all the problems that beset the United States of America during the century from the Declaration of Independence to the end of Reconstruction, the most pervasive concerned disagreements about the nature of the Union and the line to be drawn between the authority of the general government and that of the several states. At times the issue bubbled silently and unseen beneath the surface of public consciousness; at times it exploded; now and again the balance between general and local authority seemed to be settled in one direction or another, only to be upset anew and to move back toward the opposite position, but the contention never went away. Even though the country was passing through profound material and demographic changes, those changes were conditioned throughout the period by preoccupation with the tensions inherent in the concept of states' rights. Moreover, the tensions continued to be felt as the twentieth century came to an end.

And yet, despite the enormous volume of literature about American history in general and about aspects of the states' rights controversy, no one as far as I am aware has attempted to fashion a general survey of the subject. Works abound on various chapters of the story—the Hamilton-Jefferson rivalry, the Virginia and Kentucky Resolutions, New England's resistance to Jefferson's foreign policy and the War of 1812, the nullification controversy, Andrew Jackson's war against the Bank of the United States, secession and Civil War. Almost as numerous are technical legal and constitutional disputations concerning esoteric aspects of the subject, such as the question whether a federal common law regarding criminal cases was contemplated in the constitutional scheme of things. But no book-length study of states' rights as a whole has previously appeared.

In the following pages I have attempted to fill that lacuna in the literature. I deliberately shunned the kinds of technical questions that specialists love and concentrated instead on fashioning a narrative and analytical account of the larger contours of the history of the subject. This is essentially a work of synthesis, meaning that—though I studied the primary sources, documents showing what participants in the flow of events had to say—I relied mainly on the primary research of many historians (including my own earlier work). Doubtless I overlooked some of the secondary literature, but I believe I did not miss much of it.

One of the readers of the manuscript for the University Press of Kansas opined that the subtitle, *Imperium in Imperio,* was "a bit highfalutin." For those of us who have spent most of our adult lives in the eighteenth century, there is nothing highfalutin about it. The phrase was common currency of the realm at the time of the Founding, and though my Latin is not as good as it once was, we can translate it roughly as supreme power within supreme power, sovereignty within sovereignty, the division of sovereignty within a single jurisdiction. Dividing sovereignty was generally regarded as impossible, until Americans devised a way of doing it.

I am grateful to George Rable, Tony Freyer, and James McClellan for keen critical readings and suggestions. Those readers who know me are aware that my greatest debt is to Ellen Shapiro McDonald, whose contributions to making this work possible were, as always, so vital as to justify adding her name to the title page—which, as usual, she declined.

University of Alabama   FORREST MCDONALD
October 1999

Prologue

THE PROBLEM OF
DIVIDED SOVEREIGNTY

In his celebrated *Commentaries on the Laws of England* Sir William
Blackstone defined law as "a rule of civil conduct prescribed by the
supreme power in a state, commanding what is right and prohibiting what is wrong." That prescribing "supreme power" was the sovereign. "Sovereignty and legislature are indeed convertible terms,"
Blackstone declared; "there is and must be" in every state "a supreme, irresistible, absolute, uncontrolled authority, in which the *jura
summi imperii,* or the rights of sovereignty, reside." In the abstract,
sovereign power was not boundless, for man-made laws had to be
compatible with natural law—God's law, discoverable through reason—and thus "no human laws are of any validity, if contrary to
this." Having made this concession to the higher law tradition, however, Blackstone qualified it in regard to Great Britain, saying that
"if the parliament will positively enact a thing to be done which is
unreasonable, I know of no power in the ordinary forms of the constitution, that is vested with authority to control it."[1]

As a practical matter, then, the powers inherent in sovereignty were
unlimited, and sovereignty was by definition indivisible: dividing it
would involve the self-contradictory doctrine of *imperium in imperio.*
The sovereign could, to be sure, create subsidiary units of power. Early
on, these took the form of baronies awarded for military service; later,
the subsidiary units were commonly established through corporate
charters, whether to cities, trading companies, or colonies. But, though

such units were to varying extents self-governing, they (like all powers and rights belonging to the subjects) emanated from the sovereign and remained subordinate to the sovereign.[2]

In England prior to 1688, the Crown had been sovereign, though it made law through the estates of the realm—the Lords Spiritual and Temporal and the Commons—and it enforced the law through the Court of the King's Bench and lesser courts. Since the Glorious Revolution of 1688, after centuries of struggles between the estates and the Crown, and since the Act of Settlement of 1701, by which Parliament determined the royal succession, sovereignty resided in Crown-in-Parliament. In practice, this "triumph of English liberty" meant parliamentary supremacy: Parliament could command anything that was not naturally impossible.[3]

Because of the doctrine of indivisibility, and also because its power was so hard-won, Parliament was entirely unable to compromise when, after 1763, English colonists in America began to challenge Parliament's authority to tax them or to legislate for them. Colonial challenges were unacceptable to Parliament, which made its own view clear in the Declaratory Act of 1766. Parliament, the Parliament asserted, had the power to enact binding legislation for the colonies "in all cases whatsoever."

The colonists, for their part, found the English position unacceptable. Those of them who thought about the matter accepted the indivisibility of sovereignty as an abstract theoretical proposition, but the colonies had operated for decades under what amounted to a de facto system of divided sovereignty. Crown-in-Parliament was sovereign in all matters of concern to the empire as a whole, including trade and foreign relations; the colonies, severally, exercised sovereign powers in matters of internal concern, including taxation. Granted, the royal Board of Trade had the power to review and, if it saw fit, disallow colonial legislation. All told, the board reviewed 8,563 acts of the mainland colonial legislatures and disallowed 469 of them. But this function was performed erratically and rarely constituted an interference into local matters. Similarly, in the eight colonies that had royally appointed governors, the Crown nominally had a hand in internal affairs, but long before the Revolution, most of the colonial legislatures had used the power of the purse to bring the royal governors under control.[4]

Still, having no theory of divided sovereignty, and being prone to distrust abstract theory in any form, Americans generally chose to justify their resistance to parliamentary measures on wholly different grounds. Some few, notably James Otis and Patrick Henry, made rather dangerous appeals to higher law. Most, however, either claimed that their rights were protected by their colonial charters or followed the moderate arguments formulated by the Philadelphia lawyer John Dickinson, first in the Stamp Act Congress of 1765 and then in his widely read *Letters from a Farmer in Pennsylvania,* published in 1767 in opposition to the newly enacted Townshend duties. Dickinson argued in terms of the historic rights of Englishmen, dating back to the Magna Carta and to time immemorial; those rights included the principle that no person could be deprived of property without his consent, in person or through his representatives. American colonists were represented in their own legislatures, not in Parliament, and that limited the powers of each. Some areas, such as trade within the empire, were properly the concern of Parliament, but just as a matter of convenience.[5]

Defenses like Dickinson's satisfied Americans until the last imperial crisis began in 1774, but the rights-of-Englishmen position could not be accepted by champions of Parliament, for at base it was a tacit insistence on the divisibility of sovereignty. The irreconcilability of the American and English positions was epitomized in a debate between John Adams and Thomas Hutchinson, the royal governor of Massachusetts, occurring on the eve of the last crisis. Hutchinson insisted that colonials had admitted they were bound by acts of Parliament, and Adams rejoined that colonials were bound solely by laws to which they had given their "cheerful consent." Hutchinson acknowledged "no line that can be drawn between the supreme authority of Parliament and the *total* independence of the colonies." Adams replied, "if there be no such line, the consequence is either that the colonies are vassals of Parliament, or that they are totally independent."[6]

When the issue came to such a pass, the colonies were stuck with the stance that only loyalty to the Crown held the empire together, and George III dissolved that band by declaring the colonies outside his protection. Constitutionally, then, whatever additional legal, theoretical, or substantive issues divided Americans from their mother country, what broke apart the empire was an inability to agree on the locus and nature of sovereignty.

The problem, however, did not go away with the Declaration of Independence, for the Continental Congress willy-nilly inherited responsibility, as agent for the states, for conducting the war and treating with foreign powers, but the states clearly had sovereign power as Blackstone defined the term. At first, under the immediate exigencies of the war, no one thought much about the question, but before long, Congress became sorely divided between delegates who favored the expansion (or usurpation) of the central power by legal or extralegal means, on the one hand, and those who jealously guarded the privileges and prerogatives of the states, on the other.

As time passed, several leading patriots came to a way of thinking about sovereignty that would make it logically divisible. That way was both subtle and simple: governments at various levels had certain responsibilities, and inherent in those responsibilities was the power to carry them into execution. More specifically, Congress had sovereignty, the supreme lawmaking power, in regard to the matters entrusted to it; the states had sovereignty in regard to matters entrusted to them; and the people reserved sovereignty in still other matters, refusing to entrust it to government at any level. Alexander Hamilton, James Wilson, and Oliver Ellsworth had reached that view before 1787, but the position could have little or no meaning prior to that time, for the Articles of Confederation gave Congress no coercive power to carry out its assigned duties.

The Constitution did give the general government broad powers within a limited sphere and thereby institutionalized a system of divided sovereignty. The result was a mixed blessing, for it gave rise to the doctrine of states' rights. Historically, champions of states' rights insisted that their doctrine was necessary to prevent the concentration of power in a leviathan central government. To such ardent states' righters as John Taylor of Caroline and John Randolph of Roanoke, power concentrated in some remote center was the very definition of tyranny. On the opposite side, to such ardent nationalists as John Quincy Adams and Nicholas Biddle, vigorous action at the center was vital if the nation was to fulfill its promise and its destiny, attaining wealth and stature among the family of nations. Each position had merit, and in the event the United States, after a century of independence, managed both to remain unburdened by oppressive central authority and to take long strides toward greatness.

1

THE COMPACT

In defending their decision to declare independence from Britain in 1776, American revolutionaries ceased to regard as relevant questions of sovereignty, as well as arguments based upon colonial charters and historic rights of Englishmen. Instead, they relied upon the readily available body of doctrine most suitable to the purpose, namely, the natural rights and compact theories associated with John Locke. Those ideas were not original with Locke—they can be traced back at least as far as the 1320s, when the Italian political philosopher Marsilius of Padua published his *Defensor pacis,* and they were commonplace in patriotic sermons—but it was Locke's work that inspired the Declaration of Independence, as a comparison of the language of the document with Locke's *Second Treatise of Civil Government* abundantly testifies.[1]

In Locke's scheme of things, the compact that establishes and legitimizes a political society is between a prince or governing body and the people, between the ruler and the ruled. If the ruler fails to protect the people in their lives, liberties, and estates, and does so repeatedly and by design, the sovereign power reverts to the people, who, having returned to a "state of nature," become free to reconstitute a government on such principles (in the language of the Declaration) "as to them shall seem most likely to effect their Safety and Happiness."[2]

But, though Locke's formulation was easily adaptable to the revolutionaries' purpose, it did not quite accord with their circumstances. The colonies did not have a single hypothetical compact with the king

of Great Britain; they had thirteen real compacts in the form of charters that gave them existence as political societies. Two of these compacts established corporations, those of Connecticut and Rhode
Island; three placed an intermediate proprietary authority between
Crown and colony, those of Pennsylvania, Delaware, and Maryland;
and the rest had governors directly responsible to the Crown. Thus if
the king had, as the Declaration averred and sought to prove, performed "a long Train of Abuses and Usurpations" designed to
"reduce them under absolute Despotism," sovereign authority would
have devolved not upon the colonists as a whole but upon the people
of New Hampshire as one political society, those of Massachusetts
as another, and so on.[3]

The revolutionaries took awhile to work out a way of establishing governments appropriate to their declared principles. The corporate colonies continued to govern themselves under their old
charters. Elsewhere, existing legislatures or rump sessions of legislatures drafted constitutions and simply announced that they were
in effect. Not until 1780 was a proper method devised: the people of
Massachusetts, assembled in town meetings, elected delegates to a
convention for the express purpose of drawing up a state constitution, and the finished document was referred back to the people for
ratification. That became the normal practice.[4]

One peculiarity of the arrangements wants notice. The revolutionary state constitutions, however they were framed and adopted,
were assumed to be based upon popular consent, and the governments they established, representing the sovereign people, were
themselves sovereign in Blackstone's sense of the term. That is to
say, the state governments were authorized to exercise any power
that was not expressly forbidden to them by the several constitutions. The precise opposite situation pertained in regard to Congress,
which, before and after the adoption of the Articles of Confederation, had no powers except those that were expressly granted to it.

When, in 1787, existing constitutional arrangements became
manifestly inadequate, a new compact became necessary, but because of prior commitments, this one would have to be something
unprecedented. The Constitution would be a compact not among

sovereign states, as was the 1781 Articles of Confederation, nor a Lockean compact between ruler and ruled, nor even a compact of the whole people among themselves. It would be a compact among peoples of different political societies, in their capacities as peoples of the several states. Such a compact was undreamed of in political philosophy.[5]

Abraham Lincoln thought otherwise. In his message to Congress on July 4, 1861, he insisted that "Originally some dependent colonies made the Union, and, in turn, the Union threw off their old dependence for them, and made them States. . . . The Union, and not themselves separately, produced their independence and liberty. . . . The Union is older than any of the States, and, in fact, it created them as States." That view has been supported by some historians, and it is supported by some facts, notably that the Declaration was issued by the Second Continental Congress, that it spoke of Americans as "one people," and that in May 1776 Congress passed a resolution urging the colonies to adopt permanent governments.[6]

But this "nationalist" interpretation, as it has been called, is untenable. Congress merely "recommended" that the colonies make permanent governmental arrangements, for the members of Congress were there as agents of existing political societies, and in the nature of things, agents cannot authorize their principals to do anything. Besides, the resolution urging the colonies to act was approved by delegates from only six of the thirteen colonies. As for the response to the resolution, two colonies had already made arrangements before the adoption of the resolution, and just three reacted by formulating new political structures. And according to Lockean principles, the people of the colonies could not have returned to a state of nature unless their legislatures had gone out of existence, which they had not. Most importantly, the understanding of participants made the plural nature of the events unmistakably clear in the three documents that brought the United States into existence—the Declaration of Independence, the Articles of Confederation, and the 1783 Treaty of Paris in which Britain recognized the independence of each state.[7]

The Declaration consists of three parts. The first is a two-paragraph preamble, setting forth in ringing, almost poetic, phrases the Lockean version of the origin and purposes of government and the circumstances under which a regime may be dissolved. The second and longest part is an itemized indictment of "the present King of Great Britain," a catalog of the injustices and usurpations committed by that monarch against his American colonists. The third part is the actual declaration proper, in which the precise language is crucial: "We, therefore, the Representatives of the united States of America . . . do, in the Name, and by Authority of the good People of these Colonies, solemnly publish and declare" themselves to be "FREE AND INDEPENDENT STATES," and as such "they have full Power to levy War, conclude Peace, contract Alliances, establish Commerce, and to do all other Acts and Things which Independent States may of right do." The plural language is used throughout. In addition, in keeping with an eighteenth-century convention, nouns in the document are capitalized, and what the delegates represent are united States—that being not a name, but "united" being merely an adjective describing the stance of the states in opposition to Britain.[8]

The next founding document referred to itself as "articles of Confederation and perpetual Union between the States of Newhampshire, Massachusetts-bay, Rhodeisland and Providence Plantations," and so on down to Georgia. Article two of the instrument declared that "Each state retains its sovereignty, freedom and independence" in every power, jurisdiction, and right "which is not by this confederation expressly delegated" to the states in Congress assembled. Article three described the confederation as "a firm league of friendship." In general, Congress was given exclusive authority to conduct relations with foreign powers, including war, and to settle boundary disputes between states. Congress was not given power to levy taxes or coerce individuals, and in voting on any question, each state had a single vote. Amendments to the Articles had to be unanimous, inasmuch as it was for practical purposes a treaty.[9]

The Treaty of Paris, which can be regarded as the document that granted or recognized independence, was, like the Articles, cast in plural form: "His Brittanic Majesty acknowledges the said United

States, viz. New Hampshire, Massachusetts Bay," and the rest, "to be free, sovereign and independent States." In subsequent references to America, the peace treaty used the phrase "the said States." (The 1778 Franco-American treaty of alliance also used the plural: "The Most Christian King and the United States of North America, to wit: New Hampshire, Massachusetts Bay, Rhodes Island. . . .")[10]

Patriots of all stripes accepted the primacy of the states as a fact of political life, but they were far from unanimously happy about it. Considerable numbers of public men ardently favored an increase in the powers of Congress, but even more people jealously guarded the prerogatives of the states. Which way people leaned was a function of an interplay between circumstances and ideology.

The most impelling circumstances arose from the war. Enthusiasm for the Union and the proximity of the enemy were closely correlated. The middle states—New York, New Jersey, Pennsylvania, and Delaware—and from 1779 onward the lower South were overrun by the British army, and denizens of those areas were keen in their support of Congress. That attitude was bolstered by internal conditions, the tranquility of the areas being disrupted by political radicalism, ethnic animosities, or hostile Indians. In New England, by contrast, there was virtually no fighting after the spring of 1776, and there was almost none in the upper South until the climactic campaigning that led to the American victory at Yorktown in 1781. Moreover, the states in those regions had none of the internal problems that plagued the middle states and lower South. Leaders in New England and the upper south were ardent champions of the rights of the states and nearly paranoid in their vigilance against usurpation by Congress.[11]

Predilections based upon circumstances were reinforced by ideological dispositions. Patriot leaders in New England and Virginia eagerly embraced republican principles of political theory, which included opposition to and fear of concentrated power, active participation in public affairs, and suspicion of moneyed men. And, following the teachings of Montesquieu, who held that republics could be viable solely in small territories, they equated republicanism with local control. Nationally oriented groups in the middle states and lower South tended to be aristocrats (Hudson Valley patroons in New York, rice plantation families in the lower South) or wealthy merchants in Philadelphia who regarded states' rights republicans as radical democrats posing a genuine threat to social and political stability. The two groups had hardened into hostile factions in Congress before the end of 1776, and their enmity and mutual distrust continued until after the war. Leadership of the New England–Virginia coalition clustered around John and Sam Adams of Massachusetts and the Lees of Virginia (the "Lee-Adams Junto"); that of the middle states and lower South revolved around John Dickinson and, as time went by, the Philadelphia merchant Robert Morris and the Rutledges of South Carolina.[12]

The states' rights republicans dominated Congress from 1776 until 1780. They managed to supply the armies in the field, at first through loans from patriotic citizens, then with loans from the Netherlands and France, but mainly by printing unsecured paper money that rapidly depreciated to almost nothing. Along the way, various congressmen engaged in blatant corruption and profiteering, more demonstrated an utter lack of competence, and most displayed an ongoing distrust of the military that was defending them. The officers and men of the Continental Line grumbled and cursed Congress, many soldiers deserted and others mutinied, but George Washington remained unswervingly loyal to Congress and the cause, and he held the army together.[13]

During the winter of 1780–1781 nationalists came into control of Congress and forthwith set out to strengthen it. To obtain funds, they passed and sent to the states for ratification an amendment to the not-yet-ratified Articles of Confederation that would have given Congress power to levy a 5 percent impost on imported goods. They overhauled the central administrative machinery, scrapping the cumbersome and ineffectual committee system under which Congress had operated and creating three administrative departments—foreign affairs, war, and finance—each to be headed by a superintendent.[14]

Robert Morris, the superintendent of finance, had grand plans that he meant to set in motion once the impost amendment was adopted, but he was diverted in the meantime by a pressing need to supply Washington's army for the impending action at Yorktown. He managed to do so through financial wizardry, and then he returned to his larger scheme. Americans, he knew, shared an enormous burden in the form of public debt, amounting to about as much as all the commercial property in the country, and an enormous asset in the form of western lands that had been ceded to Congress, amounting to about twice as much acreage as the settled land in the country. Most people who thought about this asset and this burden proposed to use the land to cancel the debts. Morris proposed instead to use both as the basis for establishing semipermanent administrative agencies, one to service the debt and the other to sell the land. That would greatly expand the activities of the central authority and give many thousands of people a stake in its continued strength.[15]

When the scheme fell through as a result of the machinations and speculations of politicians in Rhode Island and Virginia, Morris and his circle undertook a truly audacious venture. During the winter of 1782–1783 the army was encamped at Newburgh, New York, awaiting the arrival of the peace treaty. The officers, not having been paid for years and facing the prospect of returning home and losing their property for nonpayment of debts and taxes, were disgruntled about Congress's inability to grant them relief. Morris and his friends conceived the notion of stirring up agitation in the army and employing the threat of a military coup to frighten Congress into passing and the states into ratifying amendments to the Articles giving Congress expanded sources of revenue. The effort got out of hand, and a mutiny nearly erupted before Washington was able to restore order.[16]

The situation, and indeed the affairs of the nation, rapidly unwound. News of the peace treaty arrived, the officers were mollified by the promise of a bonus of five years' pay, they were given notes for three months of back pay, and they were sent home on leave instead of being formally discharged. Congress fled Philadelphia after a group of drunken Pennsylvania soldiers threatened the delegates, adjourning to the tiny town of Princeton, New Jersey. So few of them actually went there that Congress barely had a quorum to ratify the treaty. Congress did, however, propose a set of revenue amendments and send them to the states. On the fate of the amendments rested the fate of the Confederation.[17]

During the next four years, as the states leisurely took up the amendments, the Union all but dissolved. Congress had a quorum about half the time, and the republicans who again dominated it were not particularly concerned that it do anything, apart from somehow retaliating for commercial restrictions that Britain had imposed after 1783. Congress did have accomplishments, notably auditing the accounts that constituted the public debts and providing for the survey and ultimate governance of the public domain, the Northwest Territory. It also negotiated a commercial treaty with Prussia, but that, like the Treaty of Paris, was limited by the absence of a capacity to give treaties the force of law.[18]

The mood of Congress in the postwar years is captured by two vignettes. In 1785 the Massachusetts legislature instructed its delegates to seek a general convention to revise the Articles. They refused, declaring that "plans have been artfully laid" to change "our republican Governments, into baleful Aristocracies," and a convention would provide the conspirators with a fresh opportunity. The next year Superintendent of Foreign Affairs John Jay negotiated with the Spanish minister, Diego de Gardoqui, and proposed to forgo American rights to navigate the Mississippi in exchange for lucrative commercial concessions; when the proposal came to a vote in Congress, heated debate along sectional lines stimulated mutterings of breaking the Union into two or three regional confederations.[19]

While Congress was floundering, the states were conducting their several experiments in independence. The smaller and weaker fared poorly, the larger tolerably well, but the course of state policies generally tended toward dissolving the bands of union. Thus it came as no surprise that, when the abortive Annapolis commercial convention of September 1786 issued a call for a general convention to amend the Articles, the reaction was lukewarm. Congress referred the proposal to a committee of three, which referred it to a committee of thirteen, which was never appointed. The Annapolis convention had sent its recommendation directly to the states as well as to Congress, but by the end of the year, only four states—Virginia, New Jersey, Pennsylvania, and North Carolina—had voted to send delegates to the proposed convention.[20]

Then, early in 1787, came two developments that electrified friends of the Union into action. The first was Shays's Rebellion, an armed uprising in central and western Massachusetts that was essentially a taxpayers' revolt at base but was widely perceived as an anarchistic and leveling movement that threatened to destroy social order in America. The second was news that New York had definitively rejected the 1783 revenue amendments, thereby dooming the Confederation Congress to bankruptcy. Stirred by these turns, the legislatures of every state except Rhode Island voted to send delegates to the Constitutional Convention.[21]

The convention was scheduled to meet in Philadelphia on Monday, May 14, but not enough delegates arrived to constitute a quorum until two weeks later. As delegates drifted in, two or three a day, it seemed evident that archnationalists would dominate the proceedings. The radical republicans of 1776 were conspicuously absent: neither of the Adamses was there, nor was John Hancock; none of the Lees attended, nor did Patrick Henry or Thomas Jefferson or Thomas Paine. George Washington, who did not make up his mind to attend until a few weeks before the convention, presided over the deliberations. Robert Morris was present, along with his close allies James Wilson and Gouverneur Morris; so were John Rutledge and some ardent younger nationalists, including James Madison and Alexander Hamilton.[22]

The nationalists' apparent dominance was indicated by the first substantive vote that was taken—a motion "that a *national* Government [ought to be established] consisting of a *supreme* Legislative, Executive & Judiciary." One state delegation, Connecticut's, voted against the proposal, one was divided, and six voted aye. That vote, however, did not mean that nationalists would have an entirely free hand, for the delegates had already rejected a proposal that the states should be given votes in the convention in proportion to their populations. Instead, the one-state, one-vote rule of Congress was adopted.[23]

That decision was pivotal, for the nationalists, though numbering a majority of the delegates, did not control a majority of the delegations. Consequently, they were unable to have the principle of confederation abandoned in the legislative branch they proposed to reconstitute and empower. Early on, the "small states"—those without claims to western lands—conceded that representation should be proportional to population in one of the two proposed legislative branches, but they insisted that the states retain equal votes in the other branch. More than a month of disagreement ensued—during which, to be sure, progress was made toward shaping a constitution— and efforts at reconciliation failed. Finally, on July 16, after considerable backstage wheeling and dealing, the convention adopted a compromise proposal offered by a committee chaired by Benjamin Franklin: equality in the second branch, but bills for raising and spending money would originate in the popular branch.[24]

Since the members of the Senate would be elected by the state legislatures, the constitutional system would, as Oliver Ellsworth of Connecticut described it, be "partly national; partly federal," one branch representing the people of the several states, the second representing states directly as states. Moreover, given the ways that additional features of the proposed constitution were subsequently worked out, the system would be further mixed in two important ways. The president was to be elected by electors chosen by the voters or by the legislatures, as the individual legislatures should determine, and the number of electors allocated to each state would be the combined number of its representatives and senators. And the Senate, representing the residual sovereignty of the states, would share with the president the power to appoint ambassadors and make treaties.[25]

Sovereignty was thus being divided in the makeup of the proposed government, and it was divided in the allocation of powers, too. The central government would have supreme power in the limited areas that were entrusted to it: the conduct of foreign relations;

the raising and command of armed forces; the regulation of interstate and foreign commerce; the levying of various kinds of taxes, including an exclusive power to tax imports; and assorted miscellaneous concerns such as the granting of copyrights and patents and the punishment of counterfeiting. Supremacy in regard to all nondelegated powers remained in the states or the people.[26]

Almost, but not quite. As nationalists saw things, reorganizing and empowering the central authority was not enough. The excesses of the state governments must also be curbed. The sovereign states had persecuted loyalists by enacting bills of attainder and ex post facto laws. They had confiscated estates and refused to return them, in violation of the Treaty of Paris, and they had prevented the collection of bona fide prewar debts, again in violation of the treaty. They had passed legal tender laws, such as South Carolina's notorious Pine Barren Act, permitting the payment of debts (in the case of South Carolina, largely owed by wealthy planters) with worthless lands. They had issued unsecured paper money that rapidly depreciated, enabling governments to expunge public debts and individuals to wipe out private debts. They had interfered systematically with private commercial transactions and suspended the obligations of private contracts. They had levied taxes at rates ten to twenty times any that had been levied during the colonial period and had increased the volume of legislation on a scale that dwarfed the increase in taxes.[27]

The delegates in the Philadelphia convention attributed these misdeeds precisely to the fact that state governments were close to the people. "The evils we experience," said Samuel Adams's erstwhile protégé Elbridge Gerry, "flow from the excess of democracy. The people do not want virtue; but are the dupes of pretended patriots." Edmund Randolph of Virginia declared that the origin of the evils was to be found "in the turbulence and follies of democracy: that some check therefore was to be sought agst. this tendency of our Governments." And they were not alone in having these sentiments.[28]

The most radical proposal for restraining the states came from Charles Pinckney of South Carolina and James Madison. During the second week of the convention, Pinckney moved that the national legislature be empowered to veto state laws that it judged to be "improper." Madison seconded the motion, declaring it to be imperative. "This prerogative of the General Govt. is the great pervading principle that must controul the centrifugal tendency of the States; which, without it, will continually fly out of their proper orbits and destroy the order & harmony of the political system." After discussion, Madison conceded that the power might be entrusted to the upper house, in order that "the more numerous & expensive branch therefore might not be obliged to sit constantly." The motion was overwhelmingly rejected, three state delegations being in favor, one divided, and seven against. The question came up again on July 17 and August 23 and was rejected both times. Yet, even after the convention had ended, Madison remained convinced that the absence of a negative on state laws was a flaw that might prove fatal to the Constitution.[29]

What the convention did instead was incorporate a number of particular restrictions on the states into article 1, section 10, of the Constitution. States are forbidden to enter into international agreements, tax imports or exports except in special circumstances, keep troops (except militias) or ships of war in time of peace, or otherwise interfere in foreign relations. In internal matters, they are not allowed to "coin Money; emit Bills of Credit; make any thing but gold and silver Coin a Tender in Payment of Debts," pass bills of attainder and ex post facto laws, grant titles of nobility, or pass any "Law impairing the Obligation of Contracts."[30]

A few additional provisions regarding the relations among the several states and between the states and the general government were placed in the Constitution. One concerned the electorate. Many and perhaps most of the delegates in Philadelphia wanted to require a property qualification for voters for the House of Representatives, the branch of the government chosen directly by the people of the states. A uniform qualification, however, was impracticable because of the wide disparities in wealth from state to state. What would have been sufficient to continue the dominance of the planter class in a wealthy state like South Carolina, for example, would have disfranchised all but a handful of people in a poor state like New Hampshire. The delegates settled instead upon a stipulation in article 1, section 2, that voters for members of the House "shall have the Qualifications requisite for Electors of the most numerous Branch of the State Legislature." Among the unintended consequences of that provision was that in several states only Christians could vote for representatives. More to the point, it meant that the states retained control over who chose the representatives.[31]

Relations among the states—reciprocity in recognizing one another's laws, extradition of fugitives, and the like—are covered in article 4, along with a limitation upon how the sovereign people may exercise power: "The United States shall guarantee to every State in this Union a Republican Form of Government." Article 5, the amending clause, permits amendments to be originated in either Congress or a convention requested by the state legislatures, and their ratification to be made by three-fourths of the state legislatures or state conventions. Finally, article 6 makes the Constitution, laws passed in accordance with it, and treaties made under its authority the supreme law of the land, irrespective of the constitutions and laws of the individual states.

The nature of the compact that the Philadelphia convention sent out for ratification is evident in a number of its aspects. The proposed system of government, for present purposes, is best described in Madison's *Federalist* 39. Though he had been skeptical of Ellsworth's formulation, "partly national; partly federal," Madison now rang the changes on the idea as if it were his own. First he considered the foundation of the constitutional order. This was the assent of the people, but "not as individuals composing one entire nation, but as composing the distinct and independent States to which they respectively belong." The act of establishing the Constitution, therefore, "will not be a *national,* but a *federal* act." The members of the House of Representatives would derive their powers from the people of the states, the senators from the state governments; in the one respect the government was national, in the other federal. The executive power derived from a "very compound" source, a mixture of federal and national. By the criterion of the operation of the government, it acted uniformly upon all individuals in the country and thus was of a national character.[32]

Next, Madison gave a clear explication of the way the Constitution established a system of divided sovereignty, though he did not use the term on this occasion. The idea of a national government, he wrote, involves "an indefinite supremacy" over the legitimate objects of lawful government. Among communities united for particular purposes, supremacy "is vested partly in the general and partly in the municipal legislatures." In the former, "all local authorities are subordinate to the supreme; and may be controlled, directed, or abolished by it at pleasure. In the latter, the local or municipal authorities form distinct and independent portions of the supremacy" and are no more subject, "within their respective spheres, to the general authority, than the general authority is subject to them, within its own sphere." In this sense, the proposed government could not properly be called national, "since its jurisdiction extends to certain enumerated objects only, and leaves to the several States a residuary and inviolable sovereignty over all other objects."[33]

Madison's analysis carries weight, but equally authoritative and definitive evidence of the nature of the compact is contained in the procedure recommended by the convention for the ratification of the Constitution. The Articles of Confederation specified a means of amendment—amendments recommended by Congress had to be ratified by the legislatures of every state—but the convention determined to get around that provision by seeking the approval of ratifying conventions especially elected for the purpose. In a manner of speaking, it did comply with the Articles by sending the Constitution to Congress with a recommendation that Congress send it to the state legislatures and that the legislatures call ratifying conventions. Inasmuch as Congress and (ultimately) the thirteen legislatures complied with the request, their actions in effect constituted an amendment to the Articles' amending process.[34]

The crucial features were that popularly elected conventions, not the legislatures, would make the decisions, and that when the conventions of nine states, not thirteen, had voted to ratify, the Constitution would become binding on those states. The rest would be free to ratify or not ratify as they saw fit.

The reasons for following that procedure were several. Obviously it would make ratification easier. Many delegates at Philadelphia distrusted and feared the influence of the "demagogs" who dominated some of the legislatures. Of special concern was Rhode Island, whose actions to defraud creditors had won it the sobriquet Rogues Island and whose legislature had killed the impost amendment. Of similar concern was New York, which had killed the 1783 revenue amendments. Another reason was that, if the legislatures were to ratify the Constitution, it would be a mere treaty. As Madison and others pointed out, if any party to a treaty violated it, the treaty ceased to bind the remaining parties. Alternatively, ratification by a legislature would be a mere act that could be repealed by an act of a subsequent legislature. Either way, the Constitution would be on tenuous footing.[35]

The most fundamental reason had to do with constitutional and legal niceties. Each of the states already had a constitution (if the charters of Rhode Island and Connecticut be reckoned as such). The Constitution amended the state constitutions in several ways, particularly in article 1, section 10. Thus the Constitution could not be ratified by the people of the United States as a whole, for if it were, the people in a given state would be altering the constitutions of other states. Altering a state's constitution, in the nature of things, was an action that could be taken only by the sovereign people of that state.

An objection to this interpretation was made at the time, but it is spurious. The preamble to the Constitution reads, "We the People of the United States," but, unlike the Articles and the British and French treaties, does not enumerate the states. That can be taken to mean that the act of establishing the Constitution was done by the people as a whole. Indeed, in the Virginia ratifying convention, Patrick Henry, who strongly opposed ratification, seized upon the language of the preamble as proof that the Framers intended to create a "consolidated" national government. Defenders of the Constitution treated the objection as trivial and did not bother to answer it, though

Madison did point out that if no more than a majority of the whole people were necessary for ratification, a convention in Virginia would not have been necessary, for by the time the Virginia convention met (June 1788), a majority of the people of the United States had already voted to ratify.[36]

But the answer to Henry is that the Framers could not have said, "We the People of the United States, viz. New Hampshire, . . ." for in the summer of 1787, no one could predict which states would ratify and which would not, and it was expected that a few would refuse for a long time and perhaps forever. The course of events bore out that expectation. New Hampshire's convention refused to ratify when it met in February 1788, though it did approve when it reconvened in June. As it happened, New Hampshire thus became the ninth state to ratify, activating the Constitution for those nine that had approved. Virginia and New York followed shortly afterward, creating a union of eleven members. But North Carolina flatly rejected the Constitution and did not vote to join the reconstituted entity until several months after the government had been in operation. The Rhode Island legislature at first refused even to call a ratifying convention, and the state did not ratify until May 1790.

Moreover, on the few occasions when the language of the Constitution grammatically calls for referring to "the United States" in the singular or in the plural, the plural is used. Thus in article 3, section 2, the jurisdiction of the courts of the general government includes cases arising under "the Laws of the United States, and treaties made . . . under their Authority." Again, article 3, section 3, defines treason as "levying War against them, or in adhering to their Enemies." Yet again, article 1, section 9, declares that "No Title of Nobility shall be granted by the United States: And no Person holding any Office of Profit or Trust under them" shall accept presents or offices or titles from foreign governments.

The Constitution was deemed to be incomplete upon its formal adoption, for the campaigns over ratification had been accompanied by demands for a bill of rights. The Philadelphia convention had rejected a motion to include a bill of rights, ten delegations to none, and though debate concerning the subject was minimal, several delegates subsequently made the reasons clear. James Wilson said in the Pennsylvania ratifying convention that itemizing rights would be dangerous; no one could list all human rights, and the failure to include some could be used as an excuse to violate them. Charles Cotesworth Pinckney made a particular assessment in the South Carolina ratifying convention. "With regard to the liberty of the press," he said, "the general government has no powers but what are expressly granted to it; it therefore has no power to take away the liberty of the press. . . . and to have mentioned it in our general Constitution would perhaps furnish an argument, hereafter, that the general government had a right to exercise powers not expressly delegated to it." Alexander Hamilton had analyzed the matter in similar fashion in *Federalist* 84. A bill of rights, he wrote, "would contain various exceptions to powers not granted; and, on this very account, would afford a colorable pretext to claim more than were granted." Bills of rights made sense in regard to the British government and the state governments, which had all powers not forbidden them, but not to a government of delegated powers.[37]

Despite the logic of the Federalists' position, however, political considerations led many to change their minds. The agitation for a bill of rights emerged as a campaign to hold a second general convention, ostensibly to amend but possibly to undo the work of the first. If such a convention materialized, state particularists would be better prepared than in 1787, and they just might succeed. Federalists were unwilling to risk that outcome. On a personal level, the anti-Federalist Patrick Henry, who had firm control of the Virginia legislature, saw to it that the state would send two anti-Federalists to the first Senate and also that James Madison's home county was placed in a congressional district with six anti-Federalist counties. To save his political career, Madison campaigned hard for a seat in the House, his central campaign promise being that if he were elected, he would see to the introduction of a bill of rights.[38]

He followed through on his promise, and Congress generally supported him. With characteristic thoroughness, Madison studied the amendments that had been proposed, finding that more than two hundred proposals had come in, one way and another, from nine different states. He eliminated the least popular and least practicable and reduced the rest to nineteen substantive proposals in May 1789. In the form in which they passed the House as seventeen amendments, some provisions would have applied to the states as well as to the general government. The Senate removed that applicability (so that, for example, states would remain free to tax their citizens for the support of established churches, as Connecticut did until 1818 and Massachusetts did until 1833). Otherwise, the Senate largely concurred, though a joint committee meeting on September 25 consolidated the amendments further into twelve. The first two, concerning the number of congressmen and their salaries, were not approved at that time. The others, known collectively as the Bill of Rights, were ratified and became part of the Constitution on December 15, 1791.[39]

Two amendments in the Bill of Rights are especially relevant to questions of rights and sovereignty, the so-called declaratory amendments. The Ninth Amendment took care of James Wilson's objection by providing that "the enumeration in the Constitution, of certain rights, shall not be construed to deny or disparage others retained by the people." The Ninth was understood as integral to a system of divided sovereignty. By refusing to nationalize unenumerated rights, the Ninth left the question of the protection of such rights to the states or to the people of the states. The Tenth Amendment, which Thomas Jefferson called "the foundation of the Constitution," provides that "the powers not delegated to the United States by the Constitution, nor prohibited by it to the States, are reserved to the States respectively, or to the people." In his *Commentaries on the Constitution of the United States,* Joseph Story asserted that the "sole design" of the Tenth Amendment was "to exclude any interpretation, by which other powers should be assumed beyond those, which are granted." During the congressional debates concerning the amendments, Thomas Tudor Tucker of South Carolina proposed that the language be "powers not expressly delegated," but the proposal was rejected. A few days later, Elbridge Gerry attempted to insert the word "expressly" but failed by a thirty-two to seventeen vote. Over the course of time, however, champions of states' rights would come to argue repeatedly as if the word "expressly" had been inserted.[40]

2

THE FEDERALIST ERA

For about two years after the summer of 1788—when the ninth, tenth, and eleventh states ratified the Constitution—America was engulfed in a wave of nationalism that rivaled in intensity the Spirit of Seventy-six. Congressional elections were held with minimal rancor, and friends of the Constitution gained a comfortable majority of the seats. Congress convened barely five weeks behind schedule and promptly got down to business. In addition to the Bill of Rights, it passed legislation providing a rudimentary revenue system, establishing the executive departments (state, war, and treasury), and creating a system of federal courts on lines that would prevail for more than two centuries. All this happened in the first session of the First Congress and was accompanied by little friction, though some representatives were uneasy about having a single person in charge of the Treasury Department, lest the office evolve into a British-style prime ministership.[1]

Meanwhile, to no one's surprise, George Washington was unanimously elected president, and though few people understood how reluctantly, he agreed to serve. His journey from Mount Vernon to take the oath of office in New York was leisurely, dignified, and triumphant, attended by adoring throngs every step along the way. In his relations with the public, he was careful to adopt rules to strike a balance between "too free an intercourse and too much familiarity," which would reduce the dignity of the office, and "an ostentatious show" of monarchical aloofness, which would be unseemly in a republic. His major appointments met with widespread approval.

When Congress adjourned, Washington toured New England, where he was wildly cheered.

Harmony's end began in 1790. At issue was Secretary of the Treasury Alexander Hamilton's proposal to provide permanent funds for servicing the outstanding public debts accumulated during the Revolutionary War, including the debts of the states. At stake were sundry vested interests, especially those of Virginia. What was portentous for states' righters was that Hamilton's program, when fully in place, would bind the nation together far more firmly than could that "mere parchment," the Constitution.

Within a year, after Hamilton had proposed the creation of the Bank of the United States, the opposition hardened into something permanent. At first the opponents tried to work within the system, which is to say within the framework of the checks and balances built into the national authority by the Constitution. That effort failing, Hamilton's enemies went outside the system, organizing an extraconstitutional political party. As the decade wore on and the party spirit reached a fever pitch, opposition increasingly took the form of advocacy of states' rights. Both parties claimed to be the true defenders of the Constitution.

At last, in 1801, the party professing to be the champion of states' rights ousted the nationalists and gained control of the central government. The question was whether they would adhere to their principles once power was in their hands.

Acting on instructions from the House of Representatives, Hamilton prepared his plan for servicing the public debts and presented it to the House in January 1790. He proposed to open a loan, subscriptions to which would be payable in old evidences of debt at their face value plus arrearages of interest. The new certificates would bear three different rates of interest, the highest being 6 percent, and the holders would have first claim on the government's revenues. In addition to "funding" the debt in that manner, the United States would assume responsibility for the unpaid war debts of the states. The newly created public debt would be made semipermanent by placing a limit on the amount that could be redeemed in a given year. A sinking fund would be established to make purchases on the open market and thus to raise the certificates' market value and stabilize the price at or near par. In that way, Hamilton sought to make the debt into a basis for paper money, at once solving an endemic shortage of cash and capital in America and making economic activity dependent upon the success and durability of the central government. The nationalistic implications were profound and, to states' righters, profoundly unsettling.[2]

The plan was widely praised, but barriers to its enactment arose from an unexpected quarter, namely, Hamilton's quondam coauthor of *The Federalist,* James Madison. At issue was not the entire proposal but the provision for the assumption of state debts. Several states, including Virginia, had substantially retired their debts, often by means that verged on repudiation, and they were not willing to be taxed to service other states' debts. Furthermore, Virginians were anxious to have the permanent national capital located on the Potomac, and Madison intended to use the assumption question as a means of trading for votes. He organized enough opposition to defeat assumption by a narrow margin, and the funding bill was passed without it. Hamilton was beside himself with concern, for he regarded all the pieces of the program as essential to the accomplishment of his broader aims.[3]

That set the stage for a famous deal. At a dinner hosted by Secretary of State Thomas Jefferson, Madison and Hamilton came to an agreement. Madison would use his influence among southern congressmen to swing enough votes to bring about passage of assumption. Hamilton would reciprocate by influencing sufficient New England congressmen to ensure that the location of the permanent capital would be on the Potomac instead of in Philadelphia, though the temporary capital would remain in Philadelphia for ten years. As a bonus, Hamilton agreed that certain claims of the United States against Virginia, arising from the nonpayment of wartime requisitions, would in effect be waived.[4]

Congressional Virginians had made a handsome bargain for their state, but Virginians at home were less than happy with the strengthened ties of nationalism the Hamiltonian fiscal system presaged. Three months after the funding and assumption bill was signed into law on August 4, 1790, the Virginia general assembly, under the leadership of Madison's and Jefferson's archenemy Patrick Henry, adopted a pair of resolutions condemning the measures. One resolution renounced assumption as "repugnant to the Constitution of the United States, as it goes to the exercise of a power not expressly granted to the General Government." The other said that the act "demands the marked disapprobation of the General Assembly." ("This is the first symptom," Hamilton wrote to John Jay, "of a spirit which must either be killed or will kill the constitution of the United States.")[5]

That spirit subsided, but it was to be rekindled. When the First Congress convened for its final session in December, resistance to the Hamiltonian system seemed to have vanished—indeed, it was extremely popular in most parts of the country—and Congress appeared receptive to his proposal for a national bank. Even Madison and Jefferson were favorably disposed at first. But a tangential matter arose. Pennsylvania's congressmen began declaring openly "that they had never intended to aid in a removal" of the capital from Philadelphia, and then the state's house of representatives appropriated funds to construct permanent quarters for the general government. Hamilton's Bank of the United States was to have its central branch in Philadelphia, and its charter was to run for twenty years. Madison feared that if the Bank operated for that long a period, moving the capital in 1800 would be almost impossible. Accordingly, he worked quietly but diligently to gather support for limiting the charter to a ten-year term so that the Bank would expire and the capital would be removed simultaneously. That failing, and being unable to round up sufficient votes to defeat the incorporation of the Bank, Madison determined to reverse a position he had previously held and to challenge the Bank on constitutional grounds.[6]

Three eminent Virginians gave their opinions in the ensuing debate, each formulating his arguments as if the word "expressly" had been included in the Tenth Amendment's reservation "to the States respectively, or to the people" all "powers not delegated to the United States by the Constitution." Madison, on the floor of the House, was unable to bring Congress to his way of thinking, but his reasoning gave Washington pause. Before deciding whether to sign the Bank bill, Washington asked the opinion of Attorney General Edmund Randolph, whose argument was much the same as Madison's.[7]

Then Washington consulted Jefferson, who in a lengthy opinion liberally sprinkled with legalese penned the classic justification for the strict construction of the Constitution. After considering the "specially enumerated" powers and dismissing incorporation of a bank as among them, Jefferson focused on the word "necessary." Inasmuch as the enumerated powers could be executed without a bank, "a bank, therefore, is not *necessary.*" He refused to conflate "*convenience*" with necessity, lest doing so "break down the most ancient and fundamental laws of the several states." Jefferson clearly framed the issue in a states' rights perspective. He closed by urging the president to veto the measure, since "the negative of the President is the shield provided by the Constitution to protect" the states and the state legislatures from "invasions" by Congress. The current instance, according to Jefferson, "is the case of a right remaining exclusively with the states, and is, consequently, one of those intended by the Constitution" to be protected by the presidential veto.[8]

Washington turned to Hamilton, who responded with the definitive statement of the nationalist, loose-construction interpretation, which included an analysis of the principle of divided sovereignty. "Every power vested in a Government," he wrote, "is in its nature *sovereign,* and includes by *force* of the *term,* a right to employ all the *means* requisite, and fairly *applicable* to the attainment of the *ends* of such power," and which are not forbidden by the Constitution, "or not immoral, or not contrary to the essential ends of political power." As for the division in the United States between general and state governments, that meant merely "that each has sovereign power as to *certain things,* and not as to *other things.*" To Hamilton it was self-evident that creating corporations was inherent in sovereignty, for anything a government could legitimately do it could require or permit natural or artificial persons, corporations, to do. Whether Hamilton's argument or something else persuaded Washington, the president signed the bill.[9]

Despite the heat that the Bank controversy engendered, however, personal and political relations between Hamilton and Jefferson remained cordial for a time: their break would be triggered by a minor episode several weeks later. On an April evening in 1791 Jefferson hosted a dinner party at which the guests were Hamilton and Vice-President John Adams. After discussing various matters of business, the three turned to political theory. Adams spoke glowingly of the British system and said, "Purge that constitution of its corruption, and give to its popular branch equality of representation, and it would be the most perfect constitution ever devised by the wit of man." Upset though he was at hearing his old friend and revolutionary ally openly praise a government consisting, as Jefferson recorded it, of "two hereditary branches and an honest elective one," he was not surprised. But Hamilton's comment shook him deeply. "Purge it of its corruption," Hamilton casually remarked, "and give to its popular branch equality of representation, and it would become an *impracticable* government: as it stands at present, with all its supposed defects, it is the most perfect government which ever existed." Hamilton was not advocating either monarchy or corruption for America but was echoing a remark that David Hume had made in an essay, and he meant the same thing—namely, that since the House of Commons controlled the purse strings, balance could be maintained only if the Crown protected itself by using patronage to influence voting in the Commons.[10]

Brooding upon the remark, Jefferson came to the conclusion that Hamilton intended to establish a British-style ministerial system in America and ultimately a monarchy. Jefferson confided his suspicions to Washington, hoping the president would disown his secretary of the treasury, but Washington, who considered Hamilton's establishment of public credit as a veritable miracle, scoffed at the suggestion. Jefferson next told Madison, who did believe him, and the two forged an alliance with erstwhile anti-Federalists in New York to build a political party that could gain control of the government and undo Hamilton's work.[11]

While these efforts were being launched, Jefferson did something that foreshadowed the states' rights position he and Madison would take in 1798–1799. Apropos plans to open a branch of the Bank of the United States in Richmond, he urged that the Virginia legislature "should reason thus. The power of erecting banks & corporations was not given to the general government it remains then with the state itself. For any person to recognize a foreign legislature"—that is, the Congress of the United States—"in a case belonging to the state itself, is an act of *treason* against the state," and any person acting under the "authority of a foreign legislature—whether by signing notes, issuing or passing them, acting as director, cashier or in any other office relating to it shall be adjudged guilty of high treason & suffer death accordingly."[12]

On another front, a number of assorted matters concerning the balance between the general and state governments were being worked out, sometimes to the advantage of the one, more tellingly on the side of the other. At issue early on was the enforcement of congressional acts. In 1793 Congress passed a fugitive slave law. Having no effective enforcement apparatus, Congress required state and local officials to enforce the return of slaves who fled into free states. That might have elicited howls of protest from states' righters, except that the most vocal spokesmen for states' rights (save those in New York) were then concentrated in the South, at whose instance the law had been enacted.[13]

A related subject was the effort of the Washington administration to enforce the Neutrality Proclamation. When the wars of the French Revolution broke out, France did not seek American military help, for the Franco-American alliance was limited to defensive wars, and France, having declared war on its enemies, was the nominal aggressor. The revolutionary regime, however, sent Edmund Genet to the United States on a complex mission that might have entangled America in the conflict. Specifically, Genet was to commission privateers to prey on British and Spanish shipping and to issue commissions for volunteer armies to attack Spanish possessions in Louisiana and Florida. Against the advice of his secretary of state, Washington issued a proclamation on April 22, 1793, warning American citizens against committing hostile acts toward any belligerent and ordering the prosecution of "all persons who shall, within the cognizance of the courts of the United States, violate the law of nations with respect to the powers at war, or any of them."[14]

Debate about how to implement the proclamation exacerbated the strained relations among the cabinet members. Hamilton proposed that customs officers, who were operating in every major port, be authorized to report violations of neutrality to him. Jefferson denounced the idea, saying that it was aimed at creating a "corps of spies or informers against their fellow citizens, whose actions they are to watch in secret, [and] inform against in secret to the Secretary of the Treasury." States' righters had been spreading rumors that revenue officers were already "a corps, trained to the art of spies." It was agreed that the collectors should be instructed to report neutrality violations to the attorney general instead of the secretary.[15]

Attorney General Randolph did not have an easy time of it. No federal statutes were involved, and to prevent recruitment for voluntary armies or privateering, he found it necessary to bring indictments for the common-law offense of disturbing the peace. Convictions were not forthcoming. He turned to the states for help in prosecuting offenders, with mixed results. Many state judges strongly objected to the prosecutions; most governors supported them. In one significant instance, the Supreme Court became involved. French consuls in American cities had constituted themselves as courts to adjudicate prizes captured by the privateers that Genet had commissioned. In *Glass* v. *Sloop Betsy,* the Court ruled that the consuls' admiralty jurisdiction "is not of right," and that the legality of captures and the legal effect of breaches of American neutrality were exclusively within the jurisdiction of courts of the United States.[16]

The Supreme Court was also at the center of an early clash between proponents of states' rights and defenders of central authority. The principle at issue was whether states could be sued in federal courts. Article 3 of the Constitution vested the judicial power with jurisdiction over controversies "between a State and Citizens of another State." Anti-Federalists had objected that this would open the courts to suits by foreign creditors, loyalists, and anyone having claims against a state, but Federalists insisted otherwise. Events proved the anti-Federalists to be right. In the February term in 1791, a firm of Dutch bankers filed a Supreme Court suit as creditors against the state of Maryland. The next year suits were brought by an individual against New York and by a land company against Virginia.[17]

The protests were vehement. An anonymous Philadelphia newspaper article that was widely reprinted declared that if the actions were maintained, "one great National question will be settled—that is, that the several States have relinquished all their Sovereignties, and have become mere corporations, . . . for a sovereign State can never be sued or coerced by the authority of another government." Another writer asserted that the actions "involved more danger to the liberties of America than the claims of the British Parliament to tax us without our consent." They would lead "to the consolidation of the Union for the purpose of arbitrary power, to the downfall of liberty and the subversion of the rights of the people." Still another wrote that the "craft and subtility of lawyers" had placed the relevant clause in the Constitution as part of a "plan of all aristocrats to reduce the States to corporations," and yet another predicted that "if the sovereignty of the States is to be thus annihilated, there must be a consolidated Government and a standing army."[18]

Similar suits were brought against South Carolina and Massachusetts, but the pivotal case involved Georgia. In *Chisholm* v. *Georgia,* two citizens of South Carolina, executors of a deceased Georgia loyalist whose estate had been confiscated, sued the state for recovery of a bond that had been given before the Revolution. Georgia refused to appear when the case was heard by the Supreme Court, and the Court ruled for the plaintiffs by default. Georgia denounced the decision and refused to accept it; indeed, its house of representatives passed a bill providing that any federal marshal or other person who attempted to execute the decision would be "guilty of felony and shall suffer death, without benefit of clergy, by being hanged." The bill was not passed by the upper house, but several states, including Massachusetts and Virginia, adopted resolutions condemning the decision and calling for a constitutional amendment exempting states from suits.[19]

Such an amendment was proposed in Congress immediately after the decision was handed down, and it was modified and passed by the requisite two-thirds majorities in both houses a year later: "The Judicial power of the United States shall not be construed to extend to any suit in law or equity, commenced or prosecuted against one of the United States by Citizens of another State, or by Citizens or Subjects of any Foreign State." In considering ratification of the amendment, state legislators may have been moved by concern for the principle of sovereign immunity, but of equal moment was economic interest. As a newspaper ironically said of the decision, "Nothing remains but to give the key of our treasury to the agents of the Refugees, Tories and men who were inimical to our Revolution, to distribute the hard money now deposited in that office to persons of this description." In any event, the twelve states necessary to ratification (Vermont, Kentucky, and Tennessee having been added to the original thirteen) approved within four years, making the Eleventh Amendment part of the Constitution.[20]

The amendment was not enough, however, to protect an important interest group that had previously been shielded against foreign plaintiffs by state action. Prior to the Revolution a large number of tobacco planters had run up sizable debts to British merchants. The Treaty of Paris stipulated that no legal impediments should be erected against the collection of such debts, but Virginia had closed its courts to suits for recovery. In *Ware* v. *Hilton* the Supreme Court declared Virginia's action unconstitutional. That decision did nothing to endear the Court to Virginians.[21]

The next major challenge to the authority of the general government came not from states as such but from organized bands of private citizens, and it resulted in a triumph for the administration. Even before Genet arrived, backcountrymen in Pennsylvania, Kentucky, and the Carolinas had resisted payment of the excise tax on whiskey that Congress had levied at Hamilton's request, and some in the area flirted with secession. Washington issued a stern warning to "refrain and desist from all unlawful combinations and proceedings . . . having for object or tending to obstruct the operation of the laws." That proclamation, together with patience, persuasion, and moderation in enforcement procedures, resulted in a temporary pacification of the rebellious areas.[22]

Then Genet came, and as part of his mischief he promoted the organization of radical political clubs called democratic-republican societies. Of the thirty-odd organizations known to have existed, two or three were probably subversive, pro-French conspirators. The vast majority were radical critics of the Washington administration, particularly of what they regarded as its pro-British foreign policy, yet they were loyal to the country, constituting the extreme left wing of the nascent Jefferson-Madison Republican party. But three of the societies located in the Pittsburgh area were lawless and rebellious.[23]

In July 1794 their defiance of federal law became open and rampant. Of the twelve hundred distilleries in the area, thirty-seven were delinquent in their excise taxes, and the excise inspector, accompanied by a marshal, set out to serve them with writs. A party of about forty men, many of them armed, attacked the inspector's home. Repulsed, and one of their own killed, the gang rounded up five hundred additional men and resumed the attack. By that time the inspector had brought in seventeen soldiers for defense. A rebel leader was killed, several soldiers were wounded, the other soldiers were captured, and the house was burned to the ground, though the inspector and the marshal escaped. For the next few weeks, the area teemed with impassioned meetings, inflammatory speeches, and violent acts. The local militia was incited to attack the government fort in Pittsburgh. A mob of five or six thousand men gathered to march on the town. In the meantime, armed bands tarred and feathered excise officers, destroyed the property of the distilleries that had complied with the law, and robbed the mails. State and county officials either supported the rebels or ignored what they were doing.[24]

The administration moved swiftly to suppress the uprising. The militia act of 1792 authorized the president to mobilize the militia if the laws of the United States were opposed "by combinations too powerful to be suppressed by the ordinary course of judicial proceedings," and Washington obtained certification to that effect from

Supreme Court Justice James Wilson in August. A little time was wasted in futile efforts to negotiate with the insurgents, but then a militia force of 12,950 men—half from Pennsylvania, the rest from New Jersey, Maryland, and Virginia—was called up, and to the chagrin of rebels and Republicans in general, the response to the call was enthusiastic.[25]

The venture was a success. The troops set out on September 30; Washington himself headed the force for three weeks before turning command over to Governor Henry Lee of Virginia. In the face of the government's display of will and strength, the insurrection simply vanished. Not a shot was fired, but two thousand troublemakers fled down the Ohio River to Kentucky. Several dozen people were arrested and treated badly enough so that they would remember to behave in the future. Twenty were taken to Philadelphia to be tried for treason; two were convicted, and Washington pardoned both. As a justice of the Supreme Court said, the skillful way the Whiskey Rebellion was handled constituted "a lesson to Governments and People." The democratic-republican societies, blamed for the rebellion, were discredited and abandoned.[26]

The rise and fall of the democratic-republican societies was symptomatic of a shift in the focus of American politics. Before the outbreak of the wars of the French Revolution, the nascent political parties were divided by domestic issues into nationalists and states' righters. Afterward, they were also divided into Anglophiles and Francophiles. Neither party was unwavering in its position, to be sure. Friends of the administration (who increasingly referred to themselves as Federalists) tended to favor Britain, though when the British seized a number of American vessels, they prepared for war and remained in a belligerent stance until the Jay Treaty of 1794–1795 eased the tensions between the two countries. Opponents of the administration, calling themselves Republicans, favored republican France, though most temporarily turned away from the revolution during the Reign of Terror in 1793–1794.[27]

So heated did partisan animosities become that questions arose whether the opposition was entirely a loyal opposition. The doubt was especially evident in the first contested presidential election in 1796, when the rivals were Jefferson and Adams. France, angered by the Jay Treaty and by the recent recall of the Francophile James Monroe as minister to Paris, was eager that another Francophile, Jefferson, be elected president. To that end, the French minister to the United States, Pierre Adet, spent a good deal of money to influence voters in Pennsylvania, a pivotal state, and in late October and early November he published four letters in a Philadelphia newspaper. The first was a threat: thenceforth the French navy would "treat the flag of neutrals in the same manner as they shall suffer it to be treated by the English." The second ordered French citizens in the United States to wear the revolutionary tricolor cockade—an ominous order, for a French fleet was reportedly heading to New York. The third announced the severance of diplomatic relations. The fourth was a review of Franco-American dealings, replete with praise of Jefferson's pure republican principles.[28]

When Adams was elected president and Jefferson, by virtue of a peculiar feature of the Constitution, was elected vice-president, Adams conceived a clever plan. France had refused to receive Charles Cotesworth Pinckney as the American minister replacing Monroe, and Adams proposed to send two additional commissioners to join Pinckney in Paris, one of them to be Jefferson. If Jefferson agreed, he might be able to manage an amicable settlement with France, and if the mission failed, Republicans could not blame the Adams administration. Jefferson refused, and instead Adams appointed John Marshall and Elbridge Gerry, a pro-French Republican but a personal friend.[29]

The outcome of the mission was the notorious "XYZ affair," which ignited a three-year quasi-war with France. French officials, identified in the diplomatic correspondence as W, X, Y, and Z, demanded that the American commissioners pay a bribe of $240,000 before they be allowed to see the French foreign minister, Maurice de Talleyrand. When Adams read the commission's report of the demand, he was furious. He released the correspondence to the newspapers, whereupon most of the country was swept by a frenzy for war. Congress did not declare war, but it enacted taxes to pay for a war, authorized an increased provisional army, and created the Navy Department. American and French ships engaged in sporadic combat on the high seas until 1800.[30]

Southerners in general and Virginia and North Carolina Republicans in particular were alarmed by the course of events, believing or professing to believe that the real purpose of the military preparation was to suppress them out of fear that they would join the French should war come and the United States be invaded. Hamilton, who was in active charge of raising the army as second in command to Washington, the nominal commander in chief, did not believe that a French invasion was likely. He did, however, entertain thoughts of seizing New Orleans from France's ally Spain. That undertaking would entail marching the troops through Virginia and North Carolina, subjecting the locals to the kind of show of force that had been used against the whiskey rebels. The Virginia legislature resolved to put the state on a war footing to resist and appropriated money to buy five thousand stands of arms. An influential Virginia Republican, St. George Tucker, declared that if a land war with France broke out, 100,000 Americans, himself included, would join forces with the French.[31]

Meanwhile, the legislatures in both states seriously considered seceding from the Union and forming a separate confederacy. Jefferson counseled against secession, arguing that control of the government by a coalition of New England "anti-republicans" could not last. "A little patience," he wrote to John Taylor, "and we shall see the reign of witches pass over, their spells dissolve, and the people, recovering their true sight, restore their government to it's true principles." But what Jefferson and Madison did advocate was just a step removed from secession.[32]

The occasion was the passage of the Alien and Sedition Acts, which Federalists considered part of the preparation for war. Four acts were involved. The Alien Enemies Act, authorizing the president to deport alien enemies during wartime, was never invoked because war went undeclared. The Alien Act, authorizing similar power in peacetime, was poorly drawn, and only one person was deported under it. The Naturalization Act extended the time required for citizenship from five to fourteen years; it was aimed mainly against radical Irish immigrants who had been expelled from their own country. The Sedition Act prescribed fines and imprisonment for persons who combined to prevent the enforcement of federal laws or published "false, scandalous, or malicious" statements about the government, the president, or Congress. The terms of the statute, permitting truth as a defense and requiring proof of malicious intent, were more lenient than those of the common-law offense of seditious libel that prevailed in every state. The objectionable feature, from the Republicans' point of view, was not that it limited freedom of the press but that it made seditious libel a federal offense.[33]

Jefferson's and Madison's responses to these acts, embodied in the Virginia and Kentucky Resolutions, brought the issue of states' rights back to center stage. The first Kentucky Resolutions, drafted by Jefferson and steered through the state legislature by John Breckenridge, were adopted on November 16, 1798. The resolves declared that the Constitution was a compact and that "to this compact each State acceded as a State, and is an integral party, its co-States forming, as to itself, the other party." The government created by that compact could not be "the exclusive or final judge" of its own powers. Rather, "as in all other cases of compact among parties having no common Judge, *each party has an equal right to judge for itself, as well of infractions as of the mode and measure of redress.*" Exercising that right, Kentucky declared the Alien and Sedition Acts, along with "an act to punish frauds committed on the Bank of the United States," to be unconstitutional. Quite accurately, the Kentucky Resolutions pointed out that the Constitution gave Congress power to punish treason, counterfeiting, piracies and felonies on the high seas, and offenses against the laws of nations, "and no other crimes whatever," authority over all other crimes being reserved exclusively to the states. Both the first and third resolves refer to the Tenth Amendment as the unequivocal guarantor that what is not delegated is reserved to the states. The ninth resolve assures the other states that Kentucky "considers Union for specified National purposes, and particularly for those specified in their late Federal Compact, to be friendly to the peace, happiness, and prosperity of all the States; that faithful to that compact according to the plain intent and meaning in which it was understood and acceded to by the several parties, it is sincerely anxious for its preservation." But "to take from the States all the powers of self-government, and transfer them to a general and consolidated government . . . is not for the peace, happiness, or prosperity of these States." The resolve calls upon the other states not to submit tamely "to undelegated and consequently unlimited powers" in any man or "body of men." Jealousy, and not confidence, lies at the foundation of free government, and this jealousy "prescribes limited Constitutions to bind down those whom we are obliged to trust with power."[34]

The Virginia Resolutions, drafted by Madison and introduced into the state legislature by John Taylor, were adopted on December 24, 1798. Abandoning the original understanding as he had formulated it in *The Federalist*—that the Constitution was a compact among the peoples of several states in their capacities as peoples of the states— Madison embraced Jefferson's doctrine that it was "a compact to which the states are parties." Moreover, in the third resolve, he went further than Jefferson had and proclaimed the doctrine of interposition: that the state governments "have the right and are in duty bound to interpose for arresting the progress of the evil" of the federal government's exceeding its constitutional powers, and "for maintaining within their respective limits the authorities, rights, and liberties appertaining to them."[35]

Madison was not advocating interposition as a response to every perceived encroachment by the central government, though the Virginia Resolutions did warn of "a design" ultimately "to consolidate the states, by degrees, into one sovereignty," which would transform the nation from a republic "into an absolute, or, at best, a mixed monarchy." Whether Madison meant that the immediate threat was sufficient to merit interposition is unclear. In 1830 he wrote that the Virginia Resolutions merely considered "measures known to the Constitution." Indeed, during the debate in the legislature, John Taylor discussed article 5 and the amending process, congressional repeal in response to states' reactions, and judicial remedies. In the final analysis, however, as Taylor framed it, the states had "a right to withstand such unconstitutional laws of Congress as may tend to their destruction, because 'such a power is necessary for their preservation.' "[36]

Both sets of resolutions were sent to the other states in an effort to elicit support, but no support was forthcoming, for the Alien and Sedition Acts were highly popular. Indeed, every state from Maryland north roundly condemned the resolutions. Rhode Island, which had long refused to ratify the Constitution, denounced the doctrine of interposition as fraught with "evil and fatal consequences" and insisted that the Constitution "vests in the Federal Courts, exclusively, and in the Supreme Court of the United States, ultimately, the authority of deciding on the constitutionality" of acts of Congress. New Hampshire took the same position and added as an opinion "for mere speculative purposes" that the acts were constitutional and, "in the present critical situation of our country, highly expedient."[37]

Kentucky responded to the response, reaffirming its original position and going further by pronouncing the doctrine of nullification: a state, determining that an act of Congress was unconstitutional, could lawfully declare the act null and void within its jurisdiction. The following month Madison delivered a special committee report to the Virginia legislature. The hostile reactions of the other states prompted this lengthy reconsideration. The committee especially scrutinized the third resolve and pronounced it "unexceptionally true" and both "constitutional and conclusive in its inferences." The Virginia and Kentucky Resolutions, Madison's 1799 report, and the oratory that accompanied them became known as the Principles of Ninety-eight and would for decades be regarded as almost sacred to the adherents of the states' rights faith.[38]

In 1798 it did not appear likely that the reign of the witches would pass. Congressmen who voted for the Alien and Sedition Acts and ran again in that year's congressional elections were returned to their seats, almost to a man, and most of those who opposed the measures either declined to run for reelection or were unseated. The Federalist majority in the House was increased from ten to twenty-two.[39]

Nevertheless, the Republicans began working to capture control of the government in 1800, directing their greatest efforts toward the state legislatures, which would do the deciding. The legislatures would choose the senators and almost two-thirds of the presidential electors. Seven state legislatures had chosen the electors in 1796, and between then and 1800, four states shifted from popular election to legislative election of the electors. Thus in the contest between the states' rights candidate Jefferson and the nationalist Adams, the decision would be made by the states themselves.[40]

The votes of most states were predictable. Adams was certain to carry New England's thirty-five electoral votes and twelve scattered elsewhere. Jefferson was sure to receive the votes from the South and West, a total of forty-five in all. That meant that Adams needed to pick up twenty-three from among the middle states and South Carolina, and that Jefferson needed twenty-five from those places. The pivotal states were Pennsylvania, South Carolina, and New York, in each of which electors were chosen by the legislatures. The contest in Pennsylvania was furious and indecisive. Federalists controlled one house of the legislature, Republicans the other, and for a time it appeared that the state would choose no electors. After a bitter struggle, the legislators reached a compromise: they selected eight Republican electors and seven Federalists, giving the state a net vote of one. That was a gain for Adams over 1796, when Jefferson had received all Pennsylvania's electoral votes.[41]

In the other swing states, the machinations of Aaron Burr, the Republicans' vice-presidential candidate, were decisive. The Federalists' vice-presidential candidate was Charles Cotesworth Pinckney, a native of South Carolina, so it appeared that Jefferson and Pinckney would carry the state. But Burr secretly married his daughter Theodosia to Joseph Allston, a leading member of a rich and well-connected South Carolina family, thus ensuring that electors would cast one of their two ballots for Burr. The other ballot could have gone either to Jefferson or to Pinckney. In the event, Jefferson was the man.[42]

In New York, Burr manipulated brilliantly. Party strength outside New York City was evenly divided, and in the 1799 elections Federalists had swept the city and gained control of the legislature. After Federalists had announced their slate for the 1800 legislative elections—an appropriately undistinguished list, considering the relative insignificance of the offices being sought—Burr induced a roster of big-name candidates, including ex-governor George Clinton, General Horatio Gates, and Judge Brockholst Livingston, to allow their names to be put forward as candidates, even though none seriously intended to serve. Burr's candidates won easily, giving Republicans control of the legislature for purposes of choosing presidential electors.[43]

But there was a snag: Jefferson and Burr both got majorities, but they tied at seventy-three votes. In accordance with the procedures set forth in the constitution, the election was decided in the House of Representatives. The lame-duck session of the Sixth Congress, whose term expired on March 4, 1801, had been elected during the XYZ fever of 1798, and in it, Federalists had a clear majority. But the Constitution specified that in deciding a presidential electoral tie, each state's delegation would have one vote. As it happened, the congressional delegations of eight states were predominantly Republican, those of six states were predominantly Federalist, and those of two states were equally divided. The Federalists determined to support Burr, and thus neither Jefferson nor Burr could gain a majority.[44]

A deadlock ensued. After twenty or thirty ballots split eight to six to two, it began to appear possible that no choice would be made by the end of the session, which raised a terrible spectre. Under the presidential succession statute then current, if the offices of president and vice-president became vacant, the presidency would devolve upon the chief justice—John Marshall. Jeffersonians warned that if that happened, they would seize control of the government by force. Finally, two Federalist delegations were induced to change their votes, Jefferson was elected, and the constitutional crisis was averted.[45]

At his inauguration, Jefferson delivered an address that was the epitome of moderation and conciliation. "We have called by different names," he said, "brethren of the same principle. We are all Republicans, we are all Federalists." He went on to summarize the basic tenets of American government and of a regime of liberty.

Along the way he pronounced a pivotal sentiment; among the "essential principles of our Government," he declared, was that of "the support of the State governments in all their rights, as the most competent administrations for our domestic concerns and the surest bulwarks against antirepublican tendencies."[46]

Every champion of states' rights could cherish the thought. Whether Jefferson would abide by it while holding the reins of the central authority himself remained to be seen.

3

THE JEFFERSONIANS

Though appeals to the doctrine of states' rights had, before 1800, emanated largely from the South, the localist sentiment that underlay it was widespread and deep. Programmed into the human soul is a preference for the near and familiar and a suspicion of the remote and abstract. Cultural and physical circumstances reinforced that preference in the United States. Americans were scattered in clusters of farms and villages extending over a vast area, and though they shared a common English legal heritage, with variations from state to state, they were separated by differing social norms and economic interests. New England Yankees distrusted and were ill at ease among southern plantation gentry, and the feelings were reciprocated; neither group was comfortable amidst the commercial hustle and bustle of New York and Philadelphia. Too, each state had a tradition of resistance to the authority of outsiders. Against these long-standing centrifugal forces, loyalty to the United States was relatively new and feeble. Moreover, few Americans were affected by the doings of the general government. Matters of property relations, family concerns, religion, justice, law, and order fell in the domain of state and local governments.

Indeed, the habit of faithfulness to the Constitution itself, in either a states' rights or a nationalist reading, was not yet well established, though public figures in both camps were wont to posture as the Constitution's true defenders. After another generation, when the Founders had passed into myth and legend, reverence toward the Constitution would become a veritable secular religion in America, and states' rights would be among its central dogmas. But in the meantime, the striking of constitutional stances would remain as much a function of tactics as of genuine conviction. The rule of thumb seemed to be, when one's rivals or enemies were in control of the central government, one was prone to savor states' rights, but when one's own faction was in control, the doctrine lost its zest.

This is not to suggest that the radical Republicans cynically abandoned the Principles of Ninety-eight when their party took power in 1801. They strove mightily to strip down the machinery that Hamilton and the Federalists had put in place, and to some extent they succeeded. But when the nation was swept into the maelstrom of international affairs, Republicans came by degrees to exert national authority on a scale that dwarfed the measures employed earlier by the Federalists. At that point, erstwhile Federalists embraced states' rights positions as ardently as the Republican opposition had ever done.

For a band of revolutionaries whose rhetoric in opposition had gone beyond the hyperbolic almost to the hysterical, the Jeffersonian Republicans were moderate, even cautious, as they set out to return the Constitution to its pristine moorings—according to their interpretation, meaning strict construction and states' rights. Hamilton had predicted as much when urging Federalists to support Jefferson instead of Burr. It was true, Hamilton wrote, that Jefferson had cast his lot with those who sought to reduce "the administration of this government to the *principles* of the old confederation," but unlike Burr, who would dare everything to satisfy his lust for power, Jefferson was not "zealot enough to do anything in pursuance of his principles which will contravene his popularity, or his interest." He was inclined "to temporize—to calculate what will be likely to promote his own reputation and advantage"; the probable result would be that Federalist arrangements, though Jefferson had staunchly opposed them, "being once established, could not be overturned without danger to the person who did it."[1]

Illustrative of the Jefferson administration's tendency to "temporize" was its handling of the Alien and Sedition Acts. Some Republicans wanted an all-out attack on the measures, especially the Sedition Act—not because they objected to prosecutions for seditious libel, but because to them (as to Jefferson himself), federalizing the crime struck at the heart of states' rights doctrine. These enthusiasts wanted a vehement denunciation of the constitutionality of the acts, if indeed not an endorsement of the Virginia and Kentucky Resolutions. No action was forthcoming. Instead, the acts were simply allowed to expire. Jefferson quietly pardoned the ten printers who had been convicted under the Sedition Act, and Congress quietly restored the fines they had been assessed.[2]

Jefferson's proclivity for temporizing was especially evident in the case of one of the convicted libelers, James T. Callender. That notorious scandalmonger had been hired by Jefferson to attack various Federalists and had been fined $200 and sentenced to nine months in prison for his efforts. When the restoration of his fine met with a three-month delay, he approached Jefferson in the White House, demanding what amounted to blackmail in the form of cash and the postmastership of Richmond. Though embarrassed, Jefferson discussed the matter with him cordially, gave him $50, and hoped he would go away. He did not. He wrote unmerciful newspaper attacks on the president for the next two years, making charges that smeared Jefferson's reputation indelibly.[3]

Jefferson pursued a similarly timid course regarding appointments and removals. Federalists feared that his accession to the presidency would be followed by wholesale purges of officeholders, and while the Burr-Jefferson contest was pending, some of them— notably Representative James Bayard of Delaware—negotiated with Jefferson's supporters to obtain an informal agreement that no major housecleaning would take place. Meanwhile, Republicans in places from Pennsylvania to New England were clamoring for rewards for their services in electing Jefferson, and Jefferson was disposed to accommodate them. But when, early in his presidency, he arbitrarily removed the collector of the port of New Haven and replaced him with a party faithful, merchants in New Haven drew up a powerful remonstrance, demanding that Jefferson adhere to the conciliatory policy enunciated in his inaugural address. Secretary of the Treasury

Albert Gallatin, disturbed by the remonstrance, drafted a treasury circular that would stop the removal of inferior officers but forbid them to participate in political activity. Jefferson refused to approve the circular, but he determined to tread softly in ordering removals.[4]

The policy he adopted was to use the patronage to cement his strength in New England, reward a few special supporters, and punish adherents of Burr, but otherwise to base appointments strictly on merit. He determined to fire those who were patently guilty of corruption or who, in his view, were irreconcilable monarchists, which is to say devout Hamiltonians. Federal employees he regarded as honest and loyal to "ancient whig principles" would be kept in office unless the officers themselves were detrimental to the public interest. All told, the turnover in federal jobholders during his first two years was about one-third, and about half during his whole first term.[5]

The Jeffersonians were expeditious in their efforts to undo another legacy of the Federalists, the nation's armed forces. Early in 1802, an act was passed to provide for an emasculated peacetime military establishment. The army was fixed at three regiments, two infantry and one artillery, totaling 3,350 men under the command of a brigadier general; supernumerary soldiers were discharged. That token force was far from adequate to defend the frontiers against Indian attacks, let alone defend the country against foreign invaders, but the Republicans' attitude was adamant. They embraced a hoary dogma that standing armies were the greatest possible threat to liberty, and they equally embraced the supposition—belied by history—that state militias would normally constitute an adequate defense against Indians and European professional armies. In his inaugural address, Jefferson had declared "a well-disciplined militia" to be "our best reliance in peace and for the first moments of war till regulars may relieve them," and he proposed that Congress reorganize the militia system to infuse it with discipline. Congress declined to do so, but it did follow his lead and establish the Army Corps of Engineers and a military academy at West Point. The emphasis at the academy was upon engineering, not soldiering, the result being that the nation had neither a well-disciplined militia nor well-trained regulars. Jefferson and his main advisors, Gallatin and Secretary of State James Madison, agreed that the risks to national security were worth taking in light of the savings to be effected by slashing the army.[6]

The administration intended to cut the navy even more drastically, for it was expensive to maintain. By the eve of Jefferson's inaugural, the Federalist-dominated Congress had already voted to dispose of the smaller craft that had been acquired since the creation of the Navy Department, to keep six of the thirteen frigates in active service, and to reduce appropriations to $3 million annually. The Jefferson administration laid up the remaining frigates, suspended construction and everything but minimal maintenance, and cut the appropriation to $1 million. Objecting to navies on the theory that they increased the likelihood of war, Jefferson and Gallatin proposed to scrap the seagoing vessels and defend the nation's harbors with the maritime equivalent of militias, which is to say gunboats.[7]

Reality rudely disrupted these plans. The rulers of the Barbary Coast principalities of North Africa had, from time immemorial, collected tributes from the European maritime states, bribes to refrain from committing piratical acts. The United States had been paying tribute for the better part of a decade. Then in 1801 the pasha of Tripoli learned that the United States was paying more to Algiers and Morocco than to Tripoli, and he declared war in the traditional local way by cutting down the American flag. Outraged by the gesture and opposed to paying tribute to anyone, Jefferson responded by sending a four-vessel fleet, nominally to protect American shipping, but actually to rid the Mediterranean of what he regarded as scum. American naval vessels remained in the area, off and on, for four years, and they accomplished their mission.[8]

The necessity for a navy, however, hampered the administration's efforts to achieve its cherished goal of dismantling the Hamiltonian fiscal system. Gallatin was burdened by other handicaps as well. His party was totally committed to cutting taxes, even if reducing the public debt had to be accorded a lower priority. Congress repealed almost all the internal taxes—excise, carriage, and direct property taxes— that Federalists had enacted during the quasi-war with France, leaving in place those on liquor. As a result, approximately 90 percent of federal revenues came from an external source, customs duties on imports. Gallatin's efforts were further impeded by two features that had been built into Hamilton's original funding plan: that certain certificates of the public debt bore no interest for ten years but bore 6 percent thereafter, meaning that the annual interest cost increased significantly just when Gallatin took office, and that the principal of the main debt could not legally be retired in large increments.[9]

Nevertheless, Gallatin introduced stringent spending controls, and he was blessed with swollen revenues from a tremendous boom in international trade. Consequently, he was able, during Jefferson's two terms in office, to reduce the public debt from around $80 million to $57 million and to accumulate a treasury surplus of $14 million, despite the unanticipated expenditure for the purchase of the Louisiana Territory. Had not war intervened, the debt could have been extinguished in another decade. Indeed, by 1808, Gallatin was contemplating financing a system of internal transportation projects once the expected surplus appeared, and Jefferson proposed a constitutional amendment to authorize the expenditures.[10]

The other centerpiece of the Hamiltonian system, the Bank of the United States, was still in place when Jefferson left office, having been chartered for twenty years in 1791. Gallatin had long since concluded that Hamilton had been right in holding that the Bank was "necessary" under the meaning of the necessary and proper clause of the Constitution, despite his earlier argument to the contrary, and so had Madison. But the Republican old guard was as opposed to the Bank as ever, and party men were supported by businessmen, especially in New York, who resented the financial power the Bank gave to Philadelphia. Accordingly, when the Bank's charter expired in 1811, a bill to recharter failed. The vote in the Senate was a tie, broken by the former New York anti-Federalist governor and now vice-president, George Clinton. The Hamiltonian system was at last defunct, but the United States would soon pay for that triumph of states' rights.[11]

The most formidable bastion of national authority against states' rights onslaughts was the judiciary, and Republican discontent with it had been mounting steadily. As indicated, the federal courts had opened their doors to suits by British creditors of Virginia tobacco planters and had asserted jurisdiction to try persons indicted at common law, which Republicans insisted was an unwarranted extension of federal authority. And in enforcing the Sedition Act, as well as in the treason trial of Jacob Fries, a Pennsylvanian who led an abortive revolt against the collection of the 1798 direct property tax, federal judges (especially Justice Samuel Chase) had outraged Republicans by the harshness and possible illegalities of their proceedings. Then, on the eve of the Republicans' accession to power, the outgoing Federalist Congress and president delivered what Republicans regarded as a calculated slap.[12]

They enacted, on February 27, 1801, a revision of the Judiciary Act of 1789. The law, though passed at the last moment, had actually been pending since its proposal by President Adams in December 1799, and it introduced much-desired reform. The Supreme Court justices needed relief from the onerous chore of traveling long distances over poor roads to double as circuit court judges. The act created sixteen circuit courts and established separate judgeships for each; it added to the number of marshals, attorneys, and clerks; it established a number of justices of the peace in the District of Columbia; and it extended the jurisdiction of the courts to land claims arising under grants from different states. To Republicans, the act was a bald usurpation of power. Said Jefferson, "the Federalists have retired into the Judiciary as a stronghold . . . and from that battery all the works of republicanism are to be beaten down and erased."[13]

Compounding the Republicans' antagonism at the passage of the 1801 act was Adams's appointment of as many men as possible to fill the newly created positions. Jefferson regarded the appointments made after December, when the result of the 1800 presidential election was known, as immoral and illegal, and he was determined to do whatever was necessary to unseat the "midnight judges." (Actually, the last commission was signed not at midnight but at nine o'clock on the evening of March 3, 1801, three hours before Adams's term ended.) One "midnight" judge had been appointed in January:

Secretary of State John Marshall succeeded Chief Justice Oliver Ellsworth. Marshall's appointment, though not greeted with enthusiasm by Federalists, was galling to Jefferson, who despised his distant cousin. The president was doubly galled by a feature of the 1801 act providing that when the next vacancy occurred on the Court, the seat would remain vacant, meaning that Jefferson could not fill it.[14]

Two courses suggested themselves to the president and his party, both of questionable constitutionality. The lesser course was to refuse to deliver commissions to the appointees who had not yet received them, even though they had been confirmed. That action would lead, in time, to a celebrated Supreme Court case, but it was relatively unimportant at the moment. The other course was a frontal attack on the Judiciary Act of 1801—its repeal. The Republicans had enough votes for a repeal; they had won a huge majority in the House and what appeared to be an adequate majority in the Senate, but to effect repeal, they had to swallow their strict-construction scruples. Article 3, section 1, of the Constitution expressly mandated that judges, "both of the supreme and inferior Courts, shall hold their Offices during good Behaviour." Repealing the 1801 act would abolish the sixteen new circuit judgeships and thus remove the sixteen judges without regard to their "good Behaviour." Thus, after the Seventh Congress, elected in 1800, convened for its first session in December 1801, a fight concerning repeal would clearly take place, but the outcome was uncertain.[15]

After a gentle nudge from the president in his first annual message, the Senate considered the issue, whereupon both parties struck unaccustomed stances. Federalists, heretofore champions of loose construction, insisted on a strict adherence to the letter of the Constitution. Gouverneur Morris, a highflier who had long stood for elasticity of interpretation and whose oratory, as Henry Adams put it, "was apt to verge on the domain of melodrama, exceeded himself in lamentations over the grave of the Constitution." Republicans countered that no constitutional issue was involved; citing figures supplied by the president purporting to describe the volume of court business, they insisted that the judgeships were unwarranted by the caseload and therefore could not have been constitutionally established in the first place. In the middle stood (or, more properly, sat) Vice-President Aaron Burr, determined to cause mischief for the Jeffersonians. At one point the vote on the bill was a tie, and Burr cast the deciding vote against it. After being referred back to committee, the bill returned to the full Senate, where it passed by a narrow margin. In the House, Representative William Branch Giles of Virginia, hitherto the most radical of strict constructionists, led the debate for loose construction, somehow making repeal into advocacy of states' rights. The House vote to repeal was overwhelming.[16]

Apparently, however, the Republicans feared that they were on shaky ground, judging by what they did next. In April they enacted a judiciary act, returning to six the number of Supreme Court justices, reestablishing six circuit courts over each of which a Supreme Court justice would preside, and otherwise restoring the 1789 act, including its jurisdictional features. A striking feature of the act was that it abolished the June and December terms of the meeting of the Court that had been provided under the 1801 act and revived the old February term, beginning in 1803, but not the old August term. Inasmuch as the court had sat in December 1801, the result was that it would not sit again for fourteen months. The generally perceived motive for that action was concern that if the Court met sooner it might declare the repeal act unconstitutional. The administration desired to delay such a decision until it had solidified its political strength.[17]

The Supreme Court did not tackle the issue of the constitutionality of the repeal act, but in *Stuart v. Laird* it upheld the 1802 Judiciary Act insofar as it reinstated the circuit-riding feature. It did, however, take on the administration in a tangentially related case. One of the four midnight justice-of-the-peace commissions that had been held up was to have gone to a small-time political operative named William Marbury. On behalf of Marbury and the other three, a petition was filed in the Supreme Court in December 1801 for a writ of mandamus ordering Madison, as secretary of state, to deliver the commissions. The Court granted a preliminary order requiring Madison to show cause why the writ should not be issued and set the fourth day of the next term for arguing the merits of the question. The cancellation of the Court's 1802 terms meant that arguments would not be heard until February 1803; indeed, the preliminary order was another reason for the postponement of the Court's next session.[18]

The decision was unusual, and it was momentous. Ordinarily a court's first question is whether it has jurisdiction, and then if it answers in the affirmative, it considers the merits of a case and the remedies for any wrongs it finds. Chief Justice Marshall, in writing the opinion for the Court, reversed the order. First he asked whether the petitioner had a right to the commission, to which his answer was yes. Next he asked whether the laws afforded a remedy, to which he again answered yes, a writ of mandamus against the secretary of state. Then he asked whether the Supreme Court had the authority to issue the writ in the present case, and the answer was no. The reason for the negative was that section 13 of the Judiciary Act of 1789, which gave the Supreme Court original jurisdiction in such cases, was unconstitutional.[19]

The reasoning that Marshall employed in reaching that decision was portentous. Article 3 of the Constitution lists the kinds of cases to which the judicial power of the United States extends. It says, "In all cases affecting Ambassadors, other public Ministers and Consuls, and those in which a State shall be Party, the supreme Court shall have original Jurisdiction. In all the other Cases before mentioned, the supreme Court shall have appellate Jurisdiction . . . with such Exceptions, and under such Regulations as the Congress shall make." The exceptions clause was ambiguous, being unclear whether it meant that Congress could change appellate jurisdiction into original jurisdiction or that Congress could deprive the Supreme Court of appellate jurisdiction. Marshall, ruling that Congress could not change appellate jurisdiction to original, implicitly endorsed the latter view.[20]

In the short range, the decision in *Marbury* v. *Madison* seriously imperiled the whole federal judiciary, for the Jeffersonians were outraged at Marshall's audacity and were determined to bring the courts under political control. Actually, the decision was not so bold as it seemed. Marshall was careful not to claim that the Supreme Court was the sole or final arbiter of acts of Congress, and besides, the case was exclusively concerned with the judicial branch itself, and a precedent existed for the Court's refusal to do the bidding of Congress in regard to the judiciary. But the fact remains that Marshall had maintained, albeit in obiter dicta, that the courts could order a member of the executive branch to do his duty, and the Republicans would have none of that.[21]

The weapon they chose to employ against the judiciary was impeachment. Shortly before the decision in the *Marbury* case was handed down, Jefferson sent Congress a message reporting complaints about federal district judge John Pickering of New Hampshire, whose outlandish behavior on the bench was due to chronic drunkenness and insanity. He had committed no high crimes and misdemeanors, the constitutionally stipulated causes for removal by impeachment and conviction, but on March 3, 1803, the House voted to impeach him. A year later, the Senate voted by the constitutional two-thirds majority to convict him and remove him from office.[22]

The Pickering impeachment was merely a rehearsal: the Republicans planned a grander show. On the same day that Pickering was convicted, Virginia congressman John Randolph of Roanoke moved articles of impeachment against Justice Samuel Chase. The immediate occasion for the selection of Chase as the target was a virulent charge he had made to a grand jury in Baltimore, wherein he prophesied the imminent doom of the constitutional order and laid the blame on the doctrine "that all men in a state of society are entitled to enjoy equal liberty and equal rights." That seemed a direct affront to Jefferson as the author of the Declaration of Independence, and the president himself suggested the impeachment. But deeper considerations underlay Chase's impeachment. He was politically the most vulnerable of the justices, and if he were successfully tried on political as opposed to constitutional grounds, that would open the way for clearing the entire bench.[23]

Again, partisans reversed their earlier positions. Federalists insisted that an independent judiciary was the cornerstone of the constitutional system (having previously mixed the judicial and executive functions on numerous occasions) and adhered to the literal meaning of the "high crimes and misdemeanors" clause. Giles, arguing for the Republicans, maintained that high crimes and misdemeanors were merely some of the reasons for removal and that the Senate could remove any official for any reason, at its sole discretion. As John Quincy Adams recorded his speech, Giles said that "a removal by impeachment was nothing more than a declaration by Congress to this effect: you hold dangerous opinions, and if you are suffered to carry them into effect, you will work the destruction of the Union. We want your offices for the purpose of giving them to men who will fill them better."[24]

By a supreme irony, the man who presided over the impeachment trial was the outgoing Vice-President Aaron Burr, lame duck and discredited, a fugitive from justice in New York and New Jersey for the killing of Alexander Hamilton. Jefferson, assuming that Burr was as corrupt as everyone supposed, sought in effect to bribe him into making sure the trial was political in nature, the sop being the patronage in the Louisiana Territory. Inasmuch as the plum was offered as if it had been earned—Jefferson would not have openly demanded a quid pro quo—Burr accepted it in that spirit and went on to obey his instincts. His instincts, as it turned out, dictated decorum and propriety. He had the Senate chamber decorated in velvet, obviously imitating the House of Lords when hearing impeachments, and he presided with sober austerity. That doomed the prosecution, and Chase was acquitted.[25]

Marshall and the other justices, who had been convinced that their removals were sure to follow Chase's, were relieved: the independence of the judiciary was assured. To be sure, the justices tacitly resolved to be circumspect in future, and another half century would pass before the Supreme Court saw fit to declare a second act of Congress unconstitutional. But the Court would serve as a barrier to what it perceived as transgressions by the states. In that sense, Chase's acquittal was a victory for the Constitution and, insofar as the two were in conflict, a defeat for states' rights.

The shifts of constitutional positions manifested in the confrontation between the political and judicial branches were powerfully intensified by the intrusion of foreign affairs into domestic concerns.

Early in 1802, when news of Spain's retrocession of Louisiana to France became officially known in America, the reactions of Federalists and Republicans were remarkably similar. Federalists called for assembling an army and dispatching it, with joint American and British naval cover, to seize the island on which New Orleans was located and perhaps negotiate with Napoleon for formal acquisition. Jefferson said, "there is on the globe one single spot, the possessor of which is our natural and habitual enemy. It is New Orleans." He added that if France moved to occupy the place, "From that moment we must marry ourselves to the British fleet and nation." Then, however, through misinformation, Jefferson became convinced that Napoleon would be willing to sell New Orleans and West Florida. He obtained a secret appropriation from Congress to effect the purchase, and he sent James Monroe to join Robert R. Livingston, the American minister to Paris, to consummate the deal. As a result of flukish developments, Napoleon decided to offer the entire territory to the United States for $15 million. Monroe and Livingston snapped at the opportunity. They made, as Talleyrand put it, a "noble bargain," but they also opened several cans of worms.[26]

Jefferson had doubts about the constitutionality of the acquisition. Earlier, when thinking of buying just New Orleans, he had expressed misgivings about acquiring territory, since that power was not granted in the Constitution, but his cabinet members had more or less convinced him that the power inhered in nationhood—a doctrine of inherent powers that Hamiltonian Federalists had advanced and Republicans had denounced. When Jefferson learned of the magnitude of the purchase, his doubts returned. He reluctantly accepted the idea that the government had the authority to acquire territory but thought that a constitutional amendment would be necessary to incorporate the domain into the Union, and he drafted an amendment to that end. Waiting for an amendment to pass, however, could prevent the completion of the purchase. Finally, Jefferson's doubts were overcome by the arguments of the revolutionary pamphleteer Thomas Paine. "The cession makes no alteration in the Constitution," Paine wrote him, "it only extends the principles of it over a larger territory, and this certainly is within the morality of the Constitution."[27]

Precisely that prospect, extending the Constitution over a larger territory, set off opposition in the Northeast. High Federalists from New England, led by Uriah Tracy and Roger Griswold of Connecticut and Timothy Pickering of Massachusetts, did not question the authority to acquire territory, defending it as an inherent power and maintaining that the area could be governed by the United States as if it had been a conquered nation. But they insisted that it could not be incorporated into the Union; since the Union was a compact among the states, to absorb the territory would be to alter the nature of the compact. The constitutional provision for admitting states contemplated areas that were already parts of states or the public domain—western Georgia, North Carolina, Virginia, and the Northwest Territory. Pickering argued that incorporation of the Louisiana Territory could not be accomplished even by a constitutional amendment: every state would have to approve. The "witches" whose reign Jefferson had predicted would pass had become outspoken champions of the Principles of Ninety-eight.[28]

Underlying the embrace of radical states' rights doctrine was concern about power. States carved from the Louisiana Territory would be southern and western, sharing interests and prejudices with the seaboard South and isolating New York and New England. Moreover, they would almost certainly be slave states, and because of the three-fifths rule (a slave counted as three-fifths of a person for purposes of direct taxes and representation), incorporation of the territory would give the South disproportionately greater power. Already, New York and New England had about sixty thousand more free inhabitants than did the entire slaveholding South, yet the South had thirteen more seats in the House of Representatives and twenty-one more electoral votes. If the Louisiana Territory were incorporated and opened to slaves, the imbalance would increase.[29]

In a desperate attempt to prevent that, New Englanders went beyond espousing the states' rights theory of the Union. The Massachusetts legislature proposed an amendment abolishing the three-fifths clause, and though it received little support elsewhere, it betokened sectional strains in the future. In Congress, Federalists attempted to prevent slavery in the Louisiana Territory. That effort, too, failed, but because of divisiveness among Republicans, slavery in the area was limited; no slaves were allowed to be taken there if they had been imported from abroad since 1798, and none could be taken except by bona fide owners who went as actual settlers.[30]

Fearing the perpetuation of rule of the "slaveocracy," extreme Federalists began to talk of secession. Senator William Plumer of New Hampshire declared that the eastern states would be compelled "to establish a separate and independent empire." Christopher Gore of Massachusetts despaired of the existing Union, being concerned that western and southern Republicans would "leave the Eastern States to perish . . . in poverty and disgrace." Timothy Pickering wrote, "I will rather anticipate a new confederacy, exempt from the corrupt and corrupting influence and oppression of the aristocratic Democrats of the South." Newspapers in New England brimmed with secession sentiments.[31]

In January 1804 a small group convened in Washington to devise a plan of secession. The group was led by Pickering and included Plumer, Tracy, Griswold, and James Hillhouse. Responsible Federalist leaders—the likes of Rufus King of New York and George Cabot of Massachusetts—were disturbed by the talk of secession, and they were genuinely appalled when Pickering revealed the next phase of his scheme. Believing that a New England union would not be able to survive on its own, Pickering decided that it would need New York to join it, and to that end he sought out Aaron Burr, asking the departing vice-president to run for governor of New York and presumably thereafter become president of the United States of New England. How much the ever-slippery Burr promised the conspirators is uncertain, but he did run for the governorship, and he reportedly said, "The Northern States must be governed by Virginia or must govern Virginia, and there is no middle ground."[32]

In all likelihood, the conspiracy would have failed even if Burr had been elected; popular support was limited. But regular Federalists in New York dared not take the chance. They worked almost frenziedly against Burr, and he was defeated by about seven thousand votes of a total of fifty thousand cast. The Yankees' first venture into extreme states' rights politics was stillborn.

Partisan and sectional animosities seemed to disappear for more than three years. Jefferson was triumphantly reelected, drawing 162 of the 176 electoral votes and carrying every state except Connecticut and Delaware. In 1807, Republicans gained control of the governorship and both houses of the legislature of Massachusetts, and John Quincy Adams became a Republican. American relations with both Britain and France were repeatedly strained, and revelation of Burr's alleged treason disturbed the national tranquility, but disquiet merely kindled something like a spark of unity.[33]

Harmony gave way to dissonance during the winter of 1807–1808. American shipping was squeezed between Napoleonic decrees and British policies, and by "keeping at home our vessels, cargoes & seamen," as Jefferson wrote, the embargo act of December was designed to save the United States "the necessity of making their capture the cause of immediate war." A loophole in the legislation appeared right away. The first act prohibited shipping to foreign ports, but vessels engaged in the coasting trade could divert to Europe or the West Indies after clearing their home ports. In January 1808, a second embargo act was passed to prevent such trade, and harsh penalties were prescribed for violations. By March, when a third act was passed, the aim of the legislation had changed from prohibiting shipping to prohibiting the export of goods by land or sea. The policy goal was an experiment in peaceful coercion: to force the warring powers of Europe, by depriving them of American foodstuffs and raw materials, to stop their fighting and abandon their ruinous trade restrictions. The idea was far-fetched, and if it was to have a chance of success, enforcement would have to be absolute. Accordingly, the punishments provided by the act were drastic: fines of $10,000 and forfeiture of the goods were to be levied, merchants who violated the law were forever debarred from credit on their customs duties, and captains who did so lost their ability to testify before a customs officer. The president was given broad discretionary power in enforcing or granting exemptions to the embargo.[34]

For a short time the embargo met with little resistance, partly because it was initially popular and partly because the northern ports were frozen and shipping was impossible anyway. But with the spring thaws came violations that were frequent and flagrant. Shippers left without papers, in the expectation that the British would not demand them, and a brisk trade from upstate New York to Canada began. Militias refused to cooperate in suppressing illegal trade by land, and juries refused to indict or convict shippers and owners who were apprehended by customs officers. Collectors themselves shut their eyes to violations.[35]

In the face of that resistance—and stung by Federalist charges that the embargo policy had been dictated by Napoleon—Jefferson became obsessed with enforcing the policy. On April 19 he declared northern New York to be in a state of insurrection and ordered state and federal officials and "all other persons, civil and military, who shall be found within the vicinage" to suppress the alleged rebellion "by all means in their power, by force of arms or otherwise." Six days later he signed into law an act empowering collectors to seize ships and cargoes without a warrant or the prospect of a trial, upon the formulation of a suspicion that a merchant or shipper contemplated violating the embargo. Throughout the summer and fall, the army and the navy were routinely employed not to protect American citizens but to prevent them from engaging in trade that was necessary, inasmuch as most cities had to import provisions through coasting vessels. By year's end, Gallatin, on whose shoulders direct responsibility for enforcement was placed, was telling the president that collectors must be "invested with the general power of seizing property anywhere" and of disabling any and all ships, even though "such arbitrary powers are equally dangerous and odious." Still more stringent enforcement legislation was the result.[36]

Truly, as Henry Adams put it, after this experience, if Jefferson "or his party again raised the cry of States-rights, or of strict construction, the public might, with some foundation of reason, set such complaints aside as factious and frivolous, and even . . . as treasonable."[37]

Meanwhile, opponents of the embargo were raising the cry of states' rights with a vengeance. Die-hard Federalists again talked of secession, though they received little support. Other northerners adopted the language of nullification and interposition. John Quincy Adams, who had lost his seat in the Senate for supporting the embargo, wrote that state judges and juries were actively preventing enforcement. Representative Barent Gardenier of New York explicitly endorsed the doctrines of the Virginia and Kentucky Resolutions. "Why should not Massachusetts take the same stand, when she thinks herself about to be destroyed?" Gardenier asked. Representative Samuel W. Dana of Connecticut, though disclaiming secession, asked, "If any State Legislature had believed the Act to be unconstitutional, would it not have been their duty not to comply?" He went on to say that the state legislatures, "whose members are sworn to support the Constitution, may refuse assistance, aid or cooperation" if they regarded an act as unconstitutional, and so could state officials. Unconvincingly, southerners retorted that though "there can be no doubt that the States who are parties to the compact can interpose," Virginia and Kentucky never claimed that they could "resist the law."[38]

The Republican *Richmond Enquirer* noted the irony. In headlines it proclaimed, "Things turned Topsy Turvy—Federalists turned Anti-Federalists—The Friends of Order turned Jacobin." Solemnly, it declared that "if these doctrines go into effect, the chain that binds together these States will soon be dissolved. If it be at any time within the power of a State to evade the force of the General Government . . . the Union of the States will be like a rope of sand." The *Enquirer* failed to point out that its position, too, had been turned topsy-turvy.[39]

Even as opposition to the embargo was reaching its climax, an unrelated clash between Pennsylvania and the federal government was leading toward armed conflict. At issue was a dispute about a Revolutionary War prize between the state and a sea captain named Olmstead. A prize court established by the Confederation Congress had ruled in favor of Olmstead, but the state refused to recognize its authority and had deposited the proceeds of the sale of the vessel with the state treasurer. The case lay dormant for years, but in 1803, Olmstead sued in the federal district court, where Judge Richard Peters ruled in his favor. Governor Thomas McKean sent a record of the proceedings to the legislature with an angry denial of the court's jurisdiction, and the legislature in turn instructed him to resist. Judge Peters, fearing impeachment (Justice Chase was in the process of being impeached, and Peters was said to be a prime candidate for the same treatment), declined to issue an order to carry his decision into effect. In 1808, Olmstead sought a writ of mandamus from the Supreme Court requiring Peters to execute the decision; early the next year, he got it.[40]

In response, the governor dispatched a militia force to surround the house of the former state treasurer, where his executrices were holding the disputed funds. A federal marshal was prevented from serving the process that Judge Peters had issued in accordance with the writ, and the marshal summoned a posse of two thousand men. As a violent confrontation shaped up, the governor appealed to the newly installed president, James Madison, citing Madison's own doctrines of 1798. The president turned him down. A federal grand jury indicted the commander of the militia and some of his lieutenants, and they were convicted of resisting the laws of the United States, fined, and sentenced to imprisonment. The state had to retreat, but Pennsylvanians seethed for a long time.[41]

The embargo conflict unwound with much bombast but no open breaches. The Massachusetts legislature, responding in January and February 1809 to the December enforcement act, adopted resolutions that expressly disavowed an intention to secede but nonetheless issued an ultimatum that amounted to a threat to secede. In February, Governor Jonathan Trumbull of Connecticut asserted that Congress had exceeded its constitutional authority and that it was the duty of the legislators "to interpose their protecting shield between the rights and liberties of the people and the assumed power of the general government," and the legislature resolved accordingly. Perhaps in response to these threats, northern Republicans in Congress turned against the embargo policy, and on March 1 Jefferson signed a repeal bill into law. The act, as a face-saving gesture on behalf of the discredited policy of peaceful coercion, replaced embargo with nonintercourse: American trade was opened to all nations except Britain and France and their dependencies, with a proviso that if either canceled its trade restrictions it would be exempt from the nonintercourse act. A year later, the nonintercourse act was replaced by Macon's Bill Number Two, which opened trade fully but provided that if Britain or France should abandon its objectionable policies, the United States would cut off trade with the other. Neither act had any appreciable effect upon French and British policies. As for northerners, no serious protests were forthcoming, for their trade profited enormously under the revised terms, largely at the expense of southerners and westerners.[42]

The next two years of James Madison's presidency saw a succession of blunders, culminating in the war with Great Britain. The United States was far from prepared for war when it was declared in June 1812, its army being almost nonexistent, its treasury being short of funds, and the Bank of the United States being dead. Worst of all, the nation was divided against itself, as the vote on the declaration of war indicated——seventy-nine to forty-nine in the House, nineteen to thirteen in the Senate. All states north and east of Pennsylvania except Vermont voted for peace.[43]

New Englanders protested loudly and refused to cooperate in the prosecution of the war. With congressional authorization, Madison issued a call for 100,000 militiamen, but those in New England refused to hear the call, and the governor of Massachusetts intervened to prevent their being forced into service. The Constitution vests Congress with authority "for calling forth the Militia to execute the Laws of the Union, suppress Insurrections and repel Invasions," and the general supposition was that the president or Congress would determine when the call was necessary. But the Massachusetts supreme court advised Governor Caleb Strong that the governor alone had the authority. Strong, in turn, announced that neither foreign invasion nor domestic insurrection existed and that he therefore could not comply with the president's request to send a quota of the militia into the service of the United States. Similarly, bankers in the region refused to subscribe to loans to the United States, despite the government's sore need for funds, and they exerted pressure on their clients to boycott the loans as well.[44]

But the Yankees went beyond resistance into activities that were literally treasonable, even by the Constitution's restricted definition of that crime. Through well-established connections in Canada, they conducted a lucrative trade with the enemy, and Canadian officials readily granted them British passes for carrying foodstuffs and supplies to the British army fighting the French in Spain and Portugal. So lucrative was their trade that by the winter of 1813–1814, hard currency from everywhere in the United States had gravitated to New England, where investors chose to put their surpluses into British bills of exchange "to avoid the temptation of lending money to support Madison's measures."[45]

In the meantime, the war itself was discrediting two cherished tenets of the Republican creed—belief in the militias and scorn for the navy. Three militia attacks on Canada were projected, one through Lake Champlain, another at Niagara Falls, and a third at Detroit. The militiamen marched toward the first two but got cold feet and returned home. General William Hull, through his stupidity and cowardice, was forced to surrender at Detroit. By contrast, the navy comported itself brilliantly, winning five one-on-one engagements in a row.[46]

What was more important in dividing Americans in their attitudes toward the war was a British blockade, imposed partially by the end of 1812 and made total by the middle of 1813—except for New England, which was under no British restrictions. The rest of the country suffered grievously, banks collapsed, and the general government forfeited on its interest payments and was reduced to issuing fiat money at large discounts; New England thrived. It was almost as if the area had gone beyond secession and become a

British province. Indeed, the Federalist press in Massachusetts talked of taking that course, and Timothy Pickering engaged in secret communications with British agents.[47]

But then Madison, fed up with the New Englanders, struck back. In his annual message of December 9, 1813, he denounced those who profited from trading with the enemy and angrily asked for an embargo. Three days later, the House complied, and the Senate shortly followed. No longer could the Yankees hamper and otherwise ignore the general government: they must either defy it or capitulate to it.

The situation was complicated by news that arrived from Europe about two weeks after the embargo was passed. Napoleon, his power devastated by his defeat in Russia, had been decisively beaten at the Battle of Leipzig, and his days as emperor were clearly numbered. That would free the British to unleash their entire armed might in the war against America. It also meant that the New Englanders' excuse for opposing the war—that Madison, like Jefferson before him, was a tool of the emperor—was a position they could no longer maintain.

In the circumstances, what New England did approached open rebellion. The government in Washington was desperate for money and men, and Yankees were determined that it would obtain neither. As for money, in the spring the *Boston Gazette* expressed a general attitude when it declared that "any man who lends his money to the government at the present time will forfeit all claim to common honesty and common courtesy among all true friends to the country." Vainly, government brokers advertised that the names of subscribers to a loan would be kept secret. As for men, during the summer the British launched raids on coastal areas in Maine, Connecticut, the Chesapeake, and points south, and the government issued an emergency call for militia forces. At that point, Governor Strong decided an invasion had come, and he mobilized Massachusetts' well-armed and well-disciplined militia for defense, but he was careful to avoid any hint that the troops were in national service. The force was, rather, a state army under the command of a general of its own. At the same time, Connecticut's governor withdrew the brigade of state militia that was in national service and enjoined it to obey no orders except those from the state. On the day the Connecticut regiment was denationalized, the British captured and burned the public buildings in Washington, D.C.[48]

Two months later, the Massachusetts legislature did what Pickering had been urging it to do for years: it called the other New England states to convene in Hartford toward the year's end. The legislatures of Connecticut, Rhode Island, and Massachusetts elected delegates; local conventions in Vermont and New Hampshire did likewise. The assumption, widely held, was that the convention would propose secession and the creation of a New England union, though moderate Federalists worked diligently—and, ultimately, successfully—to prevent that drastic step.[49]

But even moderate voices were scarcely subdued, as is indicated by a speech delivered by Daniel Webster, a man whose whole later career would be devoted to defending the Union against states' rights claims. When Secretary of War James Monroe proposed meeting the manpower emergency by conscription, Webster reacted with horror. Displaying flashes of the oratorical brilliance for which he would become famous, young Webster thundered, "Is this, sir, consistent with the character of a free government? Is this civil liberty? Is this the real character of our Constitution? No, sir, indeed it is not. . . . Where is it written in the Constitution . . . that you may take children from their parents, and parents from their children, and compel them to fight the battles of any war in which the folly or the wickedness of government may engage it?" After further discourse in that vein, he concluded that when government resorted to such measures, "It will be the solemn duty of the State Governments to protect their own authority over their own militia, and to interpose between their citizens and arbitrary power. These are among the objects for which the State Governments exist; and their highest obligations bind them to the preservation of their own rights and the liberties of their people."[50]

As the people of the region awaited the convening at Hartford, radical positions peppered the newspapers. Repeatedly, they invoked the doctrine of state sovereignty, held that the Constitution was a treaty, denied that the general government had any sovereignty, declared that violent resistance by the states was justified, and maintained that the states were the sole judges of their own powers as well as those of the general authority. Some suggested that New England should withdraw from the war, negotiate a separate peace with Britain, and remain neutral until the war ended.[51]

Characteristic of the radical arguments was that of a writer in the *Boston Gazette*. The Hartford Convention, he suggested, "can, if they should think proper, take for their example and the basis of their proceedings, the result of the Convention of 1788 [*sic*], of which the revered Washington was President, and form a new frame of government." That frame should be "submitted to the legislatures of the several states, for their approbation and adoption, and as was the case at that time, this new constitution can go into operation as soon as two, three, four, five, or any other number of states that may be named shall have adopted it."[52]

Moderation prevailed in the convention, which, under the leadership of George Cabot and Harrison Gray Otis, adopted a resolution endorsing interposition and proposed a number of constitutional amendments to meet New England's persistent complaints. The war had already ended when the convention adjourned, and in the burst of national feeling that followed upon Andrew Jackson's postwar victory at the battle of New Orleans, both New England and the Hartford Convention came under a cloud of disapproval.

But radical states' rights doctrines, if in temporary disfavor, were far from dead.

4

An Era of Mixed Feelings, 1815–1828

For a few years after the war, relative harmony seemed to prevail. Organized political partisanship disappeared upon the demise of the Federalists, victims of their association with the Hartford Convention as well as their ineptness. The Virginia Republican James Monroe was twice elected president, all but unanimously, giving rise to the period's enduring if misleading appellation, the Era of Good Feelings. The federal government essentially reenacted the Hamiltonian fiscal system, eliciting little protest in the doing. International trade resumed on a grand scale, the federal treasury was awash with money from import duties, and the prices for American agricultural products stayed at a high level. Land values soared, fed by speculation and by waves of immigrants arriving from war-torn Europe.[1]

To be sure, clouds were gathering on the horizon, some bursting into minor storms, others portending dire consequences. Corruption was rampant at every level of government and infested commercial activity, too. A confrontation between Virginia and the Supreme Court threatened the sovereignty of the one and the integrity of the other. A sectional crisis concerning the issue of extending slavery into the northern part of the Louisiana Territory was narrowly averted by the adoption of the Missouri Compromise but left doubts whether the Union could endure. Disputes between states and between the federal authority and state and local authorities also occurred from time to time.

The troubles truly came with the international financial panic of 1819 and the ensuing depression. Farm prices and land values collapsed, and farmers by the tens of thousands, having taken advantage of easy credit to speculate in lands, found themselves destitute, their homesteads taken by bankers, most of whom were themselves in dire straits. As economic hardships intensified, animosities flared. America had no social classes in the European sense of the term, but something akin to class hostility emerged as the dispossessed clamored for state legislatures to relieve their burdens. Debtor relief laws ran directly contrary to article 1, section 10, of the Constitution, and thus the Supreme Court was brought into collision with the democracy. Other clashes arose over the widespread hostility toward the rechartered Bank of the United States, which had been utterly useless in fending off the financial panic and which many regarded as being responsible for it.

While farmers, including slave-owning plantation masters, were returning to the localism that had made their earlier counterparts into anti-Federalists and then Jeffersonian Republicans, different interest groups were rising that saw opportunities in a strengthened and active federal authority. Three groups in particular fit that description. Westerners sought "internal improvements"—roads, canals, and the dredging of rivers—at the expense of the federal government, which is to say at the expense of taxpayers from other regions. Manufacturers, who had grown in numbers and wealth through the long period when commercial restrictions and war had kept out European products, sought to block competition by the use of protective tariffs. Capitalists sought the financial stability that a reconstituted, revitalized, and honestly managed Bank of the United States could afford. These groups, though still in the minority, were energetic, greedy, and influential.[2]

In these circumstances, advocates of states' rights had their work cut out for them, even though they represented the prevailing view of the nature of the Union. They were prevented from becoming totally dominant by an internal characteristic and by two institutions. The trait was divisiveness arising from different perceptions of self-interest: a federal action that would stimulate people in some states to protest vigorously would commonly find people elsewhere indifferent. The institutions were the Bank of the United States, which, after Nicholas Biddle took over its management in 1823, became a powerful force for financial order and union, and the Supreme Court. Though Chief Justice John Marshall and Bushrod Washington were the only Federalist appointees left on the bench, the Court remained a bulwark of Hamiltonian Federalism.

The direction or directions in which the country would move in regard to the tension between federal and state authority would depend upon the interplay of these several variables, and of one more. Even as the United States was witnessing the emergence of a nascent capitalism, it was simultaneously witnessing the emergence of a nascent democracy and a new kind of party system to harness its energies.

The short-lived but intense wave of nationalism that swept the country when the war ended was matched by President Madison's enthusiasm for preparing to fight the war now that it was over. In his message to Congress in December 1815 he abandoned the reliance on raw militiamen and the fear of standing armies that had been hallmarks of earlier Republicanism and urged a nationally imposed system of discipline for the militias, the creation of a permanent peacetime army of twenty thousand men, and a comparable naval establishment. The remnants of the Republican old guard in Congress balked at the army proposal; after acrimonious debate, a standing army of ten thousand was approved. Provision for the navy was more generous. Though the Great Lakes fleet was destroyed or sold as part of long-range plans to demilitarize the Canadian border, the oceanic navy was enlarged. During the war, Congress had authorized the construction of four ships of the line, six frigates, and six sloops of war, and after the peace, nine additional ships of the line were authorized. Most of these vessels were completed and put into service. As if to confirm the dour prophecies of the likes of John Taylor and John Randolph that sending naval vessels to sea was an invitation to become involved in war, the navy was actually at war much of the time until 1820, suppressing piracy in the Mediterranean (a permanent base was established on Majorca) and combatting piracy and the slave trade in the Caribbean. The land forces, too, were active: Andrew Jackson led an expedition into Spanish Florida that destroyed a number of Indians and provoked international tension by Jackson's hanging of two British subjects.[3]

Madison also called for sweeping nationalistic economic legislation. Specifically, he asked Congress to charter a Second Bank of the United States, designed closely on the model of Hamilton's original but having three and a half times the capital; asked for the enactment of protective tariffs to support fledgling manufactures, especially of textiles and iron products; and suggested a comprehensive program of internal improvements. Madison's proposal regarding protective tariffs went beyond what Hamilton had called for in his 1791 Report on Manufactures, which would have relied more on bounties than on tariffs. In regard to internal improvements, Madison, like Hamilton, thought that a constitutional amendment would probably be required to justify them.[4]

The response to these recommendations was mixed. Most Republicans went along with the proposals, though John Randolph of Roanoke and other purists were bitterly opposed, especially to the recharter of the Bank. Southern Republicans were largely indifferent in regard to internal improvements, westerners strongly in favor, and both, thinking that slave labor could produce manufactured goods more cheaply than free labor, liked the idea of protection.

As for the Federalists, they were temporarily once again a force to be reckoned with, having won about a third of the seats in both houses in the 1814 elections due to the unpopularity of "Jemmy Madison's War" in the North, but they were divided among themselves. A few took pleasure in twitting the Republicans for embracing nationalistic doctrines, but others feared the Republicans were going too far. Gouverneur Morris, for example, declared that "the Party now in Power seems disposed to do all that federal men ever wished and will, I fear, do more than is good to strengthen and consolidate the federal government." In addition to misgivings in principle, Federalists in New York and New England were moved by concern for their interests: their existing banking systems were adequate, and a national banking power might challenge their hegemony; they were oriented toward commerce, not manufacturing; and New York had begun construction of the Erie Canal at its own expense, which would give it incalculable advantages in tapping the western trade, whereas rival seaports needed federal assistance to compete.[5]

Accordingly, Madison's measures met resistance in Congress. The tariff, staunchly supported by Representative John C. Calhoun of South Carolina, had the easiest time, being passed by a House vote of eighty-eight to fifty-four in April 1816. It was a moderate enough measure, placing a duty of 25 percent on most cotton, woolen, and iron products; 30 percent on paper, leather, and hats; and 15 percent on remaining commodities. To keep out cheap cotton textiles from Asia, it set a minimum valuation of twenty-five cents a yard on such goods, which were worth far less.[6]

The charter of the Bank, enacted in April (by a vote of eighty to seventy-one in the House and twenty-two to twelve in the Senate), is of interest mainly because of the positions taken by congressmen who would later be central figures in states' rights controversies. The bill was introduced and steered through the House by Calhoun, who had yet to indicate that there were limits to his nationalism. The erstwhile states' rights, strict-constructionist Speaker of the House Henry Clay also supported it. Clay had opposed a renewal of the charter in 1811 on constitutional grounds, but now he stepped down from the chair to explain that the wartime experience had convinced him that the Bank was necessary under the "necessary and proper" clause. Among the outspoken opponents was Daniel Webster, who argued that the Constitution contemplated a specie-based currency and that the nation could be returned to hard money without the Bank if the federal government would require state banks to convert to a specie basis.[7]

One feature of the legislation, as passed, led indirectly to the derailment of the last of Madison's proposals. In exchange for the privileges the Bank received, it was required to pay the government a bonus of $1.5 million. On February 4, 1817, a month before Madison's second term expired, Calhoun introduced a bill setting aside that sum and all future dividends as a permanent fund to finance internal improvements. Calhoun conceded the obvious point that Congress was not expressly empowered by the Constitution to spend money for such purposes, but, employing a doctrine of construction looser than any that Hamilton had advanced, Calhoun said that building roads and canals was justified by the power to appropriate funds for the general welfare and the common defense. The bill passed by a narrow margin, the line of division being neither ideological nor partisan but sectional.[8]

As his final action in office, Madison vetoed this bonus bill. He had, in his last annual message to Congress, reiterated his call for internal improvements but reaffirmed his opinion that the absence of a constitutional power to undertake such projects "could be remedied in the 'mode' that the Constitution itself had so 'providently' supplied." In his veto message he expressly rejected Calhoun's reasoning, maintaining that to draw powers from the general welfare clause would violate "the established and consistent rules of interpretation, as rendering the special and careful enumeration of powers which follow the clause nugatory and improper." Thus ended Madison's second, short-lived flirtation with energetic nationalism.[9]

Meanwhile, in a different forum, a battle concerning state sovereignty versus federal supremacy was unfolding. The combatants were the Virginia court of appeals and the Supreme Court. More properly, they were Judge Spencer Roane of the court of appeals, a bitter enemy of Chief Justice Marshall, a son-in-law of Patrick Henry, and the man Jefferson would have appointed chief justice had he had the opportunity; and Marshall himself. Roane was abetted by almost the entire bench and bar of his state; Marshall was brilliantly abetted by Justice Joseph Story and supported by the other justices, regardless of party origins.[10]

The confrontation began with the case of *Fairfax's Devisee* v. *Hunter's Lessee,* which had developed over a long period. During the Revolution, Virginia had confiscated the huge estate of Lord Fairfax in the state's Northern Neck. Fairfax's heir, Denny Martin, protested in vain that the confiscation was invalid, and Virginia proceeded to sell parcels of the land to many buyers, including John Marshall and his brother James. Litigation concerning land titles dragged on until 1810, when the Virginia court of appeals unreservedly voided Martin's claim. Martin appealed to the Supreme Court under article 25 of the Judiciary Act, which authorized appeals if the constitutionality of a state court's decision was challenged. The hearing before the Court was strange, for Marshall, as an interested party, recused himself, as did Justice Bushrod Washington. Another justice was absent and one dissented, leaving the decision to less than a majority of the full court. Justice Story, writing for the plurality, ruled that the Fairfax estate had been protected by the terms of the Jay Treaty of 1794 and, since treaties take precedence over state laws, reversed the Virginia court and ordered it to carry out the decision.[11]

Judge Roane then did an extraordinary thing: in the spring of 1813 he summoned the state's leading lawyers to argue before the court of appeals whether the state's highest court could be ordered about by the Supreme Court in a matter concerning state law. The arguments lasted six days, and the court waited a year and a half, until December 1814, before announcing its decision. The decision of Roane and his fellow judges was that the Supreme Court had no jurisdiction in the case, that article 25 of the Judiciary Act was unconstitutional, and therefore that the court of appeals was not bound by Story's ruling.[12]

In the face of this defiance of the Supreme Court and the declaration that part of an act of Congress was unconstitutional, the case was again appealed to the Supreme Court, this time as *Martin* v. *Hunter's Lessee*. As expected, Story and the Supreme Court overruled the court of appeals, but they had no way of knowing how the state court would respond. To avert confrontation for the moment, Story returned the case not to the court of appeals but to the lower state court in which it had originally been tried. Nonetheless, as a practical matter, the Supreme Court decision was simply disregarded, and the state legislature adopted a resolution confirming the court of appeals' decision.[13]

What the Supreme Court needed, if it was to maintain the authority it had asserted, was a case from which Marshall was not disqualified, so that he could pit his prestige as well as his wits against
Roane's. Before such a case could be found, however, the dispute
ballooned into a rancorous polemical war. Virginia's die-hard Republican, John Taylor of Caroline, took the lead. The most influential
of Taylor's three tracts on the subject was an 1820 pamphlet called
Construction Construed and Constitutions Vindicated. Roane himself weighed in with a series of articles in the *Richmond Enquirer*
under the pseudonym "Algernon Sidney." Jefferson made no public
statements but wrote to numerous private correspondents expressing his growing fear that the Marshall Court was destroying the Constitution. Such sentiments were nearly universal in Virginia, and they
were not confined to the Old Dominion. The supreme court of Massachusetts, in a decision rendered shortly after the *Martin* v. *Hunter's
Lessee* verdict was handed down, declared that the constitutionality
of article 25 was "a question of much doubt and argument."[14]

At the heart of the Virginia position was a belief in constitutions,
founded on natural law and embodied in the common law and history, that antedated and were superior to the Constitution. The political societies created by these constitutions had contracted together
to establish the Constitution by delegating certain limited and specific
powers to a confederal government, reserving all others to themselves. Each level of government was supreme within its sphere, and
the judges at each level were bound by oath or affirmation to support
the Constitution. The Constitution vested the confederal court with
power over cases and controversies arising under the Constitution
itself, laws enacted in pursuance thereof, and treaties made under the
authority of the United States, but not cases arising from state laws,
which were reserved to state courts. Consequently, as Taylor put it,
"whenever the constitution operates upon collisions between individuals, it is to be construed by the [supreme] court; but when it operates upon collisions between political departments," including
different levels of government, "it is not to be construed by the court."
To allow a branch of the confederal government to be the arbiter of
either that government's own powers or the powers of the parties to

the compact that gave it existence would be to pervert the very idea of compact, the inviolability of compact or contract being one of the cardinal features of the God-given natural constitution.[15]

Marshall and friends of the Supreme Court were looking for a case—this was typical of the chief justice—in which they could win Virginia's acquiescence by giving it something it wanted but could have only if it accepted the Court's jurisdiction on appeals from state law. They thought they had found (or, more properly, arranged) such a case in what became *Cohens v. Virginia*. Congress had authorized the city of Washington to institute lotteries; the sale of lottery tickets was illegal in Virginia. Two brothers named Cohen were induced to sell lottery tickets in Virginia and were duly arrested, convicted, and fined, whereupon they appealed to the Supreme Court. Virginia's counsel argued against jurisdiction, again asserting that article 25 was unconstitutional, but refused to argue the merits of the case. Marshall, writing for the Court, held that it did have jurisdiction but that the decision of the state court should stand because the Cohens had violated state law. (The congressional act had not expressly authorized sale of tickets in the states, and the ruling did not say whether it had that power, though Marshall hinted in obiter dicta that it did.)[16]

If Marshall had believed that Virginia would accept the decision simply because the state's verdict had been upheld, he was mistaken. The *Cohens* decision was greeted by strong denunciation. "There is on this subject," Marshall complained in a letter to Story, "no such thing as a free press in Virginia, and of consequence the calumnies and misrepresentations of [Roane] will remain uncontradicted and will by many be believed to be true. He will be supposed to be the champion of State-Rights, instead of being what he really is, the champion of dismemberment." Writers in Ohio and Kentucky joined the cry of the Virginians and set in motion a campaign, which would last for a decade, to subject the federal courts to a major overhaul.[17]

But Virginians would not be among the leaders in that campaign, for two years after the *Cohens* decision, the Marshall Court gave Virginia a ruling it refused to turn down. The case was *Green v. Biddle*. In 1792, when Virginia had consented that its western part be separated and admitted to the Union as the state of Kentucky, it was

mutually agreed that grants of land in Kentucky that had already
been made would continue to be valid. But the Virginia grants had
been made while Kentucky was largely wilderness, and their precise
locations were not known; thus conflicting grants resulted. To clear
up the confusion and to benefit its own inhabitants, the Kentucky
legislature passed laws providing that Virginia claimants could not
gain possession of land to which they proved title unless they com-
pensated occupants for improvements the occupants had made. In
the absence of recompense, the occupant could gain title by paying
Kentucky the value of the land without improvements. Kentucky
courts repeatedly upheld the state laws, but in a suit between private
individuals brought in 1819, the constitutionality of the laws was
challenged on the ground that the agreement between the two states
had been a contract and that the Kentucky legislation violated the
contract clause of the Constitution.[18]

On appeal, the Supreme Court assumed jurisdiction. In 1821 it
ruled that the Kentucky legislation was unconstitutional, but Henry
Clay and the Kentucky legislature protested so vigorously that the
Court agreed to hear the case argued a second time. The second hearing was in 1822, and in 1823 the Court reluctantly returned the same
decision. Virginians, having much to gain from the decision, opted
to put interest before principle, and they accepted the Court's ruling
without protest. Bitterly, Clay wrote that the Court's action "cripples
the Sovereign power of the State of Kentucky noore [*sic*] than any
other measure ever affected the Independence of any state in this
Union, and not a Virginia voice is heard against the decision."[19]

Of the decisions rendered by the Supreme Court during this period,
those concerning the Bank of the United States elicited the strongest
resistance by states' righters. The Bank had opened branches in ten
states, and by virtue of mismanagement, ineptness, favoritism, and
corruption, it promptly won enemies everywhere. State after state
responded to the Bank's misdoings by seeking to oust it from their
borders. Indiana, for example, in its 1816 constitution, forbade the

establishment of branches of any bank not chartered by the state, and Illinois followed suit in 1818. Various states levied taxes on out-of-state banks doing business in the state: Tennessee ($50,000 annually) and Georgia (31¼ percent annually of the value of bank stock) in 1817, North Carolina ($5,000 annually on each branch) in 1818, and Kentucky ($60,000 annually per branch) and Ohio ($50,000 annually per branch) in 1819. The taxes were clearly designed to destroy the branches of the Bank. To make the war against the Bank total, the Pennsylvania legislature in March 1819 proposed a constitutional amendment prohibiting Congress from chartering a bank to operate outside the District of Columbia; the legislatures of four states supported the proposal. And Congress itself debated a motion to repeal the Bank's charter.[20]

In this atmosphere, compounded by the first devastating shocks of the panic of 1819, the Supreme Court issued its landmark decision in the case of *M'Culloch* v. *Maryland*. Maryland had levied a stiff stamp tax on notes issued by any bank chartered outside the state, which could be commuted by an annual payment of $15,000. James W. M'Culloch, cashier of the Baltimore branch of the Bank— who, incidentally, was systematically embezzling funds from the branch—refused to pay the tax, was tried and found guilty, and appealed to the Supreme Court. Marshall, for the Court, made three far-reaching pronouncements. The first upheld the constitutionality of the Bank's charter in the classic formulation of loose construction: "Let the end be legitimate, let it be within the scope of the Constitution, and all means which are appropriate, which are plainly adapted to that end, which are not prohibited, but consist with the letter and spirit of the Constitution, are constitutional."[21]

The second pronouncement was an equally famous passage, taken from the argument of Daniel Webster as counsel for the Bank. Marshall held that the Maryland tax was unconstitutional on the ground that "the power to tax involves the power to destroy," and a state could not legitimately destroy what Congress had legitimately created. (In vain did states' righters point out that the Constitution forbids states to tax certain things but by implication allows them to tax all others.

In vain, too, did they note that the Bank, though created by Congress, was a private, profit-making corporation that should be as subject to taxes as any other private, for-profit corporation.)[22]

The third pronouncement had nothing to do with the judgment in the case but was obiter dictum amounting to a direct affront to states' rights advocates. As indicated earlier, initially the Constitution had been the creation of the peoples of the individual states acting in their capacities as peoples of discrete political societies. In the Virginia Resolution of 1798, Madison had reformulated the issue by claiming that the Constitution had been created by the states as states. Now Marshall denied the states a role, claiming that the Constitution was created by the whole people, who just happened to have met in state ratifying conventions as a convenience. Thenceforth, states' righters would adhere to the Madisonian position, nationalists to that of Marshall, and the original understanding would be all but lost.[23]

Several states refused to comply with the *M'Culloch* decision, Ohio among them. The state declared that the case had been fictitious, was based upon agreed facts that did not apply to Ohio, and was hurried to the Supreme Court to save the Bank from collapse as a result of its fraudulent speculations. The Bank obtained from a federal circuit court an injunction prohibiting the state auditor, Ralph Osborn, from collecting the tax that Ohio had levied. Osburn claimed that the injunction had been served improperly and proceeded to send his assistant to the Bank's branch to enter the vaults by force, if necessary, and remove what assets he could find. The assistant removed more than $120,000 in gold and notes and placed them in the state treasury, in direct contempt of the court order.[24]

The ensuing Supreme Court decision—which was delayed three years—was *Osborn* v. *Bank of the United States*. Besides the questions of the constitutionality of the Bank and of the tax (on which the Court repeated its *M'Culloch* verdict), the case involved two issues that considerably expanded federal authority against that of the states: whether the Bank could sue in federal courts, and whether it could sue a state official in regard to the performance of his duties. The answer to the first was in the affirmative. As for the second, the

Court rejected the state's argument that the Eleventh Amendment precluded jurisdiction. The state was not officially a party of record, Marshall held, and besides, a state officer who committed a trespass under authority of an unconstitutional act could be held personally responsible. To states' rights advocates, that ruling negated the Eleventh Amendment.[25]

Kentucky's resistance to the Bank and the Court was as overt as Ohio's, and it took bizarre twists as well. Kentucky was particularly hard hit by the economic depression, and a large part of its population was being pressed for debts owed to the Bank of the United States and to in-state creditors. In 1821 the legislature responded to the cries of the debtors by enacting laws abolishing imprisonment for debt (the first state to do so); preventing the sale of a debtor's real estate for less than three-fourths its value, as determined by a jury of the debtor's neighbors; incorporating the Bank of the Commonwealth, with power to issue notes not redeemable in hard money; and staying executions for debts unless the creditor indicated his willingness to accept notes of the new bank and the existing Bank of Kentucky, which were circulating at something like half their face value. The legislation was a palpable violation of the contract clause of the Constitution, and both lower state courts and the state's court of appeals so ruled.[26]

The legislature was outraged by the courts' decisions and was determined to chastise the court of appeals. It adopted a ringing resolution denouncing the court for overturning a solemn act of the sovereign state and declared its intention to disregard the ruling. (The doctrine of judicial review was still far from having won general acceptance; the Georgia legislature had also rejected the doctrine not long before.) The Kentucky legislature considered impeaching the judges of the court of appeals, then hit upon a different expedient. It abolished the court in 1824 and passed a law creating a replacement court of appeals. The judges on the old court refused to go out of business, even though the new court seized its records. For some time, both courts continued to operate.[27]

This left creditors and debtors in Kentucky on an uneven footing. The Bank of the United States and other out-of-state creditors could sue for recovery of debts in federal courts, though those courts were inadequate to handle the volume of litigation. In-state creditors had no recourse unless they sued in a trial court and managed a successful appeal to the old court, but the lower courts generally disregarded the rulings of the old court. Moreover, there was no way to appeal to the Supreme Court, inasmuch as the old court had already ruled the stay law unconstitutional, and thus creditors could not file for a writ of error to the Supreme Court.[28]

The confrontation neared the exploding point in 1825, when the legislature asked the governor to advise it on how "to refuse obedience to the decisions and mandates of the Supreme Court of the United States considered erroneous and unconstitutional" and inquired whether "it may be advisable to call forth the physical power of the State" to resist the Court. Within another year, however, the financial crisis had blown over, the debtors had won their delays, and the new court was abolished.[29]

In two other cases decided during the period, the Supreme Court delivered opinions that affected the powers of the states but without engendering significant opposition. The case of *Dartmouth College* v. *Woodward* went almost unnoticed, though its influence was powerfully felt over the next generation and beyond. The charter of the college had been granted by George III in 1769. It named twelve persons as trustees, authorized the trustees to fill vacancies as they occurred, and entitled them to govern the institution in perpetuity. In 1816 the legislature of New Hampshire, seeking to bring Dartmouth under political control, enacted a statute placing the college under a board of overseers to be appointed by the governor. The state's superior court upheld the law, holding that the college was a public corporation performing a public service and therefore subject to public regulation. On appeal, the Supreme Court overturned the decision, on the ground that a corporate charter was a contract and thus was exempt from state interference by reason of the contract clause.[30]

The implications of the decision were enormous. Corporations had long been used for conducting charitable and governmental affairs—cities were corporations—but they also were used for private business functions, and in the realm of economic enterprise they would become a dynamic force. The advantages of the corporate form were that corporations could raise capital effectively by drawing on multiple investors and that they existed legally as single immortal persons irrespective of changes in ownership. Since 1790, several hundred corporations had been created by states to engage in insurance, banking, transportation, and manufacturing. Until 1811, they were created by special enactments of legislatures, but in that year, New York passed the first general incorporation law, permitting people to form corporations merely by going through prescribed procedures and paying certain fees. That was to be the method of the future, and the transportation and industrial revolutions just getting under way would be corporate ventures.

But if the doctrine of the *Dartmouth College* case were followed strictly, corporations once established would be outside the authority of the states that created them: the terms of corporate charters could never be amended. To be sure, as Justice Story suggested in a concurring opinion, states could circumvent the problem by providing in the charters themselves that they were susceptible to amendment. Otherwise, either the court would have to retreat from its position or corporations could run amok, and the states would be powerless against them.

Quite as important in extending the central authority at the expense of the states was the decision in *Gibbons* v. *Ogden*. Back in 1807, the inventor Robert Fulton and his financial supporter Robert R. Livingston had obtained from the New York legislature exclusive rights, for a number of years, to use steamboats on the state's waterways, provided they could produce a workable steamboat. They succeeded, and in 1808 they were given the monopoly. They soon had a number of boats in operation, but, lacking the capital to meet a rapidly growing demand, they began leasing rights to others. Among the lessees was Aaron Ogden, who obtained exclusive rights to steamboat traffic across the Hudson River between New York and New Jersey. A former partner of Ogden's, Thomas Gibbons, entered into competition with him by obtaining a federal license to ply the trade under a 1793 act regulating the coasting trade. Ogden sued him in New York courts, which upheld the monopoly, and Gibbons appealed to the Supreme Court.[31]

One might suppose that the Supreme Court would have confirmed the state court's verdict, since if the Court ruled otherwise, it would impair the "contract" between the state and the monopolists. But Marshall considered the case in a different light, basing the decision on the commerce clause rather than the contract clause. Article 1, section 8, empowers Congress "to regulate Commerce with foreign Nations, and among the several States." Attorneys for the monopoly argued that commerce meant "buying and selling, or the interchange of commodities" and did not extend to navigation or transportation. Marshall held instead that, since the power to regulate shipping was everywhere recognized as part of the power to regulate foreign commerce, interstate commerce included navigation for constitutional purposes. That holding would prove to be of great moment, for it would soon extend the regulatory power to another technological innovation, the railroad. As for the meaning of "among the several states," Congress did not have power to regulate trade carried on wholly within a state, but its authority did extend to commerce between one state and another and to the navigable waters on which interstate or foreign commerce could be carried. In time, Marshall's broad definition of interstate commerce would be broadened further and used to justify every manner of federal intrusion on the rights of the states.[32]

In relation to the case at hand, having made his sweeping pronouncements, Marshall decided on a narrower ground. The 1793 licensing act under which Gibbons claimed the right to operate, Marshall declared, was an act "in pursuance" of the Constitution, and in accordance with the supreme law clause, the act therefore took precedence over the state law creating the monopoly. The reasoning was somewhat lame, but for once a Marshall decision was popular, inasmuch as the detested monopoly was now broken.[33]

Important as the Supreme Court was as a bulwark of national authority and a restraint upon the states—it had declared laws of ten states unconstitutional by 1825—it was not in the courtroom but in the arena of politics that the significant battles between nationalists and states' righters had been and would continue to be fought. But the political game was undergoing rapid change, along with the economic activity that underlay and drove politics. That economic interest was becoming a vital political force was itself a major change. Traditionally, America had been agricultural, hierarchical, and deferential. The social order (or, more properly, orders) had been stable, status resting largely upon ownership of land. Since the 1790s, however, Americans had become increasingly preoccupied with the pursuit of wealth, the land itself having become merely a commodity. The monetization of society had been a principal goal of Alexander Hamilton's program; he wanted to shake up and energize America by making money the measure of the value of all things. Indeed, that prospect had been one reason the Jeffersonian Republicans had vehemently opposed the program. In the dozen years after the War of 1812, America became Hamiltonian in a far more profound sense than in merely embracing and extending his policies.[34]

Obvious economic changes arose from the exploitation of the steamboat. The first steamboat made the trip from Pittsburgh to New Orleans in 1811, and the first to travel upstream came four years later. By 1817, seventeen steamboats plied the Ohio and Mississippi Rivers; by 1830, almost three hundred operated on the river system. Before the steamboat, trans-Allegheny residents traded in a cumbersome counterclockwise pattern. Their products were poled downriver by raft to New Orleans, from which they were carried to the West Indies or New York and Philadelphia, whence imported or locally manufactured goods were carried overland to the interior. The steamboat dramatically improved the terms of trade for the westerners. In the immediate postwar years, farmers in Ohio and Kentucky could exchange a barrel of flour for twenty-seven pounds of sugar and a barrel of pork for thirty pounds of coffee; a decade later, their barrel of flour would buy thirty-nine pounds of sugar, and their barrel of pork would fetch fifty-two pounds of coffee. The total volume of exports and imports nearly doubled during those years.[35]

The by-products and ramifications of these developments were manifold. One area of change was demographic: a massive migration from the seaboard to the interior as farmers from the east abandoned worn-out acres for cheap virgin lands to the west. Hordes of immigrants increased the population of the West still further. That had political effects, shifting power westward, and it had psychological effects, too. People on the seaboard, especially between Baltimore and New York, having long been oriented toward Europe, shifted their focus inward, where they saw the future. Their reorientation, in turn, sharpened and intensified the rivalry among the port cities and created new alliances.[36]

Developments in manufacturing were as profound though less obvious. Manufacturers, as of 1816 and for a decade thereafter, were not concentrated groups of capitalists who owned and operated large plants. A few such existed, but for the most part, manufacturing continued to be scattered throughout the country and conducted in homes or small factories by housewives, slaves, or urban craftsmen working in guilds. As long as that situation prevailed, the South in general and Virginia in particular could develop manufacturing more profitably than the North, for the main component of the cost of manufactured goods was labor, and slave labor was about half as expensive as free labor. Thus even Jefferson could support the moderate protective tariff of 1816.[37]

But in 1825–1826, conditions suddenly changed. A credit crisis in Britain disrupted the finances of Europe. Nicholas Biddle managed the resources of the Bank of the United States so skillfully that virtually no domestic repercussions were felt, but for two or three years, international trade was generally unprofitable. Merchants in Baltimore and Philadelphia, during the downturn, directed their attention to lobbying for federal aid for internal improvements, hoping to overcome the advantages in western trade that New York had just gained by opening the Erie Canal. Those in New England, precluded by geography from obtaining a share of the western trade, turned to manufacturing. Manufacturing proved to be extremely profitable; capitalists in the region never went back into shipping on a large scale, and by the end of the decade, New England was being converted into a complex of gigantic textile mills, employing heavy machinery powered by steam and water.[38]

The transformation of New England affected the rest of the country. Almost immediately it dissolved the competitive position of southern manufacturing. Now slave labor, requiring full-time subsistence and the interest and depreciation on a sizable investment, was four or five times more costly. To put it another way, money invested in machinery was four to five times as productive as money invested in nonagricultural slaves. Prospects for diversifying the southern economy by expanding manufacturing nearly vanished south and west of Norfolk by 1830.[39]

Social and political changes accompanied the economic changes. Among the social changes, the emergence of an unskilled working class portended unrest and instability in the future, though the effects were slow to be felt, because at first many of the hands in the textile mills were girls and young women. In some mills, entire families of ex-farmers were employed as units, housed in company towns, and paid with notes negotiable at company stores. These workers fared reasonably well until a depression set in late in the 1830s.[40]

More immediately of consequence was what may be loosely described as an information revolution. A proliferation of schools continued the high rate of literacy: in 1830 an estimated 91 percent of the adult white population could read, a figure unmatched anywhere else in the world. And thanks to improvements in the technology of printing, the number of newspapers burgeoned, from ninety-two in 1790 to about twelve hundred by 1830. The aggregate circulation was greater than that in any other country. Even on the frontier, almost every family subscribed to at least one newspaper.[41]

Ordinary people were better informed than they had been before (though politicians and political newspapers strove energetically to misinform them), and that contributed to democratizing America. The breakdown of the party system hastened the process, to be sure, particularly through the intensified campaigning for the presidency in the elections of 1824, in which John Quincy Adams was elected even though Andrew Jackson had more popular votes, and of 1828, which Jackson won by forming the rudiments of a new-style party system. A general broadening of the suffrage, sporadically taking place since the 1790s, contributed as well. But the democratization that took place between roughly 1816 and 1832 involved a deeper change than expanding the electorate and having candidates compete for popular votes; it undermined the deferential local and state social orders.[42]

The nature of the transformation can be illustrated by Jefferson's description of Virginia in 1816. In a letter to John Taylor of Caroline, Jefferson declared that the lower house of the assembly was the "purest republican feature in the government of our own State," that the state senate was less so, and that the judiciary was "seriously anti-republican, because for life." He continued, "Add to this the vicious constitution of our county courts (to whom the justice, the executive administration, the taxation, police, the military appointments of the county, and nearly all our daily concerns are confided), self-appointed, self-continued, holding their authorities for life, and with an impossibility of breaking in on the perpetual succession of any faction once possessed of the bench." John Adams wrote a similar description of Massachusetts, and Connecticut was notorious for its oligarchy, the Standing Order. Arrangements like Virginia's prevailed throughout the South except in the frontier areas of Alabama, Mississippi, and Georgia.[43]

All over America, with few exceptions, such situations ceased to exist in the wake of the war. Showing the way, somewhat surprisingly, was Connecticut. As indicated, after the Revolution, Connecticut had continued to govern itself under its 1662 royal charter and retained its tax-supported Congregational Church establishment. In 1818, under the leadership of Governor Oliver Wolcott, erstwhile assistant to Alexander Hamilton and his successor as secretary of the treasury, Connecticut disestablished its church and adopted a liberalized constitution. The Standing Order was no more. New York followed with a new constitution in 1821, Massachusetts liberalized by amendments in 1821, and Virginia brought up the rear with its constitution of 1830. In between, several states enacted statutes that brought government closer to the people. Henceforth, when people took states' rights or nationalistic stances, they no longer spoke solely for elites; they spoke to and for the common man.[44]

In the increasingly democratic political arena of the 1820s, two issues to which the tension between national and state authority was central received close attention—internal improvements and protective tariffs. Internal improvements, during Monroe's presidency, generated little excitement, despite the repeated efforts of Secretary of War John C. Calhoun to influence Congress to enact a comprehensive system and the support of Henry Clay and the western congressional contingent. The reason was that Monroe, though he made it clear that he regarded such a program as desirable, remained a strict-constructionist, states' rights Republican and could not condone legislation that he regarded as unconstitutional. He did approve the construction by soldiers of a number of military roads as well as post roads, as had Jefferson and Madison before him. Regarding larger undertakings, however, he was adamant.[45]

Congress sent Monroe three major internal improvement bills. The Cumberland Road bill of 1822 provided for the collection of tolls for the upkeep of the road from Cumberland, Maryland, to Wheeling, (West) Virginia, that had been built between 1811 and 1818 and had since fallen into disrepair. Monroe vetoed it, saying that Congress had no jurisdiction. A general survey bill, passed in 1824, empowered the president to initiate surveys of roads and canals that might be needed for national military, postal, or commercial purposes. It did not authorize the building of anything, so Monroe signed it. And Monroe signed, as his last deed in office, a bill authorizing the subscription of $300,000 in stock to the Chesapeake and Delaware Canal Company.[46]

That Monroe's views on the subject were principled is beyond doubt, and many in Congress agreed with them; but equally principled people (as well as self-interested parties) stood on the other side. Among these was Nicholas Biddle. An ardent nationalist, a man of keen intelligence, and a believer in progress, Biddle had minimal tolerance for the logic of states' righters. He championed internal improvements simply because they strengthened the nation's economy and its military defenses, and because he foresaw a problem that both proponents and opponents were unable to see. The government was rapidly retiring the public debt, and Biddle believed that unless opportunities for investing the treasury surpluses in useful ventures were found, an excess of money would flow into private hands and fuel widespread speculation in land, commodities, and stocks, creating a bubble that must inevitably burst.[47]

Meanwhile, the coffers of the states were full, too, and as their credit was good, several of them launched internal improvements at their own expense. Pennsylvania had long since built a good road connecting Philadelphia and Pittsburgh, and Biddle was promoting the building of a railroad to cross the state. Maryland was equally energetic. In Ohio, more than half of all state legislation dealt with transportation, mainly roads, and the state built two canals connecting Lake Erie to the Ohio River. Indiana and Illinois also built canals. The federal government, anticipating a method that would be used to finance later railroad construction, granted both Ohio and Indiana 500,000 acres of land in the public domain to facilitate their raising of funds. A number of states got themselves dangerously in debt by taking on ever more ambitious projects.[48]

John Quincy Adams was as committed to nationalism as Biddle was, and he went further to urge (as Washington had done) the creation of a national university, where the country's brightest young men could be taught to shake off their provincialism. Urging internal improvements and protective tariffs in his first message to Congress, he called for "laws promoting the improvement of agriculture, commerce, and manufactures, the cultivation and encouragement of the mechanic and of the elegant arts, the advancement of literature, and the progress of the sciences, ornamental and profound." To refrain from exercising the full range of governmental powers "for the benefit of the people themselves," he added, "would be to hide in the earth the talent committed to our charge—would be treachery to the most sacred of trusts. The spirit of improvement is abroad upon the earth. It stimulates the heart and sharpens the faculties not of our fellow-citizens alone, but of the nations of Europe and of their rulers." Apparently oblivious to Americans' deep-seated hostility toward having Europe held up as an example, Adams followed that faux pas with another. "Were we to slumber in indolence or fold up our arms and proclaim to the world that we are palsied by the will of our constituents," he declared, as if the United States were a benevolent despotism where "the will of our constituents" was of no consequence, "would it not be to cast away the bounties of Providence and doom ourselves to perpetual inferiority?"[49]

The first voice of what would become an angry chorus of opposition was that of South Carolina. A year before, Governor John L. Wilson, perturbed by the passage of the General Survey Act, had called it "but an entering wedge which will be followed, no doubt by the expenditure of millions," and predicted that ultimately "South Carolina shall be grievously assessed, to pay for the cutting of a canal across Cape Cod." Wilson was obviously concerned with the interests of his state, but, equally obviously, he was expressing the prevailing sentiment about the nature of the Constitution. "The friends of the assumed powers" regarding internal improvements, he said, "claim them as implied," which was "an open violation of that which has heretofore universally been admitted the true rule for expounding all grants"—precisely the position that had been taken by Madison.[50]

In response to Wilson's prodding, the state senate adopted strongly worded resolutions condemning internal improvements and the protective tariff, but the house of representatives failed to concur and resolved that the legislature had no power "to impugn the Acts of the Federal Government or the decisions of the Supreme Court." In December 1825, however, the two houses agreed upon a series of resolutions roundly denouncing "a general system of internal improvements," protective tariffs, and the taxing of the citizens in one state "to make roads and canals for the citizens of another state." Virginia adopted a similar resolution early in 1827, as did Georgia late in the year, closing with the ominous declaration that Georgia "will SUBMIT to no other" interpretation of the Constitution than its own. Serious confrontations were impending, and the likelihood of a showdown was increased by a turn of events concerning the tariff issue.[51]

Constitutional grounds for objecting to improvements and tariffs rested on one's interpretation of the general welfare and common defense clause. Article 1, section 8, begins, "The Congress shall have Power To lay and collect Taxes, Duties, Imposts and Excises, to pay the Debts and provide for the common Defence and general Welfare of the United States." The phraseology beginning with "to pay" was understood at the time of the Founding to be a set of limitations on the taxing power, not a separate grant of power, and it continued to be understood in that way until advocates of a general program of internal improvements began to argue otherwise. Advocates of protective tariffs argued as if the clause did not exist, as if the taxing power was a general one that could be used for any purpose, including the promotion of manufacturing.[52]

As long as the level of protection remained modest, internal improvements was the hotter issue because it could readily be pointed to as a "transfer payment"—taking money from one citizen and giving it to another, as Governor Wilson indicated in his reference to a canal across Cape Cod—though that terminology was not yet in use. The tariffs of 1816 and 1818 were so moderate that they elicited the mildest of objections, and that of 1824, as noted, aroused the opposition of South Carolina, Georgia, and Virginia, but those states were not supported by any others until 1828.[53]

In that year, Congress passed the Tariff of Abominations, greatly increasing the duties on raw wool, iron, iron products, and hemp. The tariff was the brainchild of the wily senator from New York, Martin Van Buren, who conceived it as a means of furthering Andrew Jackson's bid for the presidency. Van Buren and his cohorts reckoned that the duties would adversely affect New England woolen manufacturers, shipbuilders, and shipowners, and that New England congressmen would join southerners to defeat the bill. Jackson men could then go out on the hustings, claiming in the South that they had defeated a northern effort to raise the tariff and claiming in the North that they had tried valiantly but in vain to raise the tariff. The plan backfired because Van Buren failed to recognize how thoroughly committed to manufacturing New England had become and to understand that the duty on raw wool did not affect manufacturers there because the domestic supply was adequate for their needs. Accordingly, under the leadership of Daniel Webster, that erstwhile states' righter and opponent of the tariffs of 1816 and 1824, the New England congressmen reversed their position and voted in favor of the tariff of 1828. They were supported by congressmen from the Middle Atlantic and northwestern states, and the tariff passed. Southern opposition to the law was vehement; leaders throughout the area began to talk of deserting the Jackson coalition and of dissolving the Union. Whether the episode altered the outcome of the election is questionable. What is not debatable is that the passage of the Tariff of Abominations dumped in Jackson's lap a set of problems that would plague him throughout his term in office.[54]

The election of Andrew Jackson in 1828 was the initial stage in the formation of the second American party system, one that suited the more democratic place the nation had become. A motley coalition put Jackson across, groups of politicians who differed in principles, policies, ideologies, and visions of the future. The one thing they shared was a desire to see Jackson elected, and as often as not, they shared that desire only as a means of advancing their own careers and interests.

The campaign was entirely personal, charges of moral turpitude being leveled on both sides. In that kind of race, Jackson, the hero of the Battle of New Orleans, had the advantage, because despite Adams's superb record as a diplomat, his image lacked glamour. Besides, Adams was viewed as an aristocrat if not a monarchist, whereas Jackson could readily (if inaccurately) be depicted as a champion of the common man against the "interests." Nothing was said on either side about what the candidates would do if they were elected, though Adams was vaguely reckoned to be a nationalist, Jackson a states' righter. They wanted to be president more than they wanted to do anything as president.[55]

That would become the norm in American politics: presidential elections grew into a quadrennial ritual that canonized or demonized candidates, avoided substantive issues or magnified bogus ones, and served as a means whereby a diverse people could come together in mock warfare so that genuine warfare would not be necessary. But in 1828 the system was in its infancy, or perhaps in its embryo form, and real issues had brought many Americans nearly to the brink of genuine warfare. In the circumstances, it was probably advantageous that no one, possibly not even Jackson himself, knew where he stood on the issues.

5

STATES' RIGHTS TRIUMPHANT

Jackson announced his positions in his first annual message to Congress in December 1829, and there were some surprises. In an address carefully calculated to appeal to as many groups as possible, he raised subjects that had not been national concerns before and offered novel approaches to others. Mainly for the benefit of the Deep South, he proposed that all Indians be removed from their present (and treaty-guaranteed) lands to a reserve across the Mississippi in what would become Oklahoma and what most white Americans thought of as the Great American Desert. For those who were displeased by the tenor of the decisions of the Marshall Court, he proposed a constitutional amendment to divide the Supreme Court into two branches, one each for the states east and west of the Appalachians. He suggested another amendment to avoid repetition of the presidential election fiasco of 1824, namely, direct popular election. As for internal improvements, he offered an original approach: drop the subject until the public debt was retired, which could be expected soon, and then the federal government would parcel out its surplus revenues to the states, thereby enabling them to finance their own internal improvements. In regard to the protective tariff, Jackson's first draft condemned it as tending to "impair, rather than foster, the great interests of this country," but Secretary of State Martin Van Buren convinced him that he should hedge his remarks on the subject, and he did so.[1]

Concerning monetary institutions, he appealed to a hostile bias that dated from the eighteenth-century English Oppositionists and had been warmly embraced by Jefferson and John Taylor of Caroline. Specifically, he attacked the Bank of the United States, declaring to Congress that "both the constitutionality and the expediency of the law creating this bank are well questioned by a large portion of our fellow-citizens, and it must be admitted by all that it has failed in the great aim of establishing a uniform and sound currency." His thinking at the time was that the Bank should be replaced by an institution wholly owned by the government.[2]

Ideologically, the message tilted strongly in the direction of states' rights, but the courses that Jackson as well as his supporters and enemies would follow were influenced, if not determined, by factors other than what the president initially considered. Given the current political game, most players took their stances not on the basis of ideology or even economic interest but on the basis of personal ambitions and the interests of their faction or party. Inconsistencies and shifts of position became commonplace, and that tendency was mightily compounded by the idiosyncrasies of Andrew Jackson. The president was a man of powerful prejudices and passions, and he identified his views with the voice of the people. Anyone who crossed him was therefore an enemy of the sovereign people, and those who did took on the burden of Jackson's contempt and hatred for life or unto the death.

The course of events during Jackson's tenure was erratic, but when his presidency was done, the federal authority was immeasurably weaker, and the states, for practical purposes, were supreme.

The first test of Jackson's credentials as a states' rights man came from Georgia, and he passed it with flying colors. Eleven days after the publication of his address, the legislature of Georgia responded to the call for Indian removal by passing a number of laws concerning the Cherokees in the state. The acts extended the state's jurisdiction to include most of the Cherokee territory, prohibited the Indians from digging for gold on their lands, nullified the treaties between the Cherokees and the United States and all Cherokee laws and constitutions adopted under the authority of those treaties, forbade meetings of the newly established Cherokee government, and extended the laws of Georgia to apply to Cherokees in or out of their territory. Each of these acts was in overt violation of the "supreme law of the land," treaties made under the authority of the United States.[3]

Georgia's actions were the culmination, but not yet the climax, of a series of events dating back to 1791. At that time the Cherokees agreed to cede to the United States a substantial portion of their land in Georgia in exchange for protection in the lands they retained. Eleven years later, Georgia ceded to the United States the portions of the state that became Alabama and Mississippi, in exchange for a promise that the Indian titles remaining in Georgia would be extinguished "as soon as it could be done peaceably and on reasonable terms." For various reasons, the federal government had not fulfilled the bargain with Georgia: by 1819 it had acquired 8 million acres of Indian lands in Mississippi and Alabama, but only about 1 million of the 5 million acres owned by Indians in Georgia. Georgians were frustrated by the inaction, and during the Adams administration the governor had mobilized the militia to wage war against the Indians, the United States, or both. A showdown was avoided when the administration negotiated a treaty to remove the Creek Indians from the state, but the Cherokees remained.[4]

Two developments concentrated and intensified white Georgia's hostility toward the Cherokees. Since the Monroe administration, the federal government had supported schools for the Cherokees, run largely by New England missionaries, and the tribe had developed a written language, started a newspaper, adopted Anglo-American property laws, and otherwise made strides toward European-style civilization. In 1827 the tribe adopted a constitution, organizing a government along the lines of the United States Constitution. The prospect of a permanent state within the state sorely rankled white Georgians. The other precipitating development was that early in 1829 gold was discovered in Cherokee territory.[5]

In response to Georgia's legislation, the Cherokees sought redress from the federal government, appealing to President Jackson for protection by the army. Jackson, however, was entirely sympathetic to the Georgians and their claim to have authority to legislate for all persons resident in the state. Accordingly, he rebuffed the Indians, declaring that "the President of the United States has no power to protect them against the laws of Georgia." Jackson's view was widely shared, namely, that "civilizing" the Indians had thrown them into the clutches of avaricious chiefs and whites who had married Indian women, and that if the commonality was freed from "the tyranny of these aristocrats," as Jackson termed them, the people would gladly emigrate. Jackson and his supporters maintained that removing the Indians was a humane policy, on the ground that if they remained and tried to assimilate they would be annihilated. (Henry Clay, no Jackson man, was more forthright; he said that "their disappearance from the human family would be no great loss to the world.")[6]

Just before the Georgia laws establishing jurisdiction were to go into effect, Congress considered Jackson's proposed Indian Removal Act, and in an acrimonious debate, members of both houses made their positions clear. Anti-Jackson men, who generally called themselves National Republicans, opposed the proposal as inhumane and motivated by greed. The president's and the bill's supporters called the northern and eastern congressmen hypocrites, since "the Indians in New York, New England, Virginia etc etc" had already been left to "the tender mercies of those States," and now they were opposing exertion of the same authority by Georgia, Alabama, and Mississippi. One National Republican added a twist to the states' rights issue by claiming that Jackson's policy was designed to usurp the rights of both the states and Congress. "The only power which stands between the Executive and the States is Congress," said Representative Henry R. Storrs of New York. "The States may destroy the Union themselves by open force, but the concentration of power in the hands of the Executive leads to despotism, which is worse. Of the two evils, I should prefer the nullifying power in the States—it is less dangerous."[7]

The Indian Removal Act was passed on May 30, 1830. Some Indians had gained allotments of land for personal use in exchange for agreeing to cede tribal claims; thus, for example, individual

Choctaws were allotted about a third of a million acres of the more than 10 million ceded by the tribe, and they remained in the area. Otherwise, the expectation was that the eastern tribes would agree to voluntary removal, for they were too weak to resist. Two northern tribes, the Sac and the Fox, did resist, and numbers of them died for their efforts. In the South the Cherokees prepared to take their case to court, and they engaged William Wirt and John Sergeant, two distinguished attorneys, to represent them.[8]

That returned Georgia to the spotlight and antagonized Jackson in the bargain. Able as their counsel were, the Cherokees showed little political sense in selecting them, for the lawyers were among the president's bitter political enemies, and their choice was ill calculated to conciliate him. In any event, Wirt and Sergeant forthwith determined to bring a bill in equity in original action in the Supreme Court, seeking an injunction to restrain Georgia from executing the laws that the plaintiff contended were illegal and unconstitutional. Rather ingenuously, Wirt wrote to Georgia Governor George R. Gilmer suggesting that the state should join the suit as a test case. Gilmer responded with a sarcastic refusal, declaring the absolute immunity of the state from suit in the federal courts and the state's right to refuse obedience to federal mandates.[9]

Before the suit began, however, a different case involving the same issues arose. A Cherokee named Corn Tassel had murdered another Indian in Cherokee territory and had been arrested by state authorities, convicted, and sentenced to be hanged. An appeal was made to the Supreme Court on a writ of error, the ground being that the applicable state law was unconstitutional. The writ was issued, but Governor Gilmer treated it with disdain. He sent it to the legislature, which was then (December 1830) in session, announcing that he would resist an attempt to enforce it with all the means at his command. If the Supreme Court could enforce such a writ, he declared, the usurpation would "eventuate in the utter annihilation of the State Governments." The legislature responded by enjoining "every officer of the State to disregard any and every mandate and process that should be served upon them." Two days later, on Christmas Eve, Tassel was executed. In the words of the distinguished

Supreme Court historian Charles Warren, this "was, in fact, practical Nullification."[10]

Many northerners were appalled by Georgia's action; Jackson and his followers thought it perfectly proper. Jackson himself wrote to his secretary of war that "the north american, Indian tribes, east of the Mississippi are a conquered and dependent people. . . . they are dependent; not on the Federal power in exclusion to the state authority, when they reside within the limits of a state, but to the sovereign power of the state within whose sovereign limits they reside." The administration's Washington newspaper, the *United States Telegraph,* commented that Georgia's action "demonstrates the absurdity of the doctrine which contends that the Court is clothed with supreme and absolute control over the States." Jacksonians in Congress, instead of remonstrating against Georgia, moved to cancel the Supreme Court's authority to hear appeals from state trial courts, but the effort failed.[11]

Two and a half months after Tassel's execution, the Court heard arguments and rendered a decision in the case Wirt and Sergeant had brought on behalf of the tribe. Friends of the Cherokees were again disappointed, for although Marshall expressed sympathy with the Indians, he ruled that the Court had no original jurisdiction because the Cherokee were not a nation under the meaning of the Constitution. He hinted strongly, however, that he would rule in favor of the Indians if a suit were brought properly.[12]

A suitable case went up a year later. A part of Georgia's 1830 legislation required whites living in Cherokee territory to obtain licenses and swear an oath of allegiance to the state. Two missionaries from New England, Dr. Elizur Butler and Samuel A. Worcester, refused to get licenses and subsequently, when ordered banished from the state, refused to go. They were arrested, tried, and sentenced to four years at hard labor. They appealed, and in October 1831 the Supreme Court—now asserting jurisdiction—agreed to hear the case and ordered Georgia's governor and attorney general to appear for the state. As they had done in the Cherokee case, they refused to appear. Arguments were heard for Butler and Worcester in February 1832, and in March, Marshall announced his decision. He declared the Georgia statute unconstitutional, holding that the federal government's jurisdiction was exclusive. The missionaries were to be released, but the implementation order was delayed, seemingly in the hope that Georgia would comply voluntarily.[13]

The state did not comply; rather, the governor and attorney general denounced the decision and declared that they were willing to employ armed force to prevent its implementation. Jackson, who sympathized with Georgia, was criticized by some for not enforcing the decision, but he was neither asked nor authorized to do so. Indeed, the Court itself was unable for technical reasons to act for the prisoners' release, and citing the Georgia officials for contempt would not have freed the missionaries. The decision, in other words, was unenforceable. After a time, Georgia agreed to release the missionaries, but only if they agreed to leave the state, which is what the state had ordered in the first place.[14]

A postscript to Georgia's defiance was added three years later, when a man named James Graves was involved in a reprise of the Corn Tassel case. He was convicted of murder, the Court ordered his release, and he was hanged. In adopting a resolution approving the action, the legislature referred to the "residuary mass of sovereignty which is inherent in each State . . . in the confederacy."[15]

Even as Georgia's open and successful defiance of federal authority was being played out, a more problematical challenge was being waged by South Carolina. Until the mid-1820s, South Carolina had been staunchly nationalistic, and its leading national figure, John C. Calhoun, had been consistently nationalistic. A severe economic downturn that coincided with the enactment of the 1824 tariff changed that stance. At the beginning of 1825, the wholesale price of cotton was 18.6 cents a pound; by 1827, it plummeted by half, to 9.3 cents a pound. The wholesale price index for all South Carolina export staples in Charleston fell during the same period from 133 to 77, while the cost of imports remained constant. As conditions worsened, local political leaders ever more shrilly demanded action against the tariff, and upon the passage of the Tariff of Abominations in 1828, cries for nullification reached fever pitch. Moreover, nullificationists were not alone: a group headed by twenty-seven-year-old Robert Barnwell Rhett, a member of the legislature, was beginning to call for more radical measures.[16]

The commotion put Calhoun in a difficult position. On the one hand, he was driven by his national ambitions. He had been Adams's vice-president when the Tariff of Abominations was passed, and later in the year he was elected vice-president again, this time under Jackson. Jackson had indicated that he would serve only one term, which would clear the way for Calhoun as the favorite candidate for president in 1832. To identify himself too openly with the radicals in his state could severely damage his prospects for the presidency. On the other hand, he had no desire to lose his power base at home, which could happen if he was lukewarm in his state's cause. Besides, he believed devoutly in the Union, and he feared that if he could not come up with a moderate but effective way of protesting the tariff, the likes of Rhett would lead South Carolina into a fatal effort at secession. Accordingly, when a legislative committee, appointed to draft a statement of grievances and a plan of protest, asked Calhoun to craft the document, he agreed. He gave the committee permission to use his name but thought it best that his authorship not be made public, and it was not.[17]

The result was the *South Carolina Exposition and Protest,* which became the standard and authoritative defense of the doctrine of nullification. First Calhoun dealt with the tariff itself, pointing out that the Constitution granted Congress the taxing power for the sole purpose of raising revenue to spend for the general welfare and the common defense. Levying tariffs for the purpose of promoting the interests of one group of people, manufacturers, was not among the enumerated powers and could not be justified by any reasonable reading of the necessary and proper clause. Thus the whole principle of protective tariffs was "unconstitutional, unequal, and oppressive," making southerners "the serffs of the system." He followed this argument with a lengthy examination of the economics of agriculture and manufacturing as they related to international trade.[18]

Then Calhoun turned to politics, with an analysis that was closely reasoned and learned. His starting premise was that irresponsible power was incompatible with liberty. The Constitution, he wrote, had been designed to restrain power by a system of checks and balances, but the restraints had broken down under the pressure of population growth and democratization. The nation now had a system of majority rule, and the Framers had recognized that unrestrained majority rule could be as tyrannical as rule by an absolute monarch. The South had become a permanent minority, at the mercy of the North. The way it could protect itself lay in the nature of the compact that had created the Union. The compact had been between the sovereign people of the sovereign states, severally, and all powers that had not been delegated or implied were reserved to the states or to the people. If the government of the United States exceeded its powers, the states had the right and duty to protect their citizens by interposing their authority between them and the United States. This was essentially the argument that Jefferson and Madison had made in the Virginia and Kentucky Resolutions and in Madison's 1799 committee report to the Virginia legislature, but Calhoun developed it thoroughly and buttressed it by reference to the Framing, the Constitution itself, and the contests over ratification.[19]

Calhoun did not recommend interposition or nullification at once. He counseled patience, for he hoped that repeal of the 1828 tariff and rejection of the protective principle could be obtained through normal political channels, but that was not to be. Advocates of tariff reform expected that Jackson and his partisans in Congress would support their efforts, but the president dashed that possibility with his equivocation in his first message to Congress. Then southerners tried a different tactic: they would forge a coalition of southern and western congressmen, the South supporting the West in its efforts to obtain a policy of free or virtually free lands in the public domain (and perhaps generous grants of those lands to the western states) in exchange for western support against protectionism.[20]

The alliance of South and West was stillborn as a result of a brilliant performance by Daniel Webster. Early in 1830, in the first session of the Congress elected with Jackson, the most celebrated debate in the Senate's history took place, mainly between Webster and Robert Y. Hayne of South Carolina. The occasion was a resolution about the public domain, but Webster cleverly shifted it to a debate about the nature of the Union. Hayne followed the argument Calhoun had laid down in the *Exposition,* and he was historically on sound ground. Webster followed the position that Marshall had pronounced in *M'Culloch* v. *Maryland*—that the Constitution was the creation of the whole people of America, a notion Marshall might well have taken from Webster's argument in the case—and his position had no grounding in fact. But Webster's oration (particularly his "second reply" to Hayne) was spellbinding; he swept up the audience, and the audience became the entire nation, for forty thousand copies of the speech were printed and circulated. For generations schoolboys memorized and recited the speech, especially its last line, aimed at Hayne's paraphrase of what would be Calhoun's toast to the Union as "next to our liberty the most dear": "Liberty *and* Union, now and forever, one and inseparable."[21]

States' righters were put on the defensive, and soon Calhoun was politically and personally on the defensive as well. The president, prodded by his favorite, the cunning Van Buren, deliberately picked a quarrel with Calhoun to force him from the party. The ostensible cause of the rift was a misunderstanding about Calhoun's stance in regard to Jackson's actions during the Seminole War in 1818: Jackson had originally believed that Calhoun was his single defender in Monroe's cabinet, but now he was told that Calhoun thought he should have been punished. A bitter exchange of letters between the two men took place in 1830, but the issue had been worked through earlier, and Jackson's raising it again was a carefully predetermined way of causing a rupture. To be sure, Jackson's hostility toward Calhoun was genuine and bitter, but the real reason was that he supposed that Calhoun's wife was the ringleader in a campaign to snub the vivacious young bride of Secretary of War John Eaton, Jackson's intimate friend and "almost adopted son." Margaret "Peggy" O'Neale Timberlake Eaton, the daughter of a tavern keeper, was the subject of vicious gossip, and that reminded Jackson of similar gossip about his beloved deceased wife. The subject became an obsession with him. He spent his first year in office trying to track down and scotch the rumors; "She is as chaste as a virgin!" he roared. When he concluded that Floride Calhoun was among Peggy's leading detractors, he declared war on Calhoun forever, convincing himself that Calhoun's aim was "to coerce me to abandon Eaton, and thereby bring on me disgrace for having appointed him, and thereby weaken me in the affections of the nation, and open the way to his preferment on my ruin." The wheels of history sometimes turn on petty pivots.[22]

Calhoun's hopes of becoming president were doomed, and though he was able to delude himself for a while, he became committed irrevocably to firming up and maintaining his base in South Carolina, and that in turn propelled him into the camp of the nullificationists. He made his public stand, over the advice of his friend and political ally Duff Green, in an article published in the Pendleton (S.C.) *Messenger* and dated July 26, 1831. The article, known as the Fort Hill Address, retraced and elaborated the argument contained in the *South Carolina Exposition,* but it added what Calhoun elsewhere would refer to as the idea of the concurrent majority. In free constitutional governments, he wrote, there are absolute majorities of the whole society, whose approval is necessary for legitimate rule, but there are also distinct classes or interests, or concurrent majorities, whose approval is also necessary when their rights are oppressed by the absolute majority. In contemporary England and ancient Sparta and Rome, the people were divided into distinct classes, and in the constitutions of those states, each was "represented in the Government, as a separate estate, with a distinct voice, and a negative on the acts of its co-estates, in order to check their encroachments." In the United States, "no artificial and separate classes of society" existed, but there was a "contrariety of interests . . . almost exclusively geographical, resulting mainly from difference of climate, soil, situation, industry and production." The geographical distinctions were embodied in the several states, which—because the Constitution itself had been created by them as thirteen concurrent majorities, not by the absolute majority of the whole people of America—necessarily retained a "negative on the acts" of the absolute majority.[23]

The Fort Hill Address was widely reprinted and elicited favorable editorial comment even in New York and New England, though it did not inspire South Carolina, just yet, to act upon its implications. Action was not, however, long in coming. Already in 1830 the state's legislative elections had turned on the issue of whether to call a special convention to nullify the 1828 tariff; proponents won in both houses, but not by the required two-thirds majority in both. Then in 1832 Congress revised the tariff slightly, but in ways that benefited northeastern manufacturing and commercial interests. Without waiting for new elections, Governor Hamilton called the South Carolina legislature into special session, and it authorized the election of delegates to a nullifying convention. In accordance with Calhoun's theories, a return to the source of sovereignty was thereby being made. The procedure was precisely the same as that by which South Carolina had ratified the Constitution in 1788.[24]

The convention adopted an Ordinance of Nullification on November 24, 1832. The ordinance declared the tariffs of 1828 and 1832 unconstitutional, null, and void and forbade the collection in the state of the duties levied by them, as of the following February 1. It provided that no appeal could be taken to the Supreme Court; required all civil and military officers of the state to enforce the ordinance and the statutes enacted under its authority; and declared that if the federal government employed force in an effort to collect the tariffs, the bonds of union between South Carolina and the other states would be dissolved. Calhoun was not happy with the last feature. He had wanted the ordinance to be enforced by the state courts through proceedings against each federal officer who attempted to collect the duties. The officer would then have to seek a writ of error from the Supreme Court, and if the court ruled in his favor, South Carolina would ignore its order. That would have made South Carolina's action exactly parallel to Georgia's, which Jackson had so recently if tacitly condoned.[25]

Irrespective of whether South Carolina had followed the course Calhoun suggested, the reaction of the president would have been the opposite of that regarding Georgia, for entirely personal reasons: South Carolina's nullification was closely identified with a man Jackson hated, and the state had refused to vote for his reelection. Jackson told his aides that he intended to have the leading nullifiers "arrested and arraigned for treason," alerted the federal troops in Charleston harbor, and sent General Winfield Scott to take command of the troops in the state. On December 10 he issued a proclamation denouncing and refuting the nullifiers, embracing the "whole people" theory of the origins of the Constitution, and appealing to South Carolinians to reject the designing leaders who had brought them to the brink of treason.[26]

South Carolina's response was defiant. The legislature enacted the nullifying convention's ordinance. The newly installed governor, former Senator Hayne, issued a counterproclamation defying the president again, and the legislature thumbed its nose at Jackson by electing Calhoun (who had resigned the vice-presidency) to the Senate in Hayne's place. Jackson countered by asking Congress for authority—a force bill—to use the army to collect the revenues and empower him to close any port at his discretion. Hayne advised the people of his state to arm themselves for resistance. The Jacksonian press undertook a vicious campaign to depict nullification as treason and Calhoun as the archtraitor. But actually, the issue divided both Jacksonians and National Republicans, for even Webster agreed that if Calhoun's analysis of the origin of the Constitution was sound, the doctrine of nullification was sound. In the ensuing senatorial debates, Calhoun decisively demonstrated the soundness of his analysis, and Webster knew it. Said the aged John Randolph of Roanoke, who witnessed Calhoun's demonstration, he saw "Webster die, muscle by muscle."[27]

As the threats and counterthreats escalated, the nation was in genuine peril, and someone with a cool head was needed to intervene. That someone was Henry Clay. Clay feared to put an army into the Old Hero's hands, for he dreaded Jackson's reckless anger, nor could he accept Calhoun's argument that nullification was the way to preserve the Union. He also perceived that a sudden and drastic reduction of the tariff could wreak havoc upon the economy. But he saw the elements of a compromise that would render nullification and a force bill academic questions. He introduced a compromise tariff that would reduce duties in two-year intervals until they reached a uniform 20 percent, and reluctantly he supported the force bill. Both measures were passed on March 1, 1833. That broke the crisis, though South Carolinians went through the motions of standing by their position. They had rescinded nullification of the earlier tariff laws as soon as they learned of Clay's proposal, and they accepted the compromise tariff with relief. But, consistent to the end, they formally nullified the force bill. A showdown was no longer necessary, and the episode ended.[28]

Jackson had the opportunity a few months later to show whether he was firm in his position that a state could not defy federal law, and he demonstrated that he had no stomach left for a contest with a defiant state. In Alabama, most Indians had agreed under the Indian Removal Act to cede their lands and leave, but Creeks still held 2 million of their 5 million acres. Federal marshals and the army were ordered to protect them, but speculators and settlers flocked onto the reserved lands and defied federal authorities. Then in July 1833, soldiers killed a county commissioner who favored the settlers, and Alabama whites started forming volunteer companies to force out the army. General Scott advised Secretary of War Lewis Cass that if he tried to use the army to enforce federal law, Georgia, Mississippi, both Carolinas, and Virginia would join Alabama in armed resistance. Cass consulted with Jackson, and they agreed that white people should not kill each other for the protection of Indians, and the force bill was not invoked.[29]

The doctrine of states' rights, as embraced by most Americans, was not concerned exclusively or even primarily with state resistance to federal authority. Rather, it was addressed mainly to keeping federal activity at a bare-bones minimum. Jackson captured its spirit well when he wrote that "our Government" was not "to be maintained or our Union preserved by invasions of the rights and powers of the several States." He continued, in "attempting to make our General Government strong we make it weak. Its true strength consists in leaving individuals and States as much as possible to themselves— in making itself felt, not in its power, but in its beneficence; not in its control, but in its protection; not in binding the States more closely to the center, but leaving each to move unobstructed in its proper orbit."[30]

Jackson resisted efforts by Congress to extend the scope of the federal government and worked diligently to reduce the activities in which it was already engaged. Not least among his goals was the retirement of the public debt. Indeed, it became one of his priorities, which explains in part why he was loath to have the tariff schedules lowered. His insistence upon frugality in government was made dramatically evident during the first Congress that met under his presidency, when he vetoed with fanfare an internal improvement project called the Maysville Road. A proposed extension of the National Road was to run from Maysville, Kentucky, to Lexington. On the ground that it was an expenditure in a single state (Henry Clay's, at that) and not for the general welfare, Jackson vetoed the bill. Congress seemed determined, he said, "to make mine one of the most extravagant administrations since the commencement of the Government. This must not be." When Congress adjourned at the end of the month, it left Jackson a last-minute barrage of additional internal improvement bills, and he killed them all, several by pocket veto—withholding his signature after Congress adjourned.[31]

His effort to minimize government culminated in his destruction of the Bank of the United States. The Bank's twenty-year charter was scheduled to expire in 1836, but in the winter of 1831–1832, its friends decided that the time was ripe to seek a recharter. Jackson was ambiguous about the Bank in his third annual message, and in February 1832, Secretary of State Edward Livingston, seemingly with the president's approval, told a leading Pennsylvania Jacksonian that Jackson would sign a recharter bill if certain modifications were made. Actually, Jackson was determined to veto a recharter no matter what the terms; he and his choice for vice-president, Van Buren, hoped merely to delay the measure until after they were elected in November. Negotiations about modification did delay the question until March, and then administration leaders in Congress stalled by demanding an investigation of charges that the Bank had violated its existing charter. No violations were found, and in June, Congress approved the recharter by substantial margins.[32]

Jackson responded on July 10 with a veto message, written largely by kitchen cabinet member Amos Kendall, that combined unrestrained anger with unrestrained demagoguery. The message asserted that the Bank was unconstitutional, despite the decision in *M'Culloch* v. *Maryland,* and echoed Jefferson's dictum that the three branches of government "must each for itself be guided by its own opinion of the Constitution." Jackson castigated Congress for enacting legislation aimed at making "the rich richer and the potent more powerful" and denounced such legislation as "grants of monopolies and exclusive privileges" that prostituted government "to the advancement of the few at the expense of the many." He chastised the Supreme Court for betraying the "humble members of society, the farmers, mechanics, and laborers," by upholding the constitutionality of the Bank and accused the Bank itself of arraying "section against section, interest against interest, and man against man, in a fearful commotion which threatens to shake the foundations of our Union."[33]

When Jackson was reelected by a considerable margin that fall, he took his success at the polls to be a mandate to destroy the "Monster," as he called the Bank, and he set out to slay it. In his December 1832 message to Congress, he recommended that the Bank be investigated on account of the "many serious charges impeaching its character" and the general fear (which no one had expressed) "that it is no longer a safe depository of the money of the people." Secretary of the Treasury Louis McLane had already, at Jackson's request, investigated the Bank, and the House Ways and Means Committee had followed on its own. Both concluded that the Bank was solvent and the deposits safe. Furthermore, the Bank had recently demonstrated that it could survive attacks, including what Jackson was determined to bring about—the complete removal of the government's deposits. During the preceding year, government deposits had exceeded $10 million at their peak, but in January 1833, as a consequence of a sizable payment toward retiring the public debt, they had fallen to less than $25,000 without causing disruption of the Bank's operations or of the national economy.[34]

The lineup regarding the proposed removal was mixed. Jackson himself and some of his intimates were so consumed by hatred and fear of moneyed institutions that they were impervious to evidence that they were wrong. Others, notably speculators who resented the financial restraint imposed by the Bank and New Yorkers who aspired to dominate the nation's banking facilities, supported any attacks on the Bank that the president might undertake. On the opposite side, the Bank was popular, it had friends in Congress, and it was supported by most members of Jackson's party and by his cabinet.

Disregarding the advice of everyone who disagreed with him, Jackson announced to the cabinet on March 19, 1833, that he intended to remove the federal deposits from the Bank and place them in selected state banks. By law, however, the deposits could be removed only by the secretary of the treasury, and then only if they were unsafe. McLane refused to order their removal. Any encouragement this might have given Nicholas Biddle was short-lived, for unbeknownst to Biddle, Jackson had decided that as of June, McLane would take Livingston's place as secretary of state and be replaced at treasury by William Duane. Duane was a strict constructionist who thought the Bank was unconstitutional, but to Jackson's astonishment, he too refused to remove the deposits. He knew the Bank was safe, and he had vivid memories of the chaos in state banking during the War of 1812; he was not willing to violate the law that charged him with responsibility for keeping government funds in safe repositories. Subjected to intense pressure, he continued to refuse, and in September, Jackson summarily dismissed him.[35]

Duane's replacement was Attorney General Roger Brooke Taney of Maryland, an old-line, states' rights, strict constructionist who shared the president's hostility toward the Bank. Pending his confirmation (which never came), he began to comply with the withdrawal order. The process took awhile: as payments by government became due, funds were withdrawn, and as revenues came in, they were deposited in the "pet" state banks. That gave Biddle time to call in outstanding loans and curtail credit, with the result that the Bank remained strong. In the short run, Jackson's policy failed.[36]

The policy, however, had unforeseen consequences. Some state banks selected as depositories were honest and sound, others were not, but they all greatly expanded their note issues on the basis of federal deposits. That set off a speculative boom that lasted through the mid-1830s. The Bank's charter expired in 1836 and was not renewed, but Biddle obtained a charter from Pennsylvania and continued to operate. But he could not, in the absence of federal deposits, exercise restraint over the entire banking system, and the bubble, attracting British investments, continued to expand.

When it burst, government policies were largely responsible. In June 1836, Congress passed the Deposit Act, requiring that after January 1 at least one bank in every state be a repository for federal funds, and providing for the distribution of surplus revenues to the states when the debt was retired, which took place before the end of the year. In July, disturbed by the inflation resulting from currency issued against land speculators' notes, the Jackson administration issued a specie circular, requiring that after August 15 gold and silver be used to pay for public lands. A contraction set in, aggravated by British withdrawal of funds and the strain on state banks created by the distribution provisions of the Deposit Act. By early 1837, prices of land and cotton had collapsed; in May, banks in New York suspended specie payment, and shortly thereafter, those in Baltimore, Philadelphia, and Boston followed suit. In the wreckage, the Bank of the United States of Pennsylvania collapsed. As he had promised, Andrew Jackson had destroyed the Bank. He had also destroyed the American financial system, setting off the longest depression in the nation's history.[37]

The other bastion of national authority, the Supreme Court, seemed at the time of Jackson's first inauguration to stand on shakier ground than did the Bank. Its unpopular decisions had not yet evoked Georgia's open defiance, but movements were afoot to curtail it by increasing the number of justices, by requiring supermajorities in cases involving the constitutionality of state actions, and by repealing article 25 of the Judiciary Act to remove jurisdiction over state court decisions. What was more, a number of the justices were growing old—Marshall was seventy-three and Gabriel Duval seventy-five—and it appeared likely that when they retired or died, Jackson would replace them with radical strict constructionists and states' righters.[38]

Perhaps because of the pressure, perhaps because the weight of the Republican appointees was beginning to take effect, the Court had already become less consistent in its nationalism and more frequently divided in reaching decisions. In 1829, for example, the Court backed away somewhat from its earlier holding in *Gibbons* v. *Ogden* that the power of Congress to regulate commerce and navigation took precedence over state laws. In that case, Marshall did not have to consider whether states could legislate on the subject in the absence of congressional enactments. In *Willson* v. *Black Bird Creek Marsh Company,* Marshall faced that question. A steamboat operator brought suit to challenge a Delaware statute authorizing the building of a dam that would close off a small but navigable creek. Marshall ruled in favor of the state. Given "all the circumstances," he wrote in an ambiguous passage, the Delaware law could not "be considered as repugnant to the power" of Congress "to regulate commerce in its dormant state"—that is, when Congress had not acted. Reconciling this "dormant state" with the general thrust of the *Gibbons* ruling would for years produce uncertainty as to what states could and could not do in regard to interstate commerce.[39]

Uncertainty also marked subsequent cases arising from the commerce clause. Maryland had passed an act that required wholesalers of imported goods to pay a license fee. One refused to pay, calling the fee a tax on foreign commerce and therefore unconstitutional. The state contended that the fee applied to wholesalers of a variety of goods, some of which had incidentally been imported. The question before the Court was, at what point in the course of trade did the jurisdiction of the state begin. Marshall answered by formulating the "original package" doctrine: as long as imported items remained in the container in which they arrived and were not "mixed up with the mass of property in the country," they were in interstate or foreign commerce and not subject to state or local taxation. The doctrine would necessitate retreating in the future, but what was more vexing was a contradictory bit of obiter dictum. States could

control or prohibit imports, he said, as part of their "police power"—
this was the first case in which the phrase was used—to promote or
protect the health, safety, or well-being of their citizens.[40]

In 1834 a case arose in which the tension between the police
power and foreign commerce was put to the test, only to have the
Court avoid the question by flatly reversing an earlier position. New
York, overrun with indigent immigrants and facing the choice
between feeding them at state expense or letting them starve, enacted
a statute requiring the masters of ships to post bonds that immigrants
would not become public charges; otherwise, they could not be
landed. The statute was both a legitimate exercise of the police power
and an interference with foreign commerce, as Marshall had defined
the terms. Marshall and three associate justices thought the act unconstitutional, but because two of his supporters had been absent
during the arguments, they could not take part in the decision. Three
justices held that the law was constitutional. Marshall, however, out-
voted three to two, postponed the decision by reversing the ruling in
Fairfax's Devisee v. *Hunter's Lessee* and holding that decisions in
constitutional cases could not be given unless four justices, a majority of the whole, agreed. The case would finally be determined in
1837, by which time Marshall was dead.[41]

In two cases arising from the contract clause, the Court retreated
somewhat in the direction of states' rights. One had a long history.
The Constitution vests Congress with power to establish a uniform
system of bankruptcy law, but except for the Bankruptcy Act of
1800, which had "remained on the statute books for three years and
eight months," it had declined to legislate. The states were not expressly forbidden to create their own bankruptcy systems, and in
1811, New York became the first state to enact such legislation. The
law was challenged and reached the Supreme Court in the case of
Sturges v. *Crowninshield*. Marshall held that a state could pass a
bankruptcy act if it did not violate the contract clause, but he also
held that this specific act did violate the clause because it relieved
insolvent debtors of the obligation to pay debts contracted before
the law was passed. In response, New York and several other states
passed bankruptcy laws that applied to debts accrued thereafter but

not to those acquired before. In 1827, New York's revised system was challenged in *Ogden* v. *Saunders.* For the sole time in his career, Marshall was in dissent. For the majority, Justice Bushrod Washington held that a bankruptcy law in force at the time a contract was made formed a part of the contract, and the contracting parties understood that to be included in their agreement. Both the majority and the minority concurred that a state bankruptcy law could not discharge a debt owed to a citizen of another state.[42]

The other contract clause case produced a relaxation of the doctrine in the *Dartmouth College* case that a corporate charter was a contract and could never be altered unilaterally by a state. In 1791, Rhode Island had granted a corporate charter to the Providence Bank, and at that time the bank was not subject to taxation under state law. In the 1820s, taxes were levied on the bank, and it sued, claiming that the tax impaired the contract in the original charter. In *Providence Bank* v. *Billings,* the Supreme Court ruled that the bank was not exempt from taxation unless its charter of incorporation explicitly granted immunity, which it had not. The broad principles of the *Dartmouth* decision, however, remained intact as long as Marshall was on the Court.[43]

One last case pertaining to states' rights was handed down by the Marshall Court in 1833. The original understanding of the Bill of Rights—or, more properly, the substantive and procedural rights proclaimed in the first eight amendments—was that it did not restrict the states. Thus, for example, although the Fifth Amendment says that private property shall not be taken for public use except by "due process of law," and that if it is taken government must pay the owner a "just compensation," state and local governments disregarded these restrictions from the beginning. In the 1830s, the owner of a wharf in Baltimore, whose property had been rendered worthless by the city's redirection of certain streams for public use, sued on the ground that the action was a taking in violation of the Fifth Amendment. The Supreme Court ruled that the Fifth Amendment as well as the other amendments constituting the Bill of Rights did not apply to the states in any way. In reaching that decision, the Court was reverting to the original intentions of the Framers: that the states reserved all powers not granted by them to the federal government or expressly denied them in the Constitution.[44]

There remains the matter of Jackson's appointments to the Supreme Court, which were more numerous than those of any predecessor except Washington. Jackson's initial appointee was Postmaster General John McLean, chosen apparently to remove him as a barrier to Jackson's proposed policy of replacing post office employees with Jackson supporters. Almost no one objected to him. The next appointment would fill the vacancy caused by Bushrod Washington's death late in 1829. The front-runner seemed to be John Bannister Gibson, chief justice of Pennsylvania and an outspoken opponent of the authority of the Supreme Court to pass upon the constitutionality of statutes. But Gibson was a favorite of Calhoun, and the Calhounites strongly opposed another eminent Pennsylvanian, Henry Baldwin; so, in accordance with his practice of letting personal dislikes dictate, Jackson chose Baldwin. Then, in January 1835, he chose a close friend and supporter, James M. Wayne of Georgia, a staunch states' righter but a firm opponent of nullification. So far, Jackson had surprised his political opponents, who had been expecting the worst.[45]

That soon changed. About the time that Wayne was being appointed, Justice Gabriel Duval resigned. To succeed him, Jackson nominated Roger Brooke Taney, whom the Senate had previously rejected as secretary of the treasury. Taney's withdrawal of federal deposits from the Bank of the United States during a recess appointment had not endeared him to the senators, and on March 3, 1835—the last day of the Congress elected in 1832—the Senate rejected Taney a second time. It would be December before Jackson had another opportunity to fill the vacancy.[46]

A complication arose in the interim, for on July 6, 1835, Chief Justice Marshall died. Brooding on the matter for months, Jackson decided to fill the associate justiceship with Philip P. Barbour of Virginia (praised by the *Richmond Enquirer* as a man of "inflexible and uncompromising State-Rights principles") and to submit Taney as the replacement for Marshall. The nominations were sent to the Senate on December 28, eliciting cries of gloom and doom from Whigs, as the National Republicans were calling themselves to dramatize their opposition to the reign of "King Andrew." Wrote Webster to a friend, "Justice Story thinks the Supreme Court is *gone,* and I think so too." At first it appeared that the nominations, or at least Taney's, would be blocked, but after two and a half months, both were confirmed.[47]

The Supreme Court was not "*gone,*" but an indication of its future course was given while the nominations were pending. The Court sat in its annual session in the meantime, Story presiding, and it decided a conflict between federal and state authority—in favor of the state. The question was whether property seized by a sheriff under a state court order could be taken by a United States marshal. No, answered the Court, in an opinion written by Jackson appointee Justice McLean. "A most injurious conflict of jurisdiction," he wrote, reversing the decision in *United States* v. *Peters* and the whole tendency of the Marshall Court, "would be likely, often, to arise between the Federal and the State Courts, if the final process of the one could be levied on property which had been taken by the process of the other."[48]

Apart from the economic disaster he bequeathed the nation through his fiscal policies, the legacy of Andrew Jackson was a mixed bag. Like most of his countrymen, he believed in minimal government at the federal level and deplored the centralizing tendencies of the administration of John Quincy Adams, and in that respect, his presidency was an unqualified success. He believed in states' rights—again, as did most Americans—and his eight years in office saw the triumph of the states' rights doctrine. He also believed in the Union, and his policies did nothing to weaken Americans' faith in the Union; perhaps, as a result of his handling of the nullification crisis, he strengthened the bonds.

Conversely, a system of divided sovereignty such as the Founders had devised requires delicate but strong balancing mechanisms if it is to remain viable, and in this respect, Jackson's doings were unfortunate. At the state level, effective governments, jealous of their prerogatives, are needed to prevent encroachments by the central authority. They must be able, if not to interpose themselves between the federal government and their own citizens, at least to retard federal measures by legal and constitutional means. Jackson did nothing to upset existing arrangements in that dimension, but he undermined the requisite balancing mechanisms from the other direction. The central authority must restrain the states by providing a uniform and stable currency system, and the destruction of the Bank made that all but impossible. The central authority must provide a legal arbiter for disputes between individuals and between states, and Jackson's appointments to the Supreme Court considerably lessened that capacity. Finally, the chief executive must embody the spirit of the nation and serve as a symbolic surrogate for a monarch. Jackson brought such disrepute to his office that that vital function of the presidency could scarcely be performed again for the remainder of the century.

6

GOVERNMENT IN LIMBO
1837–1845

The federal government, by the time Jackson departed its premises, had become virtually nonfunctional. His immediate successor, Van Buren, spent most of his efforts in office trying to make the separation of the government from economic activity in general and banks in particular permanent and complete. The Whigs, to be sure, were anxious to reestablish a national bank and cause the general government to resume an active role in promoting economic growth, and in 1840 they gained control of the White House and both houses of Congress. Unfortunately for their plans, however, their president, William Henry Harrison, died soon after he took office. He was succeeded by John Tyler, who turned out to be a more staunch states' righter than Van Buren. As a consequence, the Whigs' ambitious programs came to naught.

The government limped along, performing those minimal functions it could not shirk. It did manage to avoid a war with Great Britain over the disputed boundary between Maine and New Brunswick and to settle the issue amicably, though its armed forces were considerably expanded during the tension. Otherwise, it delivered the mail, or most of the mail, for it extralegally kept antislavery propaganda from being sent to the Deep South. It collected enough tariff revenues to service the small public debt and meet its minuscule payroll. It operated its land office to accommodate the immigrants who came in increasing numbers and the easterners who sold their old farms and migrated westward, also in increasing numbers. And that was about the sum total of what the federal government did.

Inactivity at the federal level did not, however, mean that government in America was inactive. The idea of states' rights carried with it, in the country at large, the idea of states' duties, and that implied vigorous promotion of economic activity by state governments. Inasmuch as the different states and regions had widely varying resources for promotional activity, the state-oriented order of things yielded greatly varying directions and rates of economic growth and drove the regions further apart.

Nor did the dormancy of the federal government mean that federal politics was harmonious. The national political arena became the center of heated controversy concerning the newly raised issue of slavery, a controversy that reached the flash point during the debates about the annexation of the Republic of Texas. By the time the Texas question was settled, a divisive war with Mexico was looming, and a civil war—the ultimate test of the nature of the federal Union— would be barely fifteen years away.

Martin Van Buren expressed his philosophy of government—or, rather, his view of the powers and duties of the federal government— in refusing to countenance efforts to end or alleviate the severe economic depression that beset the nation. "All communities," he said, "are apt to look to government for too much." Government's "real duty" was simply to establish a legal framework in which "private interest, enterprise, and competition" could operate, not to act positively but "to enact and enforce a system of general laws" that left each citizen free "to reap under its benign protection the rewards of virtue, industry, and prudence."[1]

The substantive measures that Van Buren did propose concerned the currency. One was a national bankruptcy act, designed to facilitate the closing of state banks and thereby to prevent the ruinous issue of unsound bank notes for speculative purposes. The proposal was a bit late, for the country has been awash in worthless notes during the years leading to the panic of 1837, but the bubble had burst, and deflation, not currency inflation, was the problem. On the ground that it was pointless to close the bank door after the money had escaped, Congress declined to act on the president's recommendation.[2] The second measure aimed at stopping the blending of "private interests with the operations of public business" by establishing an independent treasury system, whereby government funds would be kept in and disbursed from government facilities rather than banks. The effect would be to limit the credit and notes issuable by banks. Hard-money ideologues in the Jefferson-Jackson tradition, distrusting paper money of any description and holding a generally negative view of government, welcomed the independent treasury proposal. Southerners approved too, but for more tangible reasons: it would curtail government and thus hold down the need for tariff revenues. Besides, many southern planters had little need for bank credit, having credit connections directly with merchants in Britain, the destination of their agricultural staples. But despite this support, Congress did not enact the measure when Van Buren first proposed it at a special session in 1837 and rejected it again in 1838. Congress finally enacted it in the summer of 1840—and repealed it a year later.[3]

When the Whigs ousted Van Buren in the "Log Cabin and Hard Cider" elections of 1840, they thought they had gained a president who would follow their congressional leaders in reestablishing the federal government as an active participant in the nation's economic life. Whether Harrison would have gone along passively is questionable. He had no firm principles or policies, he was fuzzy regarding a national bank and took both sides regarding the tariff and internal improvements, and he was an amiable man who disliked confrontations. His brief tenure suggested that he might have had difficulty with some of the congressmen, especially the imperious Senator Henry Clay, to whom he reportedly said, "Mr. Clay, you forget that *I* am the President." But it did not matter, for shortly after midnight on April 4, 1841, only one month after he took the oath of office, he died.[4]

His successor, Vice-President Tyler, was described by John Quincy Adams as a "Virginia nullifier," but that description understates the extent of Tyler's commitment to the principle of states' rights. He rejected nullification as inexpedient and unconstitutional, arguing that the proper remedy when a state deemed an act of Congress unconstitutional was first to try all legitimate means to have the act overturned and then, those failing, to secede. While waiting to determine whether the act would be repealed, however, and while waiting to decide whether to secede, a state could not, according to Tyler, be compelled to comply with the law by force of arms, as the force bill had contemplated. In addition to holding these positions, Tyler was passionately opposed to financial institutions, to internal improvements at federal expense, and to protective tariffs.[5]

The clash between the accidental president and his party came almost immediately. Harrison had been persuaded to call a special session of Congress to convene on May 31, the purpose being to deal with the fiscal crisis that had resulted from Van Buren's inactivity. Congressional Whigs made it clear that they intended to recreate the Bank of the United States, though it would be called the Fiscal Bank of the United States, would be based in the District of Columbia, and would differ in several particulars from the Second Bank. A bill to that end was introduced in June, passed in the Senate by five votes in July, and passed in the House by a comfortable margin early in August. Tyler vetoed the bill on grounds of expedience and constitutionality. Clay Whigs in the Senate shouted "treason," but they were unable to muster the votes to override the veto.[6]

But Tyler had indicated that he would favor the creation of a suitable fiscal agent and suggested that he would support a bank if certain compulsory features—such as requiring states to permit branches within their borders—were not included. Complex negotiations, replete with misunderstandings, ensued, and a revised banking measure passed the House (August 23) and the Senate (September 3). Again Tyler vetoed the bill, giving substantially the same reasons as before, and again efforts to override the veto failed. Forthwith Tyler's entire cabinet, save for Secretary of State Daniel Webster, resigned in protest. The president received hundreds of letters threatening assassination, and congressmen began to talk of impeachment.[7]

Congress and the president continued to be deadlocked throughout the remainder of Tyler's term. The House lacked strong leadership, and of the three giants in the Senate, Webster had resigned to become secretary of state (in which capacity he negotiated the Webster-Ashburton Treaty, settling the dispute with Britain), Clay resigned to devote himself to campaigning for the Whig presidential nomination in1844, and Calhoun indicated his intention to resign and campaign for the Democratic nomination. Tyler looked toward obtaining either the Democratic nomination or nomination by a third party. No one paid much attention to the business of governing, the most interesting thing that happened being a motion by Representative John M. Botts of Virginia to impeach the president for "gross usurpation of power" and "arbitrary, despotic, and corrupt abuse of the veto power." The motion was rejected, 127 to 83.[8]

That left, if the federal government was to exert any centripetal force, the Supreme Court, with Roger Brooke Taney presiding. As it happened, the Court had a different set of ideas entirely.

Though Taney served as chief justice for more than twenty-eight years, one cannot properly refer to "the Taney Court" in the way one refers to "the Marshall Court." Marshall had introduced the practice of issuing a single opinion by the justices, frequently written by Marshall himself, instead of the earlier practice of having the justices deliver their opinions seriatim. Occasional dissents occurred during the Marshall years, but as a rule, the Court spoke as a body, perhaps on account of Marshall's personal charisma—a quality that Taney, for all his amiability, learning, and persuasiveness, lacked. During Taney's tenure, the justices, while sharing similar constitutional and legal philosophies and being more or less dedicated to strict construction and states' rights, were repeatedly divided. The Court, not uncommonly, issued as many opinions as there were judges, each following a different line of reasoning to arrive at a conclusion. Lawyers and other citizens who watched the doings of the Court found it difficult to predict what the next ruling was likely to be, even in a similar case.[9]

Taney and his brethren on the bench shared an enthusiasm for technological progress and economic growth, and they intended to use their judicial authority to promote those ends. This entailed a departure from the Marshall Court's use of the contract clause to protect vested property rights in favor of an interpretation that provided maximum opportunity for new technology and fresh ventures, and the Court removed constitutional barriers that had impeded activist state governments from vigorously supporting developments if they were so inclined. In sum, to the Supreme Court under Taney, states' rights meant state powers.[10]

This direction was evident in three decisions that the Court rendered in what contemporaries called the "judicial revolution of 1837," the first being the *Charles River Bridge* case. Back in 1785, the Massachusetts legislature had granted a corporate charter to investors who, in exchange for building a bridge over the Charles River to Charlestown on the mainland, were given a forty-year guarantee of being able to collect tolls from users of the bridge. The bridge was completed a year later, and so advantageous did it prove that in 1792 the state extended the charter for thirty years. But then in 1828 the legislature chartered the Warren Bridge Corporation to build a bridge close to and parallel to the Charles River Bridge, giving it the right to collect tolls but providing that after six years the bridge would belong to the commonwealth, and no tolls would be charged.[11]

Clearly the second bridge would deprive the Charles River Bridge proprietors of valuable, vested property rights. Under the doctrines of *Fletcher* v. *Peck* and the *Darmouth College* case, such deprivation was a violation of the contract clause. The case was argued before the Supreme Court in 1831, but one justice was absent and the others were evenly divided; no decision was rendered. The suit was repeatedly scheduled for reargument during the next five years, but each time a combination of illnesses or absences prevented a disposition.[12]

Finally, the case was argued before a full court in January 1837, and three weeks later Taney handed down his first decision—upholding the 1828 legislation. The key to the decision was that neither the original 1785 charter nor its subsequent extension explicitly granted exclusive rights to build a bridge on the site. "In grants by the public" Taney declared, "nothing passes by implication." The "object and end of all government," he added, "is to promote the happiness and prosperity of the community by which it is established; and it can never be assumed, that the government intended to diminish its power of accomplishing the end for which it was created." The crucial consideration, to Taney, was changing technology. In his own lifetime, primitive trails had been succeeded by turnpike roads, canals, and the steamboat, and the age of the railroad was well under way. The Charles River Bridge Company was claiming a monopoly over "a line of travelling," and if its claim were upheld, railroads, for example, could never be granted rights of way over routes already covered by turnpikes or canals. Such a doctrine would prevent the nation from employing the technological innovations "which are now adding to the wealth and prosperity, and the convenience and comfort, of every other part of the civilized world." Justice Story, alone in opposition, wrote a vigorous dissenting opinion in which he adhered to the older vested interest view of public contracts that there was "no surer plan to arrest all public improvements founded on private capital and enterprise, than to make the outlay of that capital uncertain and questionable, both as to security and as to productiveness." But most businessmen applauded Taney's decision; Story's was a voice from a bygone era.[13]

The second major decision of the 1837 term involved the reargument of *Mayor of the City of New York* v. *Miln,* a case that had been heard in 1834 but not decided. The day after argument in the *Charles River Bridge* case, the Court reconsidered the *Miln* case. The justices followed various courses of reasoning, but all except Story concurred that the state act restricting the landing of impoverished immigrants was constitutional. Justice Philip Barbour's opinion, recorded (inaccurately) as the majority view, pronounced a sweeping interpretation of the police power. He denied that the statute was a regulation of commerce, declaring instead that it was purely a police measure to protect the community from paupers and criminals. The state had a right as well as a "bounden and solemn duty" to "advance the safety, happiness and prosperity" of its citizens and to provide for their "general welfare, by any and every act of legislation, which it may deem to be conducive to these ends." In regulating its internal police, the state's power was "complete, unqualified, and exclusive."[14]

The third case, *Briscoe* v. *Bank of Kentucky,* substantially reversed a decision handed down by the Marshall Court seven years earlier. In that case, *Craig* v. *Missouri,* the Court had held that a state issue of paper money in the form of loan office certificates (paper lent to individuals against real estate mortgages) violated the article 1, section 10, ban on state issues of "bills of credit" and making anything but gold and silver legal tender. The ruling was technically questionable, because loan office certificates were historically quite different from bills of credit and because the Missouri law did not make the certificates legal tender. But the decision fit the Marshall Court's broad interpretation of article 1, section 10, and its intention to define state economic powers narrowly.[15]

The Court under Taney, believing that those powers should be defined broadly, ruled accordingly in *Briscoe* v. *Bank of Kentucky.* Kentucky had chartered a bank of which the state was the sole owner, and the bank issued notes that passed as currency. Justice John McLean, in the majority opinion, distinguished between an act of a state and an act of a satellite corporation created by a state and endorsed Kentucky's contention that if the Bank of Kentucky's notes were unconstitutional, so were the notes of every other state-chartered bank, "almost the entire circulating medium of the country." In vain, Story dissented again, arguing that what a state could not do, it could not authorize others to do.[16]

In a banking case decided two years later, *Bank of Augusta* v. *Earle,* the Court pronounced a doctrine that made the economic powers of the states almost absolute, though the ruling did go against a state on technical grounds. A Georgia bank had obtained bills of exchange (checks drawn by merchants on accounts with other merchants, not on bank accounts) issued by residents of Alabama, and in the depression that followed the panic of 1837, the debtors declined to pay, contending that an out-of-state corporation had no legal authority to do business in Alabama. The federal circuit court ruled in favor of the debtors, to the chagrin of businessman throughout the country. When the case was appealed to the Supreme Court,

Daniel Webster, as counsel for the bank, maintained that a corporation was a person in the eyes of the law and as a citizen of one state was entitled to "all Privileges and Immunities of Citizens in the several States," in keeping with article 4, section 2, of the Constitution. Taney, for the Court, rejected Webster's line of argument and opined that a state had full power to prevent outside corporations from conducting business inside its borders. But he went on to say that it was common practice to allow them to operate and that absent legislation expressly excluding them, it had to be assumed that the state had approved. On that narrow ground he ruled in favor of the bank, which led many people to conclude, mistakenly, that the Court had declared that a state could not keep outside corporations outside. The principle of exclusion stood, however, and in short order a number of states began to act on it. Truly, the Court seemed to be giving the states a blank check to fill in as they pleased.[17]

During the generation after the Civil war, the myth grew that, in the absence of an activist national government, the antebellum years had been a laissez-faire paradise (or hell, depending on the point of view) in which economic activity was essentially unregulated. As the myth had it, the spirit of individual pursuit of wealth swept the nation, the measure of the value of all things was money, the entrepreneur was the American par excellence, and the devil took the hindmost. The needs of the community, of society as a whole, were of little concern, and efforts to meet those needs by governmental action were disdained. In actuality, none of the above conditions ever existed, for communal concerns prevailed throughout the period, and those concerns were met by vigorous state action in every American jurisdiction.

Granted, in the three decades or so before Jackson became president, the shape of the law in the several states had been reforged to alter property relations in the direction of a capitalist system. This was the work not of politicians and legislatures but of lawyers and judges, who brought about a change in property law to favor development, replacing an older order in which property rights were regarded as existing for the enjoyment of the owner. Accompanying the transformation was a revolution in contract law that favored commercial development. Contract law had been based upon the concept that everything had a fair value and a just price; contracts violating that concept were invalid and unenforceable. The arrangement discriminated against merchants, traders, shippers, financiers, capitalistic manufacturers, and entrepreneurship in general. By midcentury, the theory that had come to prevail made the market the determinant of value. Given the embodiment of market theory in law, a modern, dynamic economy could replace the static, fixed economic system, rooted in feudalism, that had prevailed at the time of the adoption of the Constitution.[18]

But the states did not sit idly by and let capitalists run riot. Pennsylvania, for example, enacted and enforced laws abolishing child labor, limiting hours in factories and mines, and regulating working conditions. It enacted and enforced laws requiring the inspection of a wide variety of products intended for sale in external markets, including flour, beef, pork, hogslard, butter, biscuits, leather goods, tobacco, shingles, potash and pearlash, staves, lumber, pickled fish, spirituous liquors, and gunpowder. It required licenses of innkeepers, peddlers, retailers of foreign goods, liquor merchants, wharfage pilots, and auctioneers. It fixed standards of weights and measures in the absence of federal standards. The attitude underlying this activism was enunciated by Chief Justice Jeremiah Black of the state supreme court, who declared, "it is a grave error to suppose that the duty of a state stops with the establishment of those institutions which are necessary to the existence of government. . . . To aid, encourage, and stimulate commerce, domestic and foreign, is a duty of the sovereign, as plain and as universally recognized as any other."[19]

Moreover, though individual entrepreneurs could benefit from state promotional and regulatory activities, underlying them in Pennsylvania and in most other jurisdictions was a fear of and hostility toward capitalists and capitalism. A distinction was routinely made between what were called "producers"—meaning farmers, artisans, and small to medium-sized miners and manufacturers—and "capitalists," meaning large merchants, bankers, other dealers in paper transactions, and corporations, who were regarded as privileged because they enjoyed economies of scale and legal advantages not available to the middling sorts. The distinction can be seen in the Pennsylvania constitution of 1838, which set restrictions on banks by limiting charters to twenty years and reserving to the legislature the right to "alter, revoke or annul" charters if the corporation's activities were "injurious" to the public. It was the "producers" alone that Chief Justice Black had in mind when he spoke of the duty of the sovereign to "aid, encourage, and stimulate."[20]

Further manifestations of the bias against capitalists can be seen in the states' attitudes toward the granting of corporate charters, especially the incorporation of financial institutions. New York's general incorporation law in 1811 did not stimulate a rush of states eager to follow the example. Delaware mandated separate legislative acts for incorporation (until 1875) and made the process difficult by requiring a two-thirds vote in each branch of the legislature and by limiting charters to twenty years. Louisiana prohibited the creation, extension, or renewal of any corporate body having "banking or discounting privileges." In 1846, Arkansas amended its constitution to proscribe the incorporation of financial institutions; Iowa prohibited bank charters in the same article that provided for a general incorporation law. Even when states did enact general laws, as Maine did in 1819 and Pennsylvania did in the 1830s and 1840s, capitalists and promoters commonly declined to use them because of the restrictions they imposed, preferring instead to seek special legislative charters in the belief that venal politicians could be induced to give them better terms.[21]

Charters, whether obtained from legislatures or through general statutes, were normally granted with a view toward promoting the public interest of the state. Article 10 of the Illinois constitution contained five sections of restrictions on corporations, but in section 6 it ordered the general assembly to "encourage internal improvements, by passing liberal laws of incorporation for that purpose." In Pennsylvania, nearly two-thirds of the charters were for transportation, the remainder being for banks, insurance companies, manufacturing, and water and gas utilities. Mining, by contrast, could be carried out by small operators, and a fear of monopolizers thwarted the spread of corporations in that field. Monopoly and special privilege had long been regarded as inimical to the public interest and consequently were the subjects of explicit prohibitions.[22]

The kinds of special privileges that would ultimately effect a corporate revolution in America were understandably slow in being accepted. Limited liability charters, divorcing owners and directors from responsibility for the actions and debts of corporations, began to appear in the 1830s and 1840s, but some states moved in the opposite direction, creating liability where it had not existed before. Connecticut enacted an "any lawful purpose" incorporation law in 1837, permitting corporations to engage in any activity that natural persons could legally perform, and five other states passed such laws before the Civil War, but the remainder restricted corporations to performing only the functions that were enumerated in the charter.[23]

A common indicator of wariness about corporate power was the popularity of the mixed corporation, a company in which a state or, more frequently, a local government became a shareholder and active partner in the corporation's management. Beginning in Pennsylvania with the state's subscription to the stock of the Bank of Pennsylvania in 1793, mixed corporations were created in every state. The constitutions of Alabama, Mississippi, and Missouri required that the state have a percentage of the stock and a proportional number of directors of a chartered bank. Many states required a bonus in cash or stock in exchange for charters. Moreover, a number of states ventured into "socialism" by requiring that ownership of corporations revert entirely to the state after a number of years, as had been the case with the second bridge company in Massachusetts.[24]

States and localities stimulated and directed economic activity in accordance with their perceived, and popularly acceptable, notions of what would be advantageous. In some instances, notably in Pennsylvania, the result was extreme divisiveness by geographical areas; elsewhere, general policy agreements were reached. The broad-range consequence was that the nation's sections went in different directions. The systems of policy in the North generally favored commercial, industrial, and financial development, those in the South the agrarian way. Until the 1850s, the West tended to identify itself with the South, inasmuch as the lines of transportation and communication were along the north-south rivers. The construction of a network of east-west railroads would change the alignments drastically, leaving the southern states as an isolated minority.

The isolation of the South had already begun; the coming of the railroad merely completed the process. The issue was slavery. Southerners had believed that the question of slavery in national politics had been settled by the Missouri Compromise of 1820, which admitted Missouri as a slave state but otherwise prohibited slavery in the Louisiana Purchase Territory north of 36°30′, the Arkansas-Missouri border, and permitted it south of that line. In the mid-1830s, however, abolitionists began swamping Congress with petitions, and though Congress could not constitutionally interfere with slavery as a domestic institution, John Quincy Adams (who served nine terms in the House after he left the presidency) insisted on reading the petitions on the floor. That seriously disrupted business, but the right to petition was expressly guaranteed by the First Amendment. Then in 1836 the House adopted what critics called the gag rule, under which abolitionist petitions would be received but tabled without discussion.[25]

In the meantime, abolitionists, having been expelled from the South, were sending propaganda tracts into the region by the mails. In the summer of 1835, the postmaster in Charleston impounded a shipload of antislavery tracts, and a mob seized and destroyed them. When the postmaster reported the incident to Postmaster General Amos Kendall, Kendall officially informed him that there was no legal authority to ban the publications from the mails. Unofficially, he suggested, southern postmasters could intercept such materials, on the ground that "we owe an obligation to the laws, but a higher one to the communities in which we live."[26]

The issue was rekindled from an unexpected quarter and in an unexpected way. The people of Illinois were as militantly committed to the defense of states' rights as any in the country; the state's motto was "State Sovereignty and National Union." Illinoisans were also, in a vague sort of way, opposed to slavery, but what they opposed more strongly were persons of color. Indeed, in 1848 they would adopt a constitution expressly requiring the legislature to "prohibit free persons of color from immigrating to and settling in this State; and to effectually prevent the owners of slaves from bringing them into this State, for the purpose of setting them free." (Indiana adopted a similar provision three years later.) Citizens in Illinois so disliked and feared blacks that they were particularly fierce in opposing abolitionists. During 1837, unruly crowds in Alton several times vented their hostility by destroying the printing press of an abolitionist named Elijah Lovejoy. When on November 7 he attempted to defend his press, a mob murdered him. Abolitionists in New England reacted by deluging Congress with a flood of petitions, and because the gag rule had expired, congressmen from the region introduced them in the House. An angry debate ensued, at the culmination of which a combination of northern and southern Democrats adopted a stricter gag rule by a 122 to 74 majority.[27]

A week later, John C. Calhoun determined to introduce in the Senate a proslavery offensive. Of the resolutions he proposed, five were approved by comfortable margins as being in keeping with traditional Republican-Democratic stances. The first and second resolutions affirmed the state compact theory as to the origin and nature of the Union and declared that the states had exclusive jurisdiction over their internal affairs and institutions. Another specifically defined slavery as an internal institution. The resolutions concerning slavery in the District of Columbia and the admission of new states were adopted after being "toned down."[28]

But one of Calhoun's resolutions went far beyond the tradition of states' rights and, in seeking to protect slavery, actually distorted the doctrine. The South Carolinian urged that the federal government had a "positive" and "solemn" duty to provide "increased stability and security" for slavery. Northern Democrats saw the proposal as fraught with mischief and vigorously attacked it. The duty of the federal government, they insisted, was negative: nonintervention was the "true interpretation of the Constitution," the only principle consistent with the "old republican school of '98." That resolution was roundly rejected.[29]

The renewal of the gag rule defused slavery as a political issue for a time, but it resurfaced in 1842 as a result of a Supreme Court decision. The Fugitive Slave Act of 1793 had provided for the return to their owners of slaves who fled into free states, as was authorized by article 4 of the Constitution, and required state and local officials to enforce the act. After a time, a number of northern states, beginning with Indiana in 1824, passed personal liberty laws refusing to cooperate. Vermont went a step further in 1840, making it a felony for a citizen to aid in the capture of runaway slaves. A case testing the constitutionality of the personal liberty laws was arranged between officials in Maryland and Pennsylvania. A man named Prigg had carried a runaway slave woman and her child from Pennsylvania to Maryland, thus violating a Pennsylvania act prohibiting kidnapping and forbidding the removal of an alleged fugitive without a certificate from a state official. Prigg returned to Pennsylvania, where he was tried and convicted. He appealed to the Supreme Court.[30]

Justice Story delivered the opinion of the court in *Prigg* v. *Pennsylvania,* saying that the Pennsylvania law was unconstitutional, but he drew fine distinctions. Slave owners had a constitutional right to have their slaves returned, and no state could interfere in any way, for power on the subject was granted exclusively to Congress. When Congress delegated enforcement to the states in 1793, it was within its authority, but it could not require state officials to enforce federal law if state law prevented them from doing so.[31]

Six justices (Taney was absent due to illness) wrote concurring opinions, "everyone of them dissenting from the reasoning of all the rest." Thus the signal sent to antislavery people in the North was unclear. Massachusetts promptly seized upon the portion of Story's opinion that said that state officials could not be required to enforce a federal statute, and it prohibited state officials from assisting in the capture of runaways. Vermont did the same in 1843, Connecticut in 1844, New Hampshire in 1846, Pennsylvania the following year, and Rhode Island the next.[32]

A political battle involving slavery arose again concerning the annexation of Texas, though it need not have. The Texans had won their independence in 1836, and before long, President Sam Houston sought annexation by the United States. The matter became ensnarled in the complex relations of France, England, and the United States; delay followed upon delay. Abolitionists were concerned that annexation would expand the area of slavery, and defenders of slavery were concerned by rumors that the British were somehow going to end slavery in Texas. Most Americans did not particularly care about the subject one way or the other.[33]

But President Tyler strongly desired annexation, and in 1844, after several false starts, John C. Calhoun—who, through a curious train of circumstances, had become Tyler's secretary of state—completed the negotiations for annexation by treaty. Tyler favored the step as being in the national interest, but he made a passing reference to the security of the South and to the abolitionist danger posed by British interference. Calhoun wrote a long, impassioned, gratuitous, and highly publicized letter to the British minister, defending slavery as a positive good and pointing to the wretched condition of free blacks in the North. These comments roused abolitionists and alienated northern Democrats who might otherwise have been disposed to ratify the treaty. The result was that the Senate rejected it by a thirty-five to sixteen vote.[34]

Tyler persisted, however, and asked Congress to adopt a joint resolution of annexation. Finally, after Tyler had been succeeded by James K. Polk, Congress acted. The terms of the resolution were more pro-South than the treaty had been: the state would retain its public lands but be responsible for its public debts, and, most significantly, it was authorized to split itself into five states—slave states—if it chose.[35]

Confrontations between state and federal authority on issues other than slavery also disturbed Tyler's presidency. One was the prospect of a revival of the tariff war. The compromise tariff of 1833 expired in 1842 and was replaced by a tariff that restored rates to the moderately protective 1832 levels, those that had evoked South Carolina's nullification. In response, Robert Barnwell Rhett, the radical South Carolinian, instituted a campaign known as the Bluffton Movement, whose aim was to coordinate southern opposition through state conventions. Resistance would take the form of either nullification or, in Rhett's eyes the preferable course, secession. The movement attracted support in South Carolina but almost none elsewhere, and then it collapsed even in South Carolina. Calhoun, declaring his love of the Union, exerted his powerful influence on the state legislature, counseling it to await the results of an appeal to the ballot box, and the legislature acceded to his wishes. Tyler's secretary of state thus averted the threat of renewed state defiance.[36]

In one particular area, the states did defy the Constitution in a way that embarrassed the Supreme Court. During the economic depression that continued throughout the presidencies of Van Buren and Tyler, many states enacted legislation aimed at protecting debtors from their creditors, contrary to a strict reading of article 1, section 10. To allow such interferences in the obligations of contracts would weaken American credit abroad and thereby impede economic recovery and a renewal of expansion, to which the justices were strongly committed. But to declare the interferences unconstitutional would be contrary to the Court's predilection for giving the states as free a rein as possible. The course the Court took was to seek a middle position. The leading case was *Bronson* v. *Kinzie,* decided in 1843. The Federal Bankruptcy Act of 1841 had been repealed amidst protestations that it impinged upon the rights of the states, but in the *Bronson* decision, the Supreme Court ruled invalid an Illinois statute giving debtors a year to redeem property sold to pay mortgage debts and providing that the property could not be sold unless it fetched two-thirds of its appraised value. That ruling was reconfirmed a year later. But when state laws softening the methods of execution of nonmortgage debts were challenged, the Court generally upheld the statutes; when the statutes were not upheld, the state courts generally refused to follow the Supreme Court's rulings.[37]

A different sort of confrontation involved constitutional provisions that had not yet been contested. Article 4, section 3, states that "no new State shall be formed or erected within the Jurisdiction of any other State." Section 4 provides that "the United States shall guarantee to every State in this Union a Republican Form of Government" and that the United States shall protect each state, "on Application of the Legislature, or the Executive (when the Legislature cannot be convened) against domestic Violence."

These provisions might have been applied on several occasions, but each time the circumstances did not precisely invoke the article. The two Pennsylvania insurrections in the 1790s, the Whiskey Rebellion and Fries's Rebellion, were risings against federal, not state, authority; the one was suppressed by militia forces under national command, the other by a force organized by a federal marshal. The 1808 confrontation in Pennsylvania that led to *United States* v. *Peters* was between the state militia and a posse raised by a federal marshal; at issue was a federal court ruling. More recently, in 1836, Democrats in Maryland had marched on Annapolis and forced the Whig-controlled legislature to reapportion representation in the state by threatening to destroy the government. At nearly the same time, Democrats in the territories of Arkansas and Michigan had established constitutions without congressional authorization. In 1838, Democrats in Pennsylvania won control of the legislature, whereupon a Whig–Anti-Masonic coalition refused to turn over the reins of power; the Democrats expelled them by amassing a force to occupy the capital. In none of these events was federal intervention requested or provided, though future president Tyler called the Pennsylvania situation "the precursor of that revolution which is sooner or later to occur."[38]

The episode that brought the article 4 provisions into play was the Dorr Rebellion in Rhode Island, which erupted in 1842 after a long gestation. During the Revolution, as was indicated earlier, every state except Connecticut and Rhode Island had adopted a constitution, those two choosing instead to continue to be governed by their colonial charters. Though Connecticut did adopt a constitution in 1818, Rhode Island remained under its charter. The charter empowered the legislature to set the qualifications for voters, which had long been established as ownership of real estate valued at $133 or payment of $7 annual rent in tenancy. Modest as these requirements were, they disfranchised most adult males. The enormous increase in population in the tiny state meant that there was simply not enough land to go around. Moreover, since no one but freeholders could vote on calling a convention to adopt a constitution, advocates of reform were powerless to change things.[39]

Thus in an ardently democratic age, Rhode Island remained undemocratic. No more than four of ten adult white males could vote, bring a suit in court, or serve on a jury. Freemen in Providence, a city of nearly twenty-two thousand people, constituted just 6 percent of its population. Legislative apportionment was also skewed. The larger and growing towns had one representative for 2,590 people, those in static rural towns one for 1,074 inhabitants. Overall, one-third of the voting population, concentrated in the rural southern part of the western shore, governed the two-thirds who lived elsewhere.[40]

Thomas W. Dorr, heir of a Providence mercantile family and a National Republican—but nonetheless a dedicated, democratic ideologue—emerged as the leader of a reform movement in the early 1830s. Considerable numbers of workingmen formed the backbone of the movement, which demanded that the general assembly call a constitutional convention. In response, the assembly authorized one to meet in 1834, but it retained the franchise requirements and the apportionment of seats by towns in the election of delegates. The result, as anticipated, was a temporary defusing of the issue, since few voters participated and the convention dissolved itself for want of a quorum. Workingmen abandoned the movement thereafter, and Dorr, becoming a Democrat, thrashed about in an effort to form an anticharter coalition. In the meantime, a number of New York Democrats petitioned Congress to invoke the republican-guarantee clause of the Constitution and intervene in Rhode Island "to free the unfortunate Sons and Successors of Roger Williams."[41]

Then, in 1840, the First Reform Society of New York City goaded reformers to take radical steps. The society published and circulated an "Address to the Citizens of Rhode Island who are denied the Right of Suffrage," urging the inhabitants to go outside the framework of the charter, elect a popular convention to draft a constitution, and submit that document for ratification by all American citizens resident in the state. If the voters approved, the charter would automatically be defunct. If the existing government acquiesced in the popular will, no trouble would ensue. If it did not, Congress would have no choice but to back the constitution under the republican-guarantee clause.[42]

Within two years, reformers led by Dorr had followed the New Yorkers' advice. They had drawn up and ratified a constitution and held elections under it, but things did not work the way the outsiders had predicted. The general assembly, instead of accepting the legitimacy of the proposed arrangement, enacted a treason statute, began making wholesale arrests of people voted into office under the constitution, and proclaimed martial law to defend against what the assembly declared to be a violent insurrection. Dorr, who had been elected governor by the reformers, did indeed attempt to seize power by force of arms. In addition to suppressing the Dorrites, the general assembly called a convention of its own, which drafted an official constitution providing essentially for universal manhood suffrage.[43]

In the meantime, confused appeals to the outside world were raised. Dorrites sought armed help from New York and from elsewhere in New England, as well as intervention by the federal government, citing the republican-guarantee clause. The chief justice of the Rhode Island supreme court invoked another provision of the Constitution, declaring for the benefit of prospective interveners that to recognize the Dorrites would be to violate article 4, section 2, the prohibition against forming new states within the jurisdiction of existing states. The loudest call for help came from a three-man mission sent by Governor Samuel Ward King to ask for President Tyler's aid in suppressing a domestic insurrection.[44]

Tyler was impaled on a dilemma. One the one horn, as a southerner, he accepted the premise that local laws must be strictly enforced, with the help of the Union, if necessary; one of the Rhode Island emissaries, Elisha R. Potter, recorded in a memorandum that Tyler said that enforcement was necessary "to prevent negroes revolutionizing the south." On the other, as a states' righter who had opposed Jackson during the nullification controversy and who believed that force should be employed only when every other means of coping had been exhausted, he was loath to act. For the moment he hedged, telling the mission to inform Governor King that Congress had recognized the charter government as "republican" by seating its elected senators and representatives, and that until a full-fledged insurrection appeared, he could not intervene. Then he sent his own emissary, Secretary of War John C. Spencer, to evaluate the situation, after which he ordered the rebels to disperse within twenty-four hours, lest he request the governors of Massachusetts and Connecticut to mobilize militias and join the United States Army in defending Providence against them. The Dorrites attempted to seize the local armory, and when that failed, they scattered. Dorr himself was arrested and sentenced to life imprisonment, though he was released a year later.[45]

The legally sanctioned constitution went into force in 1843, and the episode was over. Its significance was not immediately evident, and opinions as to whether justice had triumphed were many and diverse. Even so, given that military force had been employed to suppress the voice of the people, that president Tyler had mobilized the power of the United States in support of suppression, and that in 1849 the Supreme Court decision in *Luther* v. *Borden* would confirm the handling of the Dorr Rebellion, one could suppose that the idea of popular sovereignty—in the sense of the Declaration of Independence's dictum that the people retain a right to alter or abolish their governments, irrespective of legal forms and norms—had been challenged and rejected. That rejection, if such it was, would bear powerfully on the federal-state confrontations to come.[46]

7

A CHANGED DYNAMIC, 1845–1852

The dynamics of the tension between federal and state authority changed abruptly during the late 1840s. The Supreme Court ceased for a time to be a divisive force and actually smoothed interstate relations. The issues that had driven national politics since the War of 1812, the ingredients that Henry Clay had called the American System—namely, a national bank, protective tariffs, and internal improvements—lost their relevance. In New England, New York, and elsewhere in the North, reformers agitated for a variety of causes, including temperance, women's rights, nativism, and abolitionism. And then, as a by-product or offshoot of a war of conquest, slavery—a subject that leading politicians had, with the exception of the gag rule controversy and Calhoun's occasional outbursts, scrupulously kept out of partisan debate—erupted as the dominant issue in that arena. So disruptive was the issue that it subjected the federal Union to the greatest strain the young republic had yet known.

Despite its internal divisions and its practice of issuing multiple opinions, the Supreme Court managed during the period to deliver a number of major decisions that provoked no serious opposition and seemed instead to establish its position, among nationalists and states' righters alike, as the ultimate arbiter of constitutionality except in disputes involving direct clashes between federal and state authorities. One case represented a sharp break with tradition and set a precedent that would, for nearly a century, greatly expand the jurisdiction of federal courts as coequal with that of state courts. That it facilitated commercial expansion perhaps accounts for the minimal resistance it met. Section 34 of the 1789 Judiciary Act provided that "the laws of the several States . . . shall be regarded as rules of decision in trials at common law." The assumption had always been that state "laws" included state court rulings as well as statutes, but in *Swift* v. *Tyson,* the Supreme Court held that doctrines of the courts of New York relative to bills of exchange did not bind federal courts. On that basis, the Court began to establish a federal common law for civil cases, a general commercial law independent of state court decisions. (A previous Court opinion had adjudged that in criminal cases, there was no federal common law.)[1]

In matters having to do with foreign commerce, the Taney Court consistently held that federal authority was exclusive. In the *Passenger Cases,* the Court ruled (Taney dissenting) that states could not act in regard to foreign commerce even in the absence of congressional legislation. New York and Massachusetts had passed acts imposing a head tax on immigrants landing in their jurisdictions; the Court's majority held that the taxes were, in effect, duties on imports and were therefore unconstitutional violations of article 1, section 10, though it was careful to point out that the decision would not impair slave states in their control over blacks, free or slave. Two years later, the Court handed down a related ruling regarding admiralty law. The Constitution gave federal courts jurisdiction in maritime and admiralty cases. Under English law and American law too while Marshall was chief justice, that jurisdiction extended only to tidewater, which is to say the seas and navigable coastal rivers. The coming of the steamboat brought a large volume of traffic to the Great Lakes, and in 1845 Congress enacted a statute extending federal admiralty jurisdiction to the lakes. The constitutionality of the act was vigorously challenged, but Taney upheld it, thus reconciling, as he had done in the *Charles River Bridge* case, constitutional doctrine with changing technology.[2]

By contrast, in dealing with cases involving interstate commerce, the Court tended toward the position that the states had concurrent authority with Congress. The states of Rhode Island, Massachusetts, and New Hampshire had passed laws restricting and taxing the sale of imported alcoholic beverages. Such enactments were part of a temperance reform movement that was sweeping New England, in no small measure because of nativist hostility toward Irish immigrants, who were arriving in droves, drank prodigiously, and voted Democratic. A Democratic Boston newspaper declared that "Massachusetts by her narrow legislation has sought to nullify the laws of Congress in liquors, while she denounced South Carolina for doing the like in woolens and cottons." Nullification or no, in the *License Cases,* decided in 1847, the Supreme Court upheld the acts, though not without its usual splintering. Six different justices wrote nine separate opinions in the three cases, not one of which was supported by a majority. The chief justice and three associate justices declared in their opinions that state power respecting interstate commerce was concurrent with federal power; Justice John McLean disagreed, holding that congressional power was exclusive, but he voted to uphold the laws anyway as valid exercises of the states' power to police the morals and welfare of their citizens.[3]

A few years later, in *Cooley* v. *Board of Wardens of the Port of Philadelphia,* the full Court agreed that the states did have concurrent power in regard to interstate commerce. It turned out that Congress had long since acted on the question: the First Congress had directed harbor pilots to "continue to be regulated" in accordance with existing or future state laws "until further legislative provision shall be made by Congress." Pennsylvania's pilot act of 1803, under which the *Cooley* case was brought, had therefore been authorized by an act of Congress, indicating that the First Congress had regarded the power to regulate interstate commerce as being concurrent. The Court, agreeing with that determination, upheld the Pennsylvania act. (This time, the police power of southern states over slaves was only implicit.)[4]

An action that won the Court widespread, if short-lived, respect was its amicable settlement of a boundary dispute. Disagreements among states or between states and territories had been frequent and, on occasion, violent. In 1836, for example, Ohio and the territory of Michigan had engaged in armed hostility (the "Toledo War") over land that each claimed. About the same time, Rhode Island alleged that a mistake in the demarcation of its boundary with Massachusetts had deprived it of territory on its eastern shore, and despite the penchant of Rhode Islanders for violence, the state chose to file a suit in the federal courts. Litigation dragged on for ten years until the case was finally decided in favor of Massachusetts. Almost miraculously, no one complained, and the court was praised for the precedent it set.[5]

The precedent was applied the next year to settle a long-standing territorial wrangle between Missouri and Iowa. At issue was a strip of land containing about two thousand square miles in the northern part of Missouri and on the southern boundary of Iowa, then a territory. At one point, the governor of Missouri had called for fifteen thousand troops and had actually dispatched fifteen hundred men to protect its claims; the governor of Iowa had mobilized eleven hundred troops to confront them. At last Missouri took its case to the courts, and when the Supreme Court ruled in favor of Iowa, Missouri made no further challenge. The significance was that in the future, the parties to boundary disputes readily accepted the role of the Court as the arbiter between sovereign entities. Senator Lewis Cass said of the decisions that they were "a great moral spectacle. . . . In Europe, armies run lines, and they run them with bayonet and cannon. They are marked with ruin and devastation. In our country they are run by an order of the Court."[6]

In the political arena, the spectacular event was the Mexican War, but the war's effects upon federal-state relations, while profound, were conditioned by a series of less obvious developments. Specifically, the federal economic policies and programs that had resulted in periodic outbursts of states' rights enthusiasm were quietly defused—to be replaced by the explosive issue of the extension of slavery into the trans-Mississippi West.

Both the war and the domestic changes were primarily the doing of James K. Polk. Polk had won the presidency, beating Henry Clay in a flukish election decided by the defection of antislavery Whigs in the burned-over district of western New York to the Liberty party candidate James G. Birney. Polk was the polar opposite of Clay: an old-fashioned, states' rights, strict-construction Democrat. But, though his conception of the role of the federal government was essentially passive, his view of the presidency was vigorously active. Indeed, he took a more aggressive part in guiding legislation through Congress than his predecessors had done, and with the possible exception of Jefferson, he was the most successful in obtaining what he sought.[7]

His first priority was reducing the tariff and purging it of its protective features, an undertaking that was by no means easy. To be sure, Democrats had a huge majority in the House (143 to 77), but nearly a third of them favored at least some protection, and the Whigs were almost unanimously in favor of protection. A similar situation obtained in the Senate, where the Democrats' majority was six. Nonetheless, Polk called for a nonprotective, revenue-only tariff in his inaugural address in March 1845, and he set out to bring the reform to pass. He instructed his secretary of the treasury, Robert J. Walker, to survey importers and customs officials to learn what levels of ad valorem duties would be necessary, commodity by commodity, to produce the results Polk desired. Walker, in turn, gave the data to the chairman of the House Ways and Means Committee when Congress convened in December, along with a ringing treatise on the virtues of free trade, and he subsequently summoned appraisers and deputy customs collectors to testify before the committee. Polk, for his part, haled congressmen to the White House, exerting whatever pressure or persuasion he could bring to bear.[8]

After several months of intermittent debates, maneuvering, and pressure tactics by lobbyists, the House passed the Walker Tariff, and after a round of complex manipulations by Polk, the Senate followed suit at the end of July. The Walker Tariff remained on the books until 1857, and the subject ceased in the interim to be a political issue of consequence.

The next item on Polk's reform agenda was to divorce the federal government from any connection with banking and bank currency.

As indicated, an independent treasury system, having been enacted in 1840, was repealed in 1841. During the next five years, management of federal funds was left to the discretion of the secretary of the treasury, who routinely made the deposits in state banks. There they were used as the basis for bank note issues. Polk proposed a bill, drafted by Walker, for the construction of fireproof vaults in which federal money would be deposited, called the Constitutional Treasury, and Democrats in the House added an amendment that government revenues and expenditures would be payable only in gold and silver. In that form the bill became law by a party-line vote in both houses.[9]

Polk's third domestic policy goal, ending federal funding of internal improvement projects, could not be accomplished by a single piece of legislation. Many congressmen were anxious to enact what were called "harbors and rivers" bills for the benefit of their districts, though the lineup was more nearly partisan than sectional, many Democrats even from the West sharing Polk's constitutional scruples. All that Polk could do was exercise his veto power. The first harbors and rivers bill to be proposed during his presidency, appropriating about $1.4 million for a long list of projects, cleared the House in March 1846, largely as the work of Democrat John Wentworth of Illinois. Complications developed in the Senate, where John C. Calhoun steered through an alternative bill, limiting the funded projects to the Mississippi River system. The House refused to consider the substitute, and in late July, both houses concurred in passing what was essentially the original House version. Polk vetoed the bill, accompanying his action with a message in which he adopted the position that Congress had no constitutional authority to enact internal improvements and warned that such legislation would result in a "consolidation of power in the Federal Government at the expense of the rightful authority of the States." Congress failed to muster the two-thirds majority necessary to override.[10]

Early in 1847, however, a national convention of advocates of internal improvements met in Chicago, and partly in response to its recommendations and lobbying efforts, the Twenty-ninth Congress enacted a bill toward the end of its second session. Polk killed this one with a pocket veto, but he felt obliged to reiterate and elaborate his reasoning, which he did in a message delivered when the Thirtieth Congress convened. He also offered a suggestion that was constitutional but far from practical: Congress should permit the states, as it was authorized to do by article 1, section 10, to levy tonnage duties and use the proceeds to finance projects themselves. The flaw in the scheme was that only the seaboard states could collect duties on shipping, whereas the crying need was for projects in the interior states.[11]

Polk expected the second session to pass internal improvement laws, for Whigs now controlled the House, and he spent much of his time preparing a veto message. But the legislation did not come. He had managed to stave off additional measures for his entire term, though he had made no permanent gains. It seems possible that his arguments against the constitutionality of internal improvements carried some weight with Congress. After all, he was echoing the sentiments of political leaders as diverse and influential as Alexander Hamilton, James Madison, and Andrew Jackson.

But a pressing demand for federal aid was rising in response to technological developments that set off, in the late 1840s and beyond, a railroad mania. Everyone agreed that building railroads would produce economic gains bordering on the magical. Railroads, however, required unprecedentedly large amounts of capital, and despite foreign investment and an influx of gold after 1849, private investors in most parts of the country simply could not afford the outlay. New England was an exception. In Massachusetts, financiers and state subsidies brought such a spurt of building that, as early as 1851, the region was crisscrossed by a thousand miles of track, representing a capital investment of $52 million. New York and Ohio were also able to build abundantly. Elsewhere, however, local capital, whether public or private, was inadequate.[12]

The solution was the brainchild of Democratic Senator Stephen A. Douglas of Illinois: a grant of land from the public domain to underwrite the building of a railroad. The federal government had from time to time granted lands to states for various purposes, and since 1837, private railroad promoters in Chicago had been seeking land grants, but it was Douglas who in 1850 engineered a huge grant to the states of Illinois, Mississippi, and Alabama for building the Illinois Central Railroad, linking Chicago to the Gulf Coast. In all, the Illinois Central, via federal-through-state grants, was endowed with 2,595,000 acres, for the first half of which it received more than $10 million. By 1854, the railroad was operating from Chicago to Cairo, Illinois; the southern portions were longer in coming.[13]

That set off a rush of grants. In the seven years after 1850, the federal government donated about 26 million acres for railroad building in the Mississippi Valley region. That was universally acceptable, since it cost taxpayers nothing. Thus internal improvements, like the tariff and the banking system, had ceased to be a dividing issue in national politics.[14]

Even as Polk's domestic policies were defusing economic concerns that had charged the political atmosphere for nearly two generations, his expansionist policies triggered the volatile moral problem of slavery. Polk did not introduce the term Manifest Destiny—that was the coinage of a newspaper publisher named John L. O'Sullivan—but he epitomized its spirit. He was determined when he assumed the presidency to obtain a favorable settlement with England in regard to the disputed Oregon territory, to annex Texas, and to acquire New Mexico and California from Mexico. He believed that the Oregon question could be settled peaceably but that obtaining the Southwest would require the use of military force. He proved to be right on both counts.

The way Polk got the war started ensured that it would be vehemently protested in certain quarters. Shortly after Texas was annexed (December 29, 1845), Polk ordered General Zachary Taylor, commander of the army in Louisiana, to move to Texas to protect its southern flank on the Rio Grande. In reality, the southern flank was the Nueces, 150 miles to the north; Mexico claimed the area between the two rivers, and the pretensions of Texas and the United States were without foundation. An American reconnoitering party of sixty-three men encountered a Mexican force near the Rio Grande and was attacked. Eleven were killed, five wounded, and the rest captured. When Polk received the news, he asked Congress to appropriate funds to support Taylor, declared that the Mexicans had invaded the United States and "shed American blood on the American soil," and requested not a declaration of war but a recognition that "war exists" by virtue of Mexico's action. The Democratic majority in the House limited debate to two hours, read but a few of the documents Polk had submitted, and passed a bill calling for volunteers and appropriating $10 million. The bill's preamble mentioned that war existed "by act of the Republic of Mexico." Refusing to vote to support American troops supposedly under fire would have been a politically suicidal act of unpatriotism; just sixteen congressmen voted against the bill.[15]

Among the few in Congress who spoke against the action was John C. Calhoun. Unlike northern opponents of the war, he had strongly favored the annexation of Texas, but he thought the war was avoidable, set a dangerous precedent, and was likely to jeopardize the negotiations with Britain concerning Oregon. On the last point he was wrong, but he was a prophet in his constitutional argument against the war. The passage of the appropriations bill with its "war exists" preamble in effect transferred to the presidency Congress's power to declare war, for the president as commander in chief could order troops anywhere, provoke a fight, and present Congress with war as a fait accompli. The precedent could prove fatal, Calhoun insisted, for it "will enable all future Presidents to bring about a state of things, in which Congress shall be forced, without deliberation, or reflection, to declare war, however opposed to its convictions of justice or expediency." The precedent would, indeed, be applied to Calhoun's own state fifteen years later.[16]

The war proved to be extremely popular in much of the country, accompanied as it was by a succession of victories in the field, but it was opposed in the Northeast. Several legislatures, dominated by Whigs, adopted resolutions of disapproval. The strongest emanated from Massachusetts, which had been bitterly protesting the annexation of Texas for some time. Back in 1844, its legislature had resolved that "to unite an independent foreign state with the United States is not among the powers delegated to the general government," that

Massachusetts would "submit to undelegated powers in no body of men on earth," and that annexing Texas "may tend to drive these states into a dissolution of the union." The next year the legislature denounced "this nefarious project" of annexation specifically on the ground that it perpetuated and extended slavery in violation of the spirit of the Constitution, refused to "acknowledge" the validity of the act, and announced its determination to employ "every lawful and constitutional measure, to annul its conditions, and defeat its accomplishment."[17]

Once the war was well under way, Massachusetts politicians muted their opposition somewhat, for the same reason that Congress had reluctantly done Polk's bidding—namely, fear of appearing unpatriotic. Even so, they let their feelings be known. The Massachusetts legislature declared the war unconstitutional and charged that it was instituted by the president "for the conquest of . . . territory from which slavery has been . . . excluded, with the triple object of extending slavery, of strengthening the slave power, and of obtaining the control of the Free States." The resolves were based on a report written by Charles Sumner, who had argued that Congress should be urged to withhold supplies from the armed forces. The legislature would not go that far, but when a company of Massachusetts volunteers was raised, Governor George N. Briggs refused to commission the officers unless they promised not to march beyond the boundaries of the state, and the legislature refused to support it through appropriations.[18]

Massachusetts politicians were not alone. Private citizens in New England were especially vehement in their denunciations. Henry David Thoreau, for instance, wrote his renowned essay on civil disobedience in opposition to the war, and in the widely read *Bigelow Papers,* James Russell Lowell suggested that New England should express opposition by separating from the slave states.

In the rest of the country, however, news of each victory in Mexico kindled enthusiasm for the war anew, until it reached a euphoric state that expressed itself in an "All Mexico" movement. Expansionists began to dream of extending the country's boundaries to include California, the Oregon territory, the Great Southwest, and the entirety of North America. Polk himself wanted to acquire California and New Mexico and nothing more, but his strong stance earlier in favor of expansion created a momentum that was difficult to arrest, and it was furthered by his secretary of state, James Buchanan.[19]

The All Mexico movement sent a chill of horror along the spines of Americans of varying political opinions. Calhoun said flatly, "Ours is the government of the white man," and he saw no room in it for Mexicans. R. M. T. Hunter, a Calhounite from Virginia, echoed the sentiment, as did John Bell of Tennessee. No less vehement was Democratic Senator John M. Niles of Connecticut. Columbus Delano, an abolitionist Whig representative from Ohio, spoke an attitude common among those in his party and region and of his persuasion. The Mexicans, he declared, "embrace all shades of color. . . . They are a sad compound of Spanish, English, Indian, and negro bloods . . . resulting, it is said in the production of a slothful, indolent, ignorant race of beings." Such racism does not mean that abolitionists were insincere. What it does suggest is that many of them, though opposed to slavery as an institution—as a moral stain on a society supposedly committed to freedom and as providing disproportionate power in the national councils to freemen in the slaveholding states—were not especially concerned about the plight of the slaves as human beings. Indeed, they probably thought the slaves should be freed and then deported, lest their emancipation further increase the South's voting power.[20]

The Treaty of Guadalupe Hidalgo, ending the war with the cession of New Mexico and California to the United States in exchange for $15 million, derailed the All Mexico movement, but it did not quiet the agitation about slavery in the newly acquired territory. The controversy arose in August 1846, when a disgruntled antislavery Democrat from northeastern Pennsylvania, David Wilmot, introduced as a rider to an appropriation bill a provision that "neither slavery nor involuntary servitude shall ever exist in any part of" the territory that might be acquired from Mexico. This "Wilmot Proviso" passed in the House but was killed in the Senate, which failed to take action before the session ended. Early in 1847, the Proviso was passed again in the House and was again rejected in the Senate.[21]

Reactions were various. Polk was irritated by what he considered an irrelevant distraction from the successful conclusion of the war. Northerners in and out of Congress, rankled by the South's outsized power and by the federal largesse that the Polk administration had denied them, were angered by the rejection of the Proviso. Resolutions favoring the measure poured in to Congress, particularly from the Old Northwest. Northern congressmen declared that there would never be another slave state admitted to the Union. Columbus Delano threatened the South: "we will establish a cordon of free States that shall surround you; and then we will light up the fires of liberty on every side, until they melt your present chains, and render all your people *free*. This is no idle boast." One measure of the mood is that Whigs regained control of Congress in the 1846 elections. Southerners, by contrast, virtually yawned, for it was recognized that New Mexico and California were unsuitable for the use of slave labor.[22]

Calhoun, back in the Senate after his stint as Tyler's secretary of state, reacted strongly against the Wilmot Proviso, and characteristically, he launched a counteroffensive. On February 19, 1847, he proposed four resolutions: that territories were the joint and common property of the states; that Congress had no authority to discriminate against any state in regulating the territories; that congressional legislation concerning slavery would be a violation of the Constitution, the principle of states' rights, and the compact origins of the Union; and that the inhabitants of the territories had the right to adopt such constitutions as they saw fit, provided they had a republican form. The next day he issued a warning as shrill as Delano's had been. Insisting on the positive protection of slavery, and appealing again to states' rights and the compact theory, he assailed the "aggressive measures" of the nonslaveholding states and declared that if the sectional balance in the Senate were destroyed, "political revolution, anarchy, civil war, and widespread disaster" would follow.[23]

The wide dissemination of Calhoun's speeches, together with the publication of pro-Proviso speeches and editorials, sounded as an alarm bell in the South. Throughout the region, politicians' responses tended to be extreme. The Virginia legislature led the way with a set of resolutions rejecting federal authority over slavery, asserting the equal right of slaveholders in the territories, and pledging to resist restrictive legislation "at all hazards and to the last extremity." The Democratic convention in Alabama endorsed these resolutions and vowed to oppose any candidate in the 1848 presidential election who did not publicly renounce the Wilmot Proviso. A Democratic newspaper in North Carolina talked of disunion and civil war, "as sure as God lives in Heaven." The governor of Mississippi declared that the South would resist even to the point of secession and civil war.[24]

Abolitionists and their more moderate brethren, antislavery men, were decidedly in the minority in the North, but during the elections of 1848, they were as aggressive as Calhoun charged them with being. They organized a third party, the Free-Soil party, nominating Martin Van Buren for the presidency and a number of candidates for Congress. Van Buren received enough votes in New York to take that state away from the Democratic candidate, Lewis Cass, and thereby to make the Whig war hero Zachary Taylor president. Moreover, they won thirteen seats in the House of Representatives, preventing either major party from obtaining a majority.[25]

When the Thirty-first Congress convened in December 1849, the nation seemed to have become embroiled in a crisis of federal-state and intersectional relations. But the crisis existed primarily in the minds of professional politicians. Threats of defiance and disunion had become commonplace, and ordinary Americans did not appear to take either the Wilmot Proviso or other issues arising from the Mexican War to heart. Shortly before, Senator Thomas L. Clingman of North Carolina, commenting on Calhoun's clarion call, had declared that "out of the State of South Carolina . . . Mr. Calhoun was not sustained in any one State of this Union by five per cent. of the population. In fact," Clingman continued, "his strength at the South was about as great as that of the abolitionists at the North. His violence or denunciation was food for the abolitionists, just as their fanaticism gave him materials to work with."[26]

Politicians in Washington, however, displayed enough rancor and distrust to compensate for the relative calm in the countryside. The wrangling about the choice of a speaker of the House bespoke the mood. A trying succession of votes took place. After eight fruitless days, Democrats began talking of switching their support from Howell Cobb of Georgia to William J. Brown of Indiana, whose position favoring the annexation of Texas had won him trust among southerners; then it was revealed that he had promised Wilmot to support the Proviso. Southerner after southerner rose to proclaim that if slavery were prohibited in California and New Mexico—and also in the District of Columbia, as demanded by some abolitionists—the dissolution of the Union and war between the states would result. Finally, on December 23, Cobb was made speaker by a plurality, in violation of precedent that had been followed since 1789. The quarreling continued as the House elected its lesser officers.[27]

In the Senate, calmer voices prevailed, albeit barely, and the older members began to look for ways to compromise the matters in dispute. On January 29, 1850, Henry Clay, after consulting with Daniel Webster, introduced resolutions toward that end. They provided for the immediate admission of California as a free state, the organization of the remainder of the territory acquired from Mexico without restrictions on slavery, an adjustment of the Texas–New Mexico border, the compensation of Texas for land it would cede in that adjustment, noninterference with slavery in the District of Columbia but termination of the slave trade there, a strict fugitive slave law, and a declaration that Congress had no authority to interfere with interstate slave trading.[28]

A great debate ensued. On February 5 and 6, Clay appealed for mutual concessions out of love of country. Calhoun, so weak that he wrote his speech and had it read for him, answered on March 4. His immediate concern was that the admission of California would give free states a majority (sixteen states to fifteen) in the Senate and thus deprive the slave states of the means of protecting their interests. He reiterated his by-now familiar arguments and charges and said, "If you who represent the stronger portion cannot agree to settle . . . on the broad principle of justice and duty, say so, and let the states we both represent agree to separate and part in peace. If you are unwilling we should part in peace, tell us so, and we shall know what to do." The antislavery Whig senator from New York, William H. Seward, countered Calhoun with a radical challenge both to the South Carolinian's interpretation of the nature of the Union and to the proposition that the Constitution sanctioned slavery. The Union was one of the whole people, he said, not of states; and as for slavery, it was in violation of a higher law than mere man-made constitutions, as proclaimed in the Declaration of Independence, and was therefore null and void. Congress could and should, he implied, abolish slavery everywhere. On March 7, Webster appealed to moderation in a celebrated oration in favor of the compromises. "I wish to speak today," he declared, "not as a Massachusetts man, nor as a Northern man, but as an American. . . . I speak today for the preservation of the Union." Regarding the New Mexico territory, he pointed out what everyone already knew, that geography prevented the development of slavery there, and he "would not take pains to reaffirm an ordinance of nature, nor to re-enact the will of God." Other speeches would come from both sides, but the tide in favor of compromise was turned by Webster's convincing performance.[29]

Other factors contributed to the passage of the Compromise of 1850, which was enacted in a series of laws between September 9 and 20. Calhoun died before the end of March, depriving the South of its tenacious leader. President Taylor died in July and was replaced by Millard Fillmore, who was more favorably disposed toward the compromise. Senator Stephen A. Douglas worked assiduously to muster the necessary votes. A meeting of delegates from several states in Nashville in June, called at Calhoun's instigation to endorse an extreme position, instead was dominated by moderates. And as the summer passed, increasing numbers of southern congressmen realized that the compromise favored them in various ways and hurt them in none.[30]

In the South, extreme states' righters and protosecessionists grumbled, especially in Mississippi and South Carolina, but that opposition soon died down. Elsewhere in the region, general satisfaction or indifference prevailed. The compromise had seemingly removed the question of slavery from the national political arena, and the other major policies emanating from Washington—the tariff, the treasury system, internal improvements—were at long last to the liking of southerners. Moreover, the influx of gold from California and generous credit from abroad brought prosperity to the area: the price of cotton, having dipped to a disastrous four and a half cents a pound in 1849, soared to more than thirteen cents, and the trend would continue. Among southerners who thought about national and political matters, contentment was widespread.[31]

Northern reactions were negative. Webster's conciliatory speech was denounced by New England antislavery leaders. They charged that he was making a calculated bid for the presidency, called him a Benedict Arnold who had betrayed his Yankee principles, and spoke of the "meanness of the lion turned spaniel in his fawning on the masters whose hands he was licking." That sort of thing was expected. What was not anticipated was the popular hostility toward the new Fugitive Slave Act, even among those who despised the abolitionists and wished that the whole subject would go away.[32]

Southerners had been clamoring for a strong law concerning runaways since the Supreme Court's ruling in *Prigg* v. *Pennsylvania* had set off a wave of state-enacted personal liberty laws. In 1850, even as the compromise was being debated, the court handed down a decision that antagonized abolitionists and called the subject to popular attention. A slaveholder in northern Kentucky owned a black minstrel show that often performed across the Ohio River in Cincinnati. One day, three of the performers crossed the river on their own and escaped to Canada. The owner sued the ferryboat's proprietor for aiding the escape, but the boatman argued that the runaways had become freemen by virtue of having previously been in Ohio, where slavery had been prohibited by the Northwest Ordinance. The Court, in *Strader* v. *Graham,* held otherwise, declaring that the ordinance ceased to be in effect once the territory was divided into states, and adding that no matter what the status of the blacks when they were in Ohio, Kentucky law pertained when they returned there, and according to Kentucky law, they were slaves.[33]

The Fugitive Slave Act, enacted on September 18 by large margins in both houses, was striking in its severity. It put fugitive slave cases exclusively under federal jurisdiction and provided for special commissioners who could, after a summary hearing in which an affidavit by the claimant was sufficient proof of ownership, issue warrants for the arrest of fugitives and their return to their masters. Accused fugitives who claimed to be freemen were denied the right of trial by jury and the right to testify in their own defense. The commissioners were to be paid a $10 fee if they found the accused to be "guilty" but just $5 if they freed him. They were authorized to require bystanders to come to their aid and to call a *posse comitatus* if necessary to enforce the law. Marshals and deputies who refused to execute warrants were subjected to a $1,000 fine, and if a fugitive escaped through a marshal's negligence, the marshal could be required to pay the slave's value to the owner. Citizens who impeded the arrest of fugitives or helped conceal or rescue them were subject to a fine of $1,000, additional civil damages of $1,000 for each fugitive lost, and imprisonment of up to six months.[34]

Denunciations of the law and resolutions calling for its defiance were heard throughout the North, though more in New England than in the Old Northwest. Opponents of the measure based their objections primarily on Christian grounds. The editor of the *Trumpet and Universalist Magazine* of Boston surveyed the reactions in the religious press and reported that the law "has roused a spirit in New England, which has scarcely been paralleled since the times of 1770 and 1775. . . . The Clergy of all denominations, in the North, are using their influence to show the people the odiousness of the law." They were "making the blood of the people boil with indignation. . . . Men who have never interferred with the subject of slavery, are aroused on this subject." The resolutions of an antislavery meeting in Dedham, Massachusetts, were typical. Anyone defending a law "so undeniably anti-Christian" or "counselling obedience to it" should be "marked and treated as a moral leper" and "branded as a traitor." The *Worcester Spy* asked if "man, legislating under the inspiration of the devil," should be obeyed; its answer was that "Congress has made the law. . . . We claim the right to disobey it."[35]

Confrontations inevitably followed. In October 1850, a man named Hughes, the jailer of Macon, Georgia, attempted to recover fugitives William and Ellen Craft in Boston. A local vigilance committee foiled his efforts and had him arrested on a charge of defamation of character. A mob broke his carriage windows and so terrified him that he fled the city while the fugitives escaped to England. The same group, a few months later, engineered the freeing of a slave named Shadrach who was about to be returned, and the judge who had attempted to enforce the law was denounced as a public enemy. In upstate New York, a mob seized a fugitive from a marshal, hurried him into Canada, and had the marshal arrested and tried under state law for kidnapping. In Pennsylvania, a master was able to recover his runaways only after a delay of two months, during which he was thrown in jail for inciting to riot and fined $1,450. In Detroit, a runaway was reclaimed and returned to his owner when military force was employed to dispel a mob; in Chicago, where the city council had declared the Fugitive Slave Act void, citizens forced a federal commissioner to free a man being held as a fugitive.[36]

The slave catchers, for their part, were often violent. Blacks were sometimes bludgeoned into unconsciousness before efforts were made to establish their identities as runaways. The estimate is that more persons were seized as fugitives during the first year after the passage of the act than had been taken in the preceding sixty years. The conviction became widespread that the pursuit of slaves had become a regular and profitable business along the whole border area. Clearly, some blacks were taken as runaways and "returned" to masters who had never owned them.[37]

The occasions of extreme violence were much publicized. In September 1851, a Maryland slave owner went to Christiana, Pennsylvania, where a number of free blacks had settled, and in the company of an officer armed with a legal warrant tried to reclaim two fugitives. A bloody fight ensued, the master was killed, and his son was badly wounded. In October, the "Jerry rescue" occurred in Syracuse, New York, a town that Daniel Webster had referred to as a "laboratory of abolitionism, libel, and treason." Jerry was a slave who had fled from Missouri to upstate New York; an agent of his owner showed up unexpectedly just as the county fair was crowding the community and the firebrand abolitionist Gerrit Smith had convened an antislavery meeting. General rioting followed, shots were fired, and Jerry was taken from the place where the commissioner had held him and spirited away to Canada.[38]

It is possible to overdraw a picture of a populace risen in indignation. The number of runaways was not large: an estimated 1,000 in 1850 of a total slave population of more than 3 million. Those who did run away were mainly from the border states of Maryland and Kentucky. According to the census of 1850, only 16 of nearly 400,000 slaves in South Carolina attempted to escape. The number of rescues was also small, and the large percentage of instances in which fugitives were peacefully returned went unreported.[39]

Yet emotions were inflamed on both sides of the Mason-Dixon line. The violence of a few of the captures and rescues made indelible impressions. Curiously, feelings were strongest among people least directly affected. Whites in the Deep South, where escapes were infrequent and nearly impossible, reacted strongly to accounts of rescues in the North. Denizens of the upper parts of Ohio, New York, and New England, where episodes were rare compared to incidents in the southern parts of Indiana, Ohio, and Pennsylvania, were aroused whenever a capture came to their attention. One effect of the Fugitive Slave Act was thereby to convert thousands of previously conservative and law-abiding northerners to the cause of abolition. It also taught them that a states' rights position was more compatible with the cause than was looking to the federal government.

The largest numbers of people were converted by the work of a schoolteacher's wife, Harriet Beecher Stowe. The first installment of what became *Uncle Tom's Cabin: Or, Life among the Lowly* was a sketch of the death of a slave named Uncle Tom. It appeared in a semiobscure Washington religious/antislavery journal called *National Era* in June 1851. The publisher announced that the sketch was the beginning of a series that would run for three months, but the pieces attracted so much notice that they ran for ten months. By that time, arrangements had been made to publish them as a book. The initial printing of 5,000 copies was sold in two days; in three weeks, 20,000 copies had been sold; by the end of the year, the total had reached 800,000; and after a year, sales topped 1,200,000. In addition, the book was translated into several languages, and a number of dramatizations were produced on stage. The magnitude of the sales—by far the greatest that had been attained by a book in such a short period of time—can be appreciated when it is realized that scarcely more than 2 million households existed in the northern United States at the time.[40]

Harriet Beecher Stowe did not attack the South or even most slave owners, depicting the former as being saddled with a curse and the latter as often kindly and well meaning. The book's most vicious character is a transplanted Yankee, Simon Legree. What *Uncle Tom's Cabin* does attack is the institution of slavery and the effects of legislation like the federal Fugitive Slave Act. The book appealed to Christian values and dramatized the pain that slavery inflicted upon families in general and upon women and children in particular.

The passions aroused by *Uncle Tom's Cabin* steadily grew, unnerving professional politicians by the turn that the popular mood was taking. Extrapartisan organizations were wrestling control of public opinion from the professionals who had grown accustomed to manipulating it for their own ends. Their instinctive reaction in the circumstances was to avoid substance and controversy, to attempt to steer the political discourse into the channels of what a later politician would call normalcy.

The Democrats, fending off a "Young America" movement aimed at winning the presidential nomination for thirty-nine-year-old Stephen A. Douglas and endorsing "southward" expansion (meaning into Cuba), took a tried-and-true ticket-balancing approach: they nominated a Yankee, Franklin Pierce of New Hampshire, for president and William R. King of Alabama for vice-president. For a platform, seeking to solidify the southern base, the Democrats endorsed the compromise of 1850 as final, rejected congressional interference in the slavery question, and announced a commitment to the Virginia and Kentucky Resolutions. The Whigs, seeing their northern base disintegrating, nonetheless condemned agitation on the subject of slavery, accepted the Compromise, affirmed the principle of states' rights, and adhered to their traditional support of federal aid for internal improvements. To compensate for the lame platform, they nominated for president yet another war hero, General Winfield Scott of Virginia, and selected William Graham of North Carolina for vice-president. The election was a disaster for the Whigs. Pierce defeated Scott by 1.6 million popular votes to 1.38 million and swept the electoral college, carrying 27 states and 254 electors to Scott's 4 states and 42 electoral votes. Democrats also carried both houses of Congress.[41]

Within two years, the Whig party would be defunct, to be replaced by a Republican party that was purely sectional and committed against slavery in the territories. During the same two years, the Democrats would arrogantly overstep their supposed mandate and adopt measures that would make disruption of the Union all but inevitable.

8

Dissolving the Union

During the Victorian Age, an aphorism held that "idle hands are the devil's workshop." In England the adage may have been coined to salve the consciences of plutocrats wallowing in wealth gained at the expense of a wretched factory proletariat, but in the United States, at least, it had broader connotations. When times were hard and the struggle to make ends meet was continuous, Yankees accepted their lots uncomplainingly, as if that was what God had destined for them. When times were good and life was easy, they became restless and infested with feelings of guilt. In such circumstances, their tendency was to look around for evil and band together to strike it out. As indicated, the years after the 1849 gold rush were a period of unprecedented prosperity that lasted almost a decade. Fads and fancies proliferated, but most commonly, Yankees focused their reforming energies upon slavery, or, more properly, upon what they perceived as the slave power.

In contrast to the cocksure self-righteousness of the Yankees, denizens of the southern states had a curious assortment of feelings. Alerted by Calhoun's repeated warnings that the admission of California as the sixteenth free state placed them in a perpetual minority, they feared the worst from the general government. And yet, everything the federal authority did during the decade of prosperity was favorable to their interests and preferences; the outlook was for a continuation of that condition. Indeed, though the southern states remained largely Democratic, the attitudes of many southerners came more nearly to approximate the constitutional views of John

Marshall than those of Jefferson and Jackson, even as Yankees were adopting a Jeffersonian and Jacksonian suspicion of the federal government and the Supreme Court.

That was while times were good. Then came the panic of 1857 and, with it, economic devastation—in the North. There, hands by the scores of thousands were forced to be idle in a way not contemplated by the aphorism. The collapse had a great deal to do with the triumph of the antislavery (though not abolitionist) Republican party in the congressional elections of 1858, and with its capture of the presidency two years later. The South, however, was unscathed by the economic depression: the production of cotton virtually doubled during the next three years, yet world market prices remained high. Thus, threatened by the prospect of federal policies that would be ruinous to them, the southerners, not as an act of desperation but rather as an act of supreme self-confidence that they would thrive on their own, resorted to the ultimate expression of the states' rights dogma, secession.

Historians have wrangled mightily about the causes and the course of circumstances that led to the Civil War. Two principal schools, each containing variations, have dominated the historiography. One holds that the breakup of the Union was an irrepressible conflict between different cultures or ways of life, the other that the rift could have been avoided but for the antics of a blundering generation of politicians. Irrespective of whether the conflict was repressible, clearly a series of colossal blunders, beginning in 1854, set in motion events that proved fatal to the federal Union as the Union had previously been understood. The 1854 blunder was the passage of the Kansas-Nebraska Act. Earlier clashes had evoked violent language and sometimes violent action, but they had never affected large numbers of states. The Kansas-Nebraska Act and the responses it elicited set self-conscious sections of the nation against each other, vying for control of the federal government. As a consequence, everybody became involved.[1]

The act provided for the organization of the territories and the opening to settlement of the lands immediately to the west of Missouri and Iowa, without restrictions as to whether the territories would permit or prohibit slavery. The absence of restrictions had also characterized the legislation creating the territories of New Mexico and Utah as part of the Compromise of 1850, and that obeisance to the doctrine of popular sovereignty accorded with a cardinal tenet of the states' rights credo. Even dedicated nationalists conceded that domestic institutions were the exclusive domain of the individual states. Domestic institutions comprehended, among other things, property relations (except as limited by article 1, section 10), family affairs, education, morality, public health, and slavery. The tenet had been infringed, after a fashion, by the adoption of the Missouri Compromise in 1820, which drew a line setting a northern boundary for slavery. Southerners had long felt, vaguely, that the Missouri Compromise line was unconstitutional; northerners felt, equally vaguely, that the line was a permanent fact of life, almost a part of the Constitution.[2]

When Stephen A. Douglas, the Democratic chairman of the Senate Committee on Territories, proposed the legislation, known at the time as the Nebraska bill, no one seemed clear whether its leaving the question of slavery to the inhabitants violated the Missouri Compromise. Implicitly, it did repeal the Compromise; implicitly, the act organizing the New Mexico territory had repealed the Compromise, for part of that territory fell within the Louisiana Purchase area north of 36°30′. But Senator Archibald Dixon of Kentucky, a Whig who had succeeded Henry Clay, pointed to a flaw in that reading. Unless the Compromise line were explicitly repealed, he said, slave owners could not take their slaves into the territory, and thus when the time arrived for residents to fashion a constitution with or without slavery, only nonslaveholders would be residents. Dixon drafted an amendment repealing the Missouri Compromise line, and he persuaded a reluctant Douglas to accept it. "By God, sir," Douglas said, "you are right, and I will incorporate it in my bill, though I know it will raise the hell of a storm."[3]

Douglas underestimated the intensity of the storm, though he had abundant warning. The bill had scarcely been reported to the Senate when a group of antislavery congressmen published a resounding denunciation. They arraigned it "as a gross violation of a sacred pledge; as a criminal betrayal of precious rights; as part and parcel of an atrocious plot" whose ultimate aim was subjugation of "the whole country to the yoke of a slaveholding despotism." They attacked Douglas with bitter invective, but the "Little Giant" treated their effort contemptuously, denouncing the authors as "the pure, unadulterated representatives of Abolitionism, Free Soilism, Niggerism in the Congress of the United States."[4]

Douglas could take that position in Congress, for he had the votes; what he misjudged was the temper of the country. Throughout the northern states, people were still rankled by the Fugitive Slave Act, and the introduction of the Kansas-Nebraska bill deepened their resentment. More tellingly, the bill convinced moderate northerners that the slaveocracy, about which abolitionists had been screaming, actually existed and was in full control of the government. During the spring of 1854, as the bill wended its way through Congress, mass meeting after mass meeting adopted resolutions condemning the measure, as did legislatures and city councils. For the first time, respectable community leaders—ministers and merchants and newspaper publishers—joined forces with the abolitionists they had previously shunned. That development was ominous, involving as it did the radicalization of people who had formerly been moderate or indifferent. One newspaper in downstate Illinois, late in the year, caught the essence of the change. "Before the repeal of the Missouri Compromise," it editorialized, "in all contests between the slaveholders and the abolitionists our sympathies were decidedly in favor of the former," but this "act of treachery" altered everything.[5]

Douglas miscalculated the reaction in the South as badly as he had misjudged that in the North. He had supposed that the measure would win him favor in the South; many thought that he was seeking to win friends in the region who would later support his bid for the presidency. Instead, southern Democrats approved it, but not eagerly, and southern Whigs viewed it with attitudes ranging from lukewarm to hostile. Southerners of all descriptions were mystified by the charge that Douglas's bill was an act of southern aggression and that the slaveocracy ruled Washington. Free states had a majority in the Senate, and despite the three-fifths clause, they had 144 of the 234 seats in the House. They cast 176 electoral votes to the South's 120, and the incumbent in the White House was from New Hampshire.[6]

And yet northern fears were not without foundation. Though California was a free state, it was dominated by southern Democrats, and its senators regularly voted with southern members. In the House, "doughface Democrats," northern men with southern principles, ensured that no legislation unfavorable to the South would be enacted. Pierce's cabinet included the fire-eater from Mississippi, Jefferson Davis, the secretary of war. Five of the nine Supreme Court justices were from the South. And writing Kansas off as unsuitable for slavery was uncertain. Cotton could not be grown in Kansas, but hemp, a slave-cultivated crop, could be, and the greatest concentration of slaveholding in Missouri was in the state's northwestern counties adjoining Kansas.[7]

If northerners needed further proof of the power and sinister designs of the slaveocracy, evidence was forthcoming in the official and unofficial manifestations of the Pierce administration's expansionist foreign policy. Three months after the passage of the Kansas-Nebraska Act, Secretary of State William Marcy instructed the American ministers to Spain, France, and Britain to meet in Ostend, Belgium, to formulate a policy for acquiring Cuba from Spain. The resulting Ostend Manifesto declared that obtaining Cuba was indispensable for the security of slavery, that the United States should attempt to buy the island, and that if Spain refused to sell, the United States should seize it by force. Nothing came of the project, nor did anything permanent result the next year when the adventurer William Walker sought to conquer Panama in a filibustering expedition. Both ventures, however, confirmed northern fears about southern intentions.[8]

The immediate yields of the turmoil were the collapse of the existing party system and the beginnings of a section-based political order. The American or Know-Nothing party burst upon the scene and gathered hordes of adherents, even though it was committed to nothing more than arresting the flow of immigrants, mainly from Germany and Ireland. The Whigs foolishly tried to embrace the Know-Nothings but succeeded only in alienating their own long-established base. By election time, the Whig party, for practical purposes, no longer existed. Fusion movements of antislavery Democrats, Free-Soilers, and northern Whigs arose spontaneously, culminating in meetings in Ripon, Wisconsin, and Jackson, Michigan, and the formation of the Republican party. Democrats in the South remained intact and gained the favor of the remnants of southern Whiggery, but they lost northern support.[9]

The results of the fall congressional elections were indecisive. A coalition of Know-Nothings and Whigs swept New York, gaining twenty-nine of its thirty-one House seats. In Pennsylvania, the margin was twenty-one of twenty-five. In Massachusetts, a fusion ticket of Know-Nothings and Free-Soilers took 80,000 votes to 27,000 for Whig candidates, 14,000 for Democrats, and 7,000 for Republicans. Fusion candidates won all the seats in upper New England; Yankee Democrats were able to hold seats only in Connecticut and Rhode Island. The story was similar in Ohio and Indiana. In the South, Democrats won the vast majority of seats, even in former Whig strongholds. The next Congress, scheduled to meet in December 1855, would see in the House 108 Republicans, 83 Democrats, and 43 Know-Nothings.[10]

The doings of proslavery people in the wake of the 1854 elections suggested that they either failed to understand the message or were contemptuous of it. Early in 1855, bands of armed Missourians crossed into Kansas and fraudulently carried the elections for a territorial representative to Congress and the territorial legislature. That legislature promptly enacted statutes providing severe punishment for antislavery agitation. Antislavery settlers responded by repudiating the legislature, drafting a constitution prohibiting slavery, and establishing a rival government. President Pierce responded by replacing the territorial governor, who sympathized with the antislavery people, by a proslavery man, and he sent a special message to Congress condemning the antislavery government as an act of rebellion. Violence broke out late in the year, and by the spring of 1856, a full-scale civil war was under way. "Border Ruffians" from Missouri joined proslavery forces in Kansas and razed the antislavery stronghold of Lawrence. Guerrilla warfare continued throughout the year, massacres being committed by both sides. Actually, the violence in "Bleeding Kansas" was not appreciably more severe than was common in newly opened frontier communities, and a lot of it involved land claims and other disputes having no bearing upon slavery. But newspapers in the Northeast carried sensational stories almost daily and portrayed the actions as representing unmitigated proslavery aggression.[11]

Then, back in Washington, came an episode that outraged and unnerved northerners, leaving many convinced that a union with southerners had no room in it for them. In May 1856, before news of the attack on Lawrence reached the capital, Senator Charles Sumner of Massachusetts gave a speech that he termed "The Crime Against Kansas." He called the treatment of Kansas "the rape of a virgin territory, compelling it to the hateful embrace of Slavery; and it may be clearly traced to a depraved longing for a new slave State, the hideous offspring of such a crime, in the hope of adding to the power of Slavery in the national government." Casting aside all reserve, he described the Missourians in the territory as "murderous robbers" and "hirelings, picked form the drunken spew and vomit of an uneasy civilization." On and on he railed, closing by attacking and insulting Senators Douglas, James Mason of Virginia, and Andrew Butler of South Carolina with bitterly sarcastic personal language not heard in the Senate since the days of John Randolph of Roanoke. Douglas and Mason were present to rebuke Sumner and did so in a spirited exchange. Butler was not present, but his nephew Congressman Preston Brooks was, and Brooks determined to exact revenge.[12]

Brooks brooded on the matter during a sleepless night. Doubtless he did not consider challenging Sumner to a duel, for according to the southern code of honor, that would be to treat the senator as an equal and a gentleman. He thought a cowhide whipping would be appropriate but rejected the idea lest Sumner, a powerful man, should wrest the whip from his hand. He settled for a caning: on the day after Sumner's insulting of Butler, Brook accosted him in an empty Senate chamber and struck him on the head repeatedly with a gutta-percha cane, knocking him unconscious. A doctor testified that examination of Sumner revealed "nothing but flesh wounds," but Sumner relished the role of martyr and recognized its contribution to the cause. (Though he stayed away from the Senate for three and a half years, protesting that his nervous system had been shattered and his brain damaged, he managed to tour Europe extensively and lead an active social life.)[13]

Reactions to the beating understandably followed a sectional pattern. Some in the South criticized Brooks on the ground of expediency, but many applauded. The *Columbia South Carolinian* went so far as to claim that a number of slaves had contributed money to buy Brooks a present for having "made the first *practical* issue for their preservation and protection in their rights and enjoyments as the happiest laborers on the face of the globe." In the North, anger and condemnation greeted the news. Robert C. Winthrop of Boston wrote, "You can have little idea of the depth and intensity of the feeling which has been excited in New England." The "masses," he added, were in "a state of fearful desperation." That desperation, said the governor of New Hampshire in a message to the legislature, was triggered by "the arrogant and aggressive demands" of the "slave power."[14]

Northerners' frustrations, which had been accumulating for the better part of eight years, were increasingly expressed in terms of states' rights, strict construction, and hostility to the Supreme Court. In 1850, for example, Senator Salmon P. Chase of Ohio, who would succeed Taney as chief justice, had assailed a decision of the Supreme Court, adopting the precise language of Jefferson and Jackson in denying that Congress was bound by the Court's decisions. Two years later, Charles Sumner made the same claim, saying that the Court "cannot control our duty as to legislation, and here I adopt the language of President Jackson in his memorable veto" of the recharter of the Bank. Soon Benjamin Wade of Ohio and Hannibal Hamlin of Maine were reiterating the sentiment.[15]

In 1854 the Court incurred the wrath of Ohio by striking down, as a violation of the contract clause, a state statute depriving a bank of exemption from taxation, which had been granted in the bank's act of incorporation. The *Cincinnati Enquirer* denounced the Court as a "silk-gowned fogydom, a goodly portion of it imbecile with age, a portion anti-republican in notions, a portion wedded to the antiquated doctrine of established precedents, no matter whether truth or fallacy." The decision (*Piqua Bank* v. *Knoop*), opined the editor, was "an invasion of State sovereignty and a great outrage upon State-Rights. . . . A crisis is here now, if it had not already been reached, and as this is the 'year of storms,' look out for the greatest one yet to come."[16]

Nor were protests limited to the verbiage of politicians and editorial writers. In 1856 the Court declared unconstitutional an Ohio constitutional amendment that attempted to do what the state had done by statute in the *Piqua* case, and it turned out that the Ohio supreme court had been refusing for two years to enter the mandate of the case. Three justices of the state court then relented and conformed to the mandate, but the chief justice dissented, saying that the decision's doctrine, in its "enormities and alarming import . . . wholly prostrates the municipal sovereignty of the people with the State." The same chief justice, sitting in district court, flatly denied the appellate jurisdiction of the Supreme Court under section 25 of the Judiciary Act and prevented appeal by refusing to perfect the record of the case.[17]

In the meantime, in 1854, the California supreme court had blatantly defied federal authority, denying a writ of error to a party seeking appeal from a state decision. The California court declared that the past acquiescence by states in the Supreme Court's exercise of appellate jurisdiction over state cases was no reason for surrendering "a power which belongs to the sovereignty we represent, involving an assumption of that power by another jurisdiction in derogation of that power." The act of Congress conferring jurisdiction in appeals from state courts, the California judges ruled, was patently unconstitutional. A year later, the state legislature passed a law requiring compliance with the federal judiciary, but only after a year of dragging their feet did the state supreme court judges agree to reverse themselves.[18]

For sheer stubbornness of resistance, no state topped Wisconsin. An abolitionist newspaper editor named Sherman M. Booth was arrested for aiding in the rescue of a runaway slave from a federal marshal, in violation of the Fugitive Slave Act. There being no federal prison in the state, he was detained in a local jail. Booth requested a writ of habeas corpus from a judge of the Wisconsin supreme court, who granted the writ on the ground that the federal act was unconstitutional. The Supreme Court, on appeal by the marshal, ordered Booth reincarcerated, and early in 1855 he was indicted, tried, convicted, and sentenced, but immediately he was released by an order of the state supreme court.[19]

Abolitionists cheered this act of defiance, amounting to nullification. Horace Greeley's *New York Tribune* said gleefully, "the North is just now taking lessons in Southern jurisprudence. South Carolina, Georgia, and little Florida have, at one time and another, displayed a glorious independence of Federal legislation, whenever it suited their purposes. . . . The example which Wisconsin has set will be as rapidly followed as circumstances admit." The editorial writer anticipated "a race among the other Free States in the same direction, till all have reached the goal of State independence." Republicans, he concluded, "naturally stand on the State-Rights doctrine of Jefferson." Indeed, Ohio and Pennsylvania, emboldened by Wisconsin's example, emulated it, but they were thwarted. Wisconsin persisted. The state was assisted by a peculiarity of the Judiciary Act that provided no appeal from criminal convictions in lower federal courts. Thus the Wisconsin court continued to issue writs of habeas corpus for Booth, the Supreme Court continued to overrule the state, and the conflict remained deadlocked until the Civil War started.[20]

To stem resistance by state courts, in 1855 Democratic Senator Isaac Toucey of Connecticut introduced a bill to give federal courts jurisdiction over suits brought in state courts against federal officers.

He was greeted by fierce opposition from antislavery senators. Echoing the doctrines of the Virginia and Kentucky Resolutions and the South Carolina nullificationists, Chase denounced the measure as "a bill to establish a great, central, consolidated Federal Government. It is a step—a stride rather—towards despotism." Benjamin Wade declared, "I am no advocate for Nullification, but in the nature of things, according to the true interpretation of our institutions, a State, in the last resort, crowded to the wall by the General Government seeking by the strong arm of its power to take away the rights of the State, is to judge of whether she shall stand on her reserved rights." The bill passed in the Senate but died in the House.[21]

The reversal of positions was observed by all. When an Ohio Whig sought to justify a measure equalizing the representation of sections in the federal courts, he cited the Virginia and Kentucky Resolutions as his justification; he was rebutted by a Virginia Democrat. When Republicans later attempted to repeal section 25 of the Judiciary Act, the *New York Times* commented that South Carolina had in the 1830s "denied the paramount authority of the Supreme Court," while Massachusetts asserted the "absolute, unqualified duty of every citizen and every State to yield implicit obedience to its decisions upon all questions."[22]

In the South, spokesmen for the Court were not unanimous, but they were nearly so. Senator James C. Jones of Tennessee said, "For purity, integrity, virtue, honor, and all that ennobles and dignifies, it stands unimpeached and unimpeachable." Andrew Butler of South Carolina, the man toward whom Sumner had directed his vitriol, declared that the "Judges are the sentinels and defenders of the Constitution; they do not decide by the 'higher law' of discretion and prejudice," as abolitionists preferred. To be sure, radical secessionists such as William L. Yancey rejected the doctrine of judicial finality in matters of constitutional law. But more common was the position expressed by the *Southern Quarterly Review* of Charleston. "Against the invading flood of aggression" by the North, said the journal, "nothing seems to be opposed but the barrier of judicial independence which the great architects of the Constitution have set up.

Gloomy will that day be for the cause of Constitutional order and State's Rights," it concluded, "when the mighty structure is levelled before the rolling waves of that angry ocean."[23]

The uneasiness on both sides was soon to grow. First came the elections of 1856, which upset southerners and northerners for different reasons. The Republican party met in Philadelphia in a convention attended by no southerners and but a handful of delegates from border states. Amidst an atmosphere of evangelical enthusiasm, it adopted a platform indicating that its whole program was the negative one of prohibiting the extension of slavery. Then it nominated for president the explorer and ersatz military hero John C. Frémont. The Know-Nothings nominated ex-president Millard Fillmore, though he had never been associated with the party and was out of the country at the time. Whatever following he might attract would almost certainly take votes away from Frémont. The Democrats nominated the Pennsylvania doughface James Buchanan. Confident of sweeping the South, they calculated that if they could capture New York or Pennsylvania and any other northern state, victory would be theirs.[24]

The campaign was marked by turbulence. News of Brooks's caning of Sumner was still fresh, reports from Bleeding Kansas poured in, and violence attended several elections, including those in Baltimore, where fourteen were killed and three hundred wounded. Many southerners declared that if Frémont were elected, secession must inevitably follow. Preston Brooks said that it would also be the duty of the South to "lay the strong arm of Southern freemen upon the treasury and archives of the government." Senator James Mason asserted that Frémont's election would mean "immediate, absolute, eternal separation." Virginia's governor, Henry Wise, invited his fellow southern governors to meet with him to plan concerned action toward secession, and Wise claimed that if secession led to war, he could "arm and equip 50,000 men the next morning, ready for revolution." Upon hearing such remarks, old-time abolitionists, who had long advocated separation, were filled with joy.[25]

Neither side was comforted by the outcome of the campaign. Buchanan won, outpolling Frémont 1.8 million to 1.3 million and collecting 174 electoral votes to Frémont's 114. But Fillmore also received 871,000 popular votes, meaning that his votes and Frémont's combined were more than half the total. To southerners, the anti-Buchanan vote suggested that the triumph of fanatical Republicanism was merely a matter of time, and not much time at that. Northerners saw the results differently. The White House would be occupied by a pro-southern president for at least another four years, and what was more, Democrats regained control of the House and the Senate. To Republicans, the slaveocracy seemed as firmly entrenched as ever.[26]

Any lingering doubts Republicans might have entertained were dispelled two days after Buchanan's inauguration, when the Supreme Court handed down its decision in *Dred Scott* v. *Sandford*. Scott was the slave of Major John Emerson, an army surgeon who in 1834 had taken him from St. Louis to Rock Island, Illinois, where slavery had been prohibited by the Northwest Ordinance, and later to the Wisconsin territory, where slavery had also been prohibited, before they returned to Missouri in 1838. In 1846, Scott brought a suit against Emerson's widow in a Missouri circuit court, claiming that his residence in free territory had made him a freeman. In January 1850, he obtained a favorable verdict, but on appeal, the state supreme court overruled the decision, holding that under the laws of Missouri he had resumed his status as a slave, no matter what had been his station when he was out of the state.[27]

Emerson's widow, who had married an abolitionist congressman from Massachusetts, C. C. Chaffee, wanted the question tested in federal courts. To that end, she transferred ownership in a fictitious sale to her brother, John F. A. Sanford of New York, establishing the ground of diverse citizenship. In November 1853, Scott brought suit in the United States circuit court on the same basis as his earlier plea in the state court. In May 1854, his suit was rejected, and the case was appealed to the Supreme Court.[28]

The Court could have settled the matter in a noncontroversial way by following the precedent it had set in 1850 in *Strader* v. *Graham* and on which the circuit court had based its decision. Apparently, most of the justices in the *Dred Scott* case intended to follow that ruling, and Justice Samuel Nelson of New York, a Tyler appointee, was assigned the task of writing the opinion accordingly. Two justices, however, John McLean of Ohio and Benjamin Curtis of Massachusetts, let it be known that they intended to write a dissenting opinion in which they would hold that the Missouri Compromise had been constitutional. That viewpoint moved the other justices to reconsider their positions. Naively believing, despite the widespread criticism of the Court, that any ruling they issued would be received as definitive, the justices determined to pronounce a sweeping statement concerning slavery and its extension. They hoped thereby to take the subject out of politics forever, and they assigned the task of writing such a decision to Chief Justice Taney.[29]

Taney began his opinion by asking, "Can a negro, whose ancestors were imported into this country, and sold as slaves, become a member of the political community . . . and as such become entitled to all the rights, and privileges, and immunities, guaranteed" by the Constitution? In answering the question, Taney said, one must construe the Constitution as it was viewed at the time of its adoption, not by later lights. At the time, he declared, not entirely accurately, blacks had been considered "as beings of an inferior order, and altogether unfit to associate with the white race, either in social or political relations; and so far inferior, that they had no rights which the white man was bound to respect." Because the Constitution had not changed since the Founding, even though public opinion had, no black could ever become a citizen of the United States. States could grant the rights of citizenship within their own limits, but not within the larger national entity. Dred Scott was therefore not a citizen of the United States and had no right to sue in its courts. Taney thus extended the concept of divided sovereignty to include divided citizenship that was not concurrent but mutually exclusive.[30]

Had a majority of the Court agreed with Taney on the point, the opinion could have ended there, but two justices explicitly disagreed, so Taney had to deal with the question whether Scott's residence in Illinois liberated him. It did not, Taney held, because his status was determined by the laws of the state in which he commenced his suit, and the Missouri courts had decided that according to state law he was a slave. On this point the judges were agreed, six to three, for the ruling was the same as in the *Strader* case. Taney could have stopped there, but instead he proceeded to another substantive issue. This one was a bombshell: the constitutionality of the Missouri Compromise and the question of congressional exclusion of slavery from the territories. The Constitution recognized slaves as property, though without using the word "slave," and the Fifth Amendment prohibited the taking of property without due process of law. From these premises, Taney reasoned that "an act of Congress which deprives a citizen of the United States of his liberty or property, merely because he came himself or brought his property into a particular Territory of the United States, and who had committed no offence against the laws, could hardly be dignified with the name of due process of law." The Missouri Compromise was therefore unconstitutional and had been all along, and any future act of Congress prohibiting slavery in the territories would be equally unconstitutional.[31]

The protest that swept the North dwarfed the reaction to the Fugitive Slave Act and reconfirmed the conviction that the Court was controlled by the slaveocracy. That conviction, however, was unjustified. Two justices who concurred in the opinion, Robert Grier and Samuel Nelson, were northerners. Of the five southerners, none was a slave owner. Taney had inherited a few slaves as a young man, but he had freed them and provided funds for the care of the elderly among them; he thought of slavery as "a blot on our national character." John A. Campbell of Alabama had some household slaves, but he freed them on being appointed to the Court. The justices can be accused of spurious reasoning, but the decision was based upon adherence to the Constitution as they understood it, not upon favoritism toward their section of the country.[32]

The decision had serious consequences. It undermined the credibility and sapped the moral capital of the Supreme Court. The finality of the Court's decisions had been questioned before, but its reputation among the general citizenry had remained high. Because the judiciary was, as Hamilton had written in *Federalist* 78, the "least dangerous" branch of government, having "neither FORCE nor WILL, but merely judgment," its authority rested solely on public trust in its impartiality and integrity. After *Dred Scott,* that trust was gone. As a result, the Court could play no decisive role in settling the issues that led to secession and those that grew out of the Civil War and Reconstruction.[33]

Another consequence of the *Dred Scott* decision was that it, in tandem with the course of events in Kansas and Washington and the aftermath of the panic of 1857, ensured that the Republican party would sweep to victory in the House of Representatives in 1858.

During August 1857, the economic boom started turning to bust. The New York branch of the Ohio Life Insurance and Trust Company, which had $5 million to $7 million in debts, could not meet its obligations because its cashier had embezzled its assets. A panic struck the financial community, stock and commodity prices collapsed, and bankruptcies triggered a succession of additional bankruptcies. A brief recovery seemed to shape up early in September, then panic began anew as depositors made runs on banks. By mid-month, every bank in the city was forced to close its doors. Banks in Boston and Philadelphia soon followed, and then those in Baltimore and the Midwest collapsed. In short order, the notes of fourteen hundred state banks became worthless, five thousand businesses failed, and western railroads went broke. And, in a reversal of the usual pattern, wherein financial dislocations in Europe set off panics in America, the panic of 1857 spread to Europe. International trade in most commodities came to a standstill.[34]

The panic was short-lived, and most banks were functioning by early 1858, but the economic depression that followed was long and harsh. In New England, cotton and woolen textile mills were idle, and workers, laid off by the thousands, were plunged into poverty. Throughout the country, railroad construction, which had carried a great deal of the boom, stopped. Land values collapsed, breaking tens of thousands of farmers who had borrowed to invest in acreage that they could no longer pay for. Female factory workers in Chicopee, Massachusetts, kept their jobs but were paid a meager $1.40 a week. In Cincinnati, half of the twenty-five thousand workers in the clothing industry were unemployed. A majority of the country's furnaces and iron mills were shut. Lumbermen in Michigan and Wisconsin, fired with almost no warning, verged on starvation. Two hundred fifty ships were tied up in Boston; a little relief to shippers came from a demand by arriving immigrants to be taken back home. Private charitable instrumentalities were inadequate to relieve the suffering, and municipalities did not have the wherewithal. The mayor of New York proposed public works projects to employ the jobless unskilled laborers, but the city council's response was minimal.[35]

Anger permeated the ranks of midwestern farmers, who sought and readily found scapegoats in the form of eastern "jobbers and speculators." From Ohio to Kansas, they blamed their troubles on manipulators in the eastern cities. Farmers in central Illinois held a convention and adopted bitter resolutions condemning "trading combinations," railroads, and banks. Other conventions alleged that stockyards and grain markets robbed the farmers, and they demanded government action. No action was forthcoming, and nothing would have helped anyway, for the farmers' plight was due to forces over which governments had no control.[36]

Urban workers did not respond to their dismissals and pay cuts in the docile way they had reacted to earlier depressions. To be sure, some of their demonstrations were peaceful. In Philadelphia, thousands held "hunger meetings," requesting the mayor to establish public works projects and promising to furnish their labor for city scrip if the city guaranteed that it would "be taken for bread and butter, tea and sugar." A mob in New York, however, threatened city hall and was turned back by three hundred policemen. Everywhere the unemployed demanded work as a right. And workers in New England textile towns, when their pay was drastically cut, went out on strikes, thronging the streets and terrifying "scabs" among their fellow employees.[37]

Manufacturers were also angry, attributing their woes to excessive importation made possible by the low import duties of the 1846 tariff and by a tariff adjustment enacted the day before Buchanan took office. Ironmasters were especially bitter, for the United States obviously had the natural resources necessary for a great iron industry, yet Britain was consistently able to undersell American producers in American markets. Textile manufacturers joined in clamoring for protective tariffs. Since 1846, imports of British printed and dyed cottons had increased eightfold to tenfold. To make matters worse, the 1857 tariff revisions had actually reduced the duties on cottons and woolens. Manufacturers across the board organized and contributed money to elect Republicans to Congress and thereby to reinstitute the protective tariff system.[38]

The cotton kingdom was almost untouched by the panic and depression. The price of cotton did drop from sixteen cents a pound in September (seasonally the peak) to nine cents by the end of 1857, but growers could wait for the rise—which came soon. Moreover, the 1857 crop was nearly a record and production during the last three years of the decade soared ever higher, while prices ranged upward from twelve cents a pound. Southerners, meanwhile, had not imported as lavishly as northerners, and thus they were essentially debt free. The prosperity of the South convinced southerners that cotton was king, that "our wealth," as *De Bow's Review* crowed, "is permanent and real, while that of the North is fictitious."[39]

And at just this time, southerners were being powerfully reminded of how much better off they would be if they were not shackled in a union with the North. Thomas Prentice Long, former editor of the *Democratic Review,* published a book called *Southern Wealth and Northern Profits,* purporting to prove something southerners suspected: that the South produced vast wealth, but the North took most of it. Using copious tables, Long reached the conclusion that the North took annually from the South $253 million in profits by means of protective tariffs, fishing bounties, commissions of brokers, interest paid to bankers, and freightage paid to shippers. Others echoed the sentiment and announced that an independent South would be a more prosperous South. "We must separate," wrote the Virginia agricultural reformer Edmund Ruffin, "and the sooner it is done, the greater will be the relative strength of the Southern party, and the more sure will be the success of the movement."[40]

Complementing this enlarged self-confidence was a persuasive book depicting slavery as a positive good. Southern clergymen had preached that slavery was justified by the Bible, so long as masters treated it as a sacred trust and in accordance with Christian duty. Now, in the year of the panic, George Fitzhugh published *Cannibals All! or, Slaves without Masters,* arguing that the masses were always enslaved, though they might not know it, and that the southern practice of slavery was far more humane than the northern. "Capital exercises a more perfect compulsion over free laborers than human masters over slaves," he wrote, "for free laborers must at all times work or starve, and slaves are supported whether they work or not." The free laborer had less practical freedom, was worse paid and provided for, and had no valuable rights. "His wants and other men's capital make him a slave without a master." According to Fitzhugh, the free labor system was a relatively new experiment that had already failed abysmally. This message warmed the hearts of slave owners and made them as smug as their Yankee detractors.[41]

The fissure separating the sections was worsened by continuing political blunders. President Buchanan, wildly miscalculating, thought that the admission of Kansas as a slave state would hurt Republicans and bring Democrats together, and he urged Congress to admit Kansas under a proslavery constitution that had been fraudulently drawn up in Lecompton. Douglas openly broke with the president, taking followers with him, which alienated southern Democrats. In a raucous debate marked by fistfights and a free-for-all, Congress rejected Buchanan's proposal by adopting a complex countermeasure. Democrats were thoroughly splintered, and Republicans had another issue to take to the voters.[42]

Republicans had additional factors working for their benefit. The Know-Nothing party was defunct except in Maryland, Illinois, and a few pockets here and there; most of its adherents drifted into the Republican camp. Republicans were energized by the adoption of popular causes, especially the protective tariff, a homestead act, and monetary reform. They were no longer a one-issue party, though they remained a one-section party primarily dedicated to halting the spread of slavery. Obviously, the Republican positions were inimical to the perceived interests of the South.[43]

During the 1858 congressional campaigns, the celebrated Lincoln-Douglas debates took place. Douglas was up for reelection, and Republicans pitted against him the Springfield lawyer and former Whig congressman Abraham Lincoln. The contest was meaningless, for the senatorial election was in the hands of the state legislature, but when Lincoln challenged Douglas to a series of debates, both men thought they could get political mileage from the encounter.[44]

Two of the orations during the campaign were of considerable significance. In accepting the nomination, Lincoln delivered his "house divided" speech. "A house divided against itself cannot stand," he said. "I believe this government cannot endure permanently half slave and half free." He did not, he added, "expect the Union to be dissolved," but "I do expect it will cease to be divided. It will become all one thing, or all the other. Either the opponents of slavery will arrest the further spread of it, and place it where the public mind shall rest in the belief that it is in the course of ultimate extinction; or its advocates will push it forward until it shall become alike lawful in all the States." Ambiguous and nonincendiary as it was, southerners read that speech as if Lincoln were a radical abolitionist.[45]

Douglas, for his part, scarcely endeared himself among southerners. His position was stoutly racist, insisting upon the inferiority of blacks ("I positively deny that [the black man] is my brother or any kin to me whatever"), but he was unequivocally committed to his doctrine of popular sovereignty. Douglas had his faults, and he was an opportunistic politician, but he was unvarying in his support of the principle underlying the doctrine of states' rights—local autonomy. That conviction led him to announce, in a debate in Freeport, Illinois, that the people of a territory could, despite the *Dred Scott* decision, legally prevent the introduction of slavery simply by passing laws prohibiting the ownership of slaves. Douglas had said that many times before, but now it was widely publicized and damned Douglas forever among southerners.[46]

The outcome of the election was that Democrats, and especially

Buchanan Democrats, were thoroughly routed. Douglas retained his post, but only because of a malapportionment of seats in the legislature. Illinois and Indiana elected Democratic majorities to their House delegations, but those were mostly pro-Douglas, anti-Buchanan Democrats. Elsewhere in the North, the Republican sweep was nearly total, even in Buchanan's home state of Pennsylvania. The Republicans captured 114 seats in the House, all from the North, and Democrats won 92 seats, overwhelmingly from the South. Know-Nothings and Whigs won 24 between them—enough to prevent a majority by either major party. Democrats retained control of the Senate by a 12-seat margin, but seemingly after one more election that would change.[47]

The defeated Democratic party promptly began to dismantle itself. In the lame-duck session of Congress that convened in December 1858, the Senate stripped Douglas of his committee chairmanship, then agitated for legislation positively protecting slavery in the territories. President Buchanan, in his annual message, again called for a militant policy toward Cuba, Mexico, and Nicaragua, as if expansion to create slave states were still a possibility. A few Democrats proposed to legalize the slave trade. Various southerners spoke of assassinating Douglas, and Douglas took the matter seriously enough to hire a noted marksman as his bodyguard. One of his allies, Senator David Broderick of California, was actually killed in a duel with a southerner that summer. Meanwhile, such firebrands as William Yancey, Edmund Ruffin, and Robert Barnwell Rhett encouraged the dissention and outlandish proposals in the hope that they would broaden popular support for secession.[48]

Until October 1859, most southerners remained loyal to the Union and were unperturbed by the election results, despite the turmoil that agitated Washington. Kansas no longer concerned them, since the settlers had made it clear that they would sooner or later enter the Union as a free state, and though the Republicans would probably seek to raise the tariff, they were likely to lose in the Senate. The news of John Brown's raid shattered that southern complacency.

Brown, a fanatical and not entirely sane abolitionist who in 1856 had led a band that slaughtered five proslavery colonists near Pottawatomie Creek in Kansas, had returned east and hatched a grand scheme. Conceiving of himself as chosen by God to be the instrument that ended slavery, he secured about $4,000 from wealthy abolitionists in the Northeast, assembled twenty-one followers, obtained two hundred Sharps rifles and a thousand pikes, and invaded the federal arsenal at Harpers Ferry in western Virginia. Believing that the whites in the mountainous area, who were hostile to slavery, would join forces with him, and convinced that slaves hated their masters, he planned to move southward and arm the slaves, who would institute a bloodbath and liberate themselves. Neither whites nor slaves answered his call. Locals from miles around formed themselves into armed companies to beseige him and his band. The next day, a detachment of Marines under Brevet Colonel Robert E. Lee captured Brown and killed most of his followers.[49]

But though the raid was a failure, Brown went a long way toward achieving his goal of destroying slavery as an institution. He was swiftly tried in a Virginia court on counts of murder, conspiracy to commit insurrection, and treason against Virginia, was convicted on all three charges, and was hanged on December 2. The trial was publicized throughout the North, and that part of the nation was overwhelmingly impressed by the dignity of his conduct and by his conscious portrayal of himself in the role of martyr to a holy cause. Abolitionists were ecstatic. Henry David Thoreau called Brown "an angel of light." Ralph Waldo Emerson referred to him as "The Saint, whose fate . . . will make the gallows as glorious as the Cross." As one observer described the northern reaction, the "events of this last month or two (including under the word events the impression made by Brown's character) have done more to confirm the opposition to slavery at the North . . . than anything which has ever happened before, than all the antislavery tracts and novels that ever were written."[50]

In the South, reaction to the raid, and to the northern response to the raid, was horror, fear, and anger. Many were convinced that groups of abolitionists were about to launch a series of Brown-like raids. The governor of Virginia fanned the flames by exaggerating the number of men who had been in Brown's party and by deploying militia to patrol the area. Papers captured from Brown suggesting that he had planned other raids were published. In the entire South, the Republican party was forthwith identified with abolitionism and John Brown's raid.[51]

An atmosphere of violence permeated the halls of Congress when it convened a week after Brown's execution. The House spent two months in acrimonious debates before it was able to organize and elect a speaker. Members in both houses carried arms; Senator James Hammond of South Carolina said that "the only persons who do not have a revolver and a knife are those who have two revolvers." Spectators in the galleries also carried weapons. Several duels were narrowly averted. Talk of secession was rife, many southerners declaring that if the Republicans won the presidency, the Union would be at an end. And the congressional session accomplished nothing in the way of constructive legislation.[52]

Congress did consider a pair of economic measures, both of which southerners regarded as contrary to their interests and as signs of what would come if the Republicans gained control of government. The first was a homestead bill, providing 160 acres of the public domain to any bona fide settler for a minimum fee of twenty-five cents an acre. Southerners opposed the bill, arguing that it would restrict slavery, stimulate a flood of European immigrants to the North and West, and increase the power of the free states. The proposal passed despite the nearly unanimous dissent of southerners, but President Buchanan vetoed it. The other measure was a moderate protective tariff, sponsored by Representative Justin Morrill of Vermont. The bill passed easily in the House but ran into a barrage of opposition in the Senate. Southerners denounced it in the kind of extreme language that had become normal among them, and northern Democrats, true to their party's low-tariff tradition, joined them and prevented passage.[53]

As the presidential election of 1860 approached, strife among Democrats resumed, but this time the conflict was carefully calculated. The Democrats met in their national nominating convention late in April. The logical candidate was Douglas, and he had a good chance of being elected, for southerners would certainly oppose the Republican candidate, thus assuring 120 of the 152 electoral votes necessary to win. But before the national convention could meet, William L. Yancey induced the Alabama state convention to instruct its delegates to withdraw if the national body refused to adopt a platform demanding that Congress protect slavery in the territories—a position Douglas could never support. As the convention gathered, the delegates from six other southern states joined Alabama's and agreed to withdraw in a body if they did not get the platform they sought.[54]

The purpose of the move was to split the party, thus ensuring a Republican victory and making it possible to inflame feelings to such an extent that secession could be brought about. The tactic worked. Douglas supporters dominated the convention and rejected the slave-protection proposal, delegates from eight states (now including South Carolina) walked out, and the convention broke up without nominating a candidate. It reconvened in Baltimore in mid-June and nominated Douglas. Ten days later, the seceders met in their own convention and nominated Vice-President John C. Breckenridge of Kentucky as their candidate. A group of former Whigs and Know-Nothings formed a Constitutional Union party and nominated John Bell of Tennessee on a platform denouncing sectional parties and supporting the Union, the Constitution, and the enforcement of federal laws.[55]

The Republicans moved shrewdly to capitalize on the disarray. They passed over William H. Seward of New York, probably the most prominent member of the party, as being too controversial and nominated the lesser-known Lincoln. They broadened their platform, adding old Whig economic issues and a homestead act to the single issue that really held them together: the absolute determination to prevent the spread of slavery in the territories. They campaigned vigorously on Lincoln's behalf but persuaded him to stay home and speak on no issues whatever.[56]

Far more important, even fateful, were the campaigns of Douglas, Breckenridge, and the Unionists. Douglas and his supporters tried to dissociate themselves from talk of disunion, but the Douglas news-paper in Atlanta declared its intention "to pave Pennsylvania Avenue ten fathoms deep with mangled bodies" if Lincoln were elected. The leading Constitutional Unionist in Georgia said that if Lincoln won, "the fact will turn out to be . . . that this Government and Black Republicanism cannot live together." Breckenridge's supporters, almost to a man, predicted that the South would secede if the Repub-licans took the White House, and politicians and editorial writers spiced their warnings with lurid accounts of abolitionist fanatics who had supposedly already invaded the region to stir up the slaves. In Georgia, Virginia, Alabama, Mississippi, and Texas, lynch mobs were formed in response to rumors of abolitionist activities.[57]

Republicans could not bring themselves to take the threat seri-ously. James Russell Lowell said that the threat was "old Mumbo-Jumbo." Horace Greeley called it "as audacious a humbug as Mormonism." John Wentworth of Chicago said that "secession talk was just 'the old game of scaring and bullying the North into sub-mission.'" The *New York Tribune* opined, "the south could no more unite upon a scheme of secession than a company of lunatics could conspire to break out of bedlam." The *Hartford Evening Press* extended that metaphor: "the threat is an empty sham," and if those who make it try to fulfill it, "their enterprise has about as good a chance of succeeding as the lunatics in the Retreat at Hartford would have of capsizing the state of Connecticut into Long Island South." Even when the legislatures of South Carolina and Alabama autho-rized the calling of secession conventions if Lincoln were elected, even when states called conventions after it was known that he had been elected, Republicans still refused to take the threat seriously. The *Boston Daily Atlas and Bee* said on November 12 that "the peo-ple of the South will take care of these agitators—if they don't, Old Abe will." The *Indiana American* on November 21 editorially asked the question, "Will there be disunion?" and answered, "Of course not. The idea of a peaceable secession is too preposterous to be entertained for a moment by any sane mind." And the *New York Tribune* declared flatly that, despite all the noise, "the secession strength in the South is overrated."[58]

And then the South, or rather the seven states of the lower South, transformed secession from a threat into a reality. South Carolina led the way; its convention met on December 17 in Columbia and unanimously adopted an ordinance declaring that the ordinance of May 23, 1788, ratifying the Constitution was "hereby repealed, and that the union now subsisting between South Carolina and other States under the name of the United States of America is hereby dissolved." Mississippi followed on January 9, 1861, Florida on January 10, Alabama on January 11, Georgia on January 19, Louisiana on January 26, and Texas on February 1. Virginia, North Carolina, Tennessee, and Arkansas did not secede at this time, but each warned that it would resist any effort by the federal government to coerce the states that had seceded.[59]

The procedure followed was carefully chosen. A convention elected by the sovereign people of a state had voted to enter the constitutional Union, and in keeping with the theory underlying the Union, the same instrumentality was used to depart from the Union. Each of the early seceding states followed that path. It has been argued that the method was adopted as a means of avoiding a popular vote, which upon due deliberation might have failed of passage. However, in Texas, which held a referendum, the vote was 34,794 in favor of secession and 11,255 against. Be that as it may, South Carolinians knew their constitutional history and acted accordingly. Their convention also published on December 24 a Declaration of Immediate Causes in which a Lockean justification of their action, complete with paraphrases of the Declaration of Independence, was added to buttress their position.[60]

Most northerners were horrified but undecided as to what could or should be done, as President Buchanan was. Mayor Fernando Wood of New York, by contrast, suggested that the city should secede and join in confederacy with the southerners. One serious effort was made to effect a compromise that would lure the seceders back into the Union and lay to rest the divisive issue of slavery. A set of six constitutional amendments was offered by Senator John J. Crittenden of Kentucky. The first would reestablish the Missouri Compromise line to the Pacific, protecting slavery in the territories south of it; the last would forbid subsequent amendments to constitutional provisions regarding slavery, such as the three-fifths clause. Historians agree that North and South would probably have approved these proposals by large margins and that they would have ended the crisis. But Lincoln was adamantly opposed to any compromise regarding slavery in the territories, and southern proslavery partisans were equally adamant on the other side. The Crittenden amendments died in committee.[61]

The Union was defunct. The events that led shortly to the firing on Fort Sumter and Fort Pickens, to Lincoln's call for seventy-five thousand volunteers to suppress the "insurrection," and to the secession of four more southern states were dramatic but also anticlimactic. The doctrine of states' rights had been stretched to and, as the Civil War would demonstrate, beyond its limits. What remained to be determined during the course of the next fifteen years was whether the doctrine itself could survive.

9

CIVIL WAR AND
RECONSTRUCTION

One result of the Civil War was to deliver from slavery nearly 4 million Americans of African descent. From the perspective of the several hundred thousand Americans of European descent who had owned bondsmen, that result was catastrophic, nullifying billions of dollars of productive property. Despite the magnitude of the change, however, leaders on both sides of the conflict were strangely loath to admit that it had anything to do with slavery.

Abraham Lincoln insisted at the outset that the war was being fought solely to preserve the Union as he conceived the Union—namely, as one among the American people, not among the states. Granted, he had said in his "house divided" speech that the government could not endure permanently half slave and half free. But Lincoln offered, after his election, to support a constitutional amendment guaranteeing slavery in those states where it already existed, so long as they desired to preserve the institution (as if an amendment were necessary, for slavery could be abolished only by an amendment to which the consent of three-quarters of the states was required).

On the rebel side, leaders insisted, at least after the fact, that the South had fought to uphold what Alexander H. Stephens, erstwhile vice-president of the Confederacy, called the "sublime moral principle" of states' rights, as a defense against the "coarse, materialistic, and erroneous" principle of unchecked majority rule that prevailed in the North. (Admittedly, Stephens had said at the beginning of the war that the cornerstone of the Confederacy was white supremacy.)[1]

Whatever the leaders of the Union and the Confederation professed to be fighting about, the presidents of both found it necessary to suppress states' rights for the nonce and to centralize power. In the short range, the "sublime moral principle" was crushed, and in the long range, its most radical tenets—secession and nullification—were permanently discredited. And yet, when postwar Reconstruction at last came to an end, and the Union was complete once again, the doctrine of states' rights reemerged, altered but as vital as ever.

For two decades before he became a Republican, Lincoln had been a Whig who embraced the party's doctrines of nationalism, loose construction, congressional supremacy, and a strictly limited executive, and in many respects, he adhered to those principles during his presidency. He accepted Congress's domestic legislation, including such traditional Whig measures as a protective tariff, a homestead act, and subsidies for internal improvements. He did propose the National Banking Act (probably the handiwork of Secretary of the Treasury Salmon P. Chase), establishing not a version of the First and Second Bank of the United States but a system of federally chartered private banks coupled with a confiscatory tax on state banks. But Lincoln regarded this as a war measure, for the act permitted national banks to issue currency against treasury bonds, thus monetizing the public debt and thereby facilitating the financing of the war. Otherwise, Lincoln did not interfere with Congress, sought its approval for his executive actions, and acquiesced in the operations and demands of the meddlesome Committee on the Conduct of the War. In regard to his department heads, the president allowed free rein in most matters.[2]

But Lincoln also extended the range of executive authority and the powers of the federal government beyond the limits accepted by his predecessors and beyond the bounds of the Constitution as it had been understood. He took seriously the oath of office charging him, and no other official, with the duty to "preserve, protect, and defend the Constitution"; he saw the preamble's phrase "to form a more perfect Union" as the vital portion of the charge; and he regarded the president's power as commander in chief as the primary means for fulfilling the charge. If it proved necessary, in his judgment, to break a host of minor laws or constitutional provisions and to trample on the rights of loyal citizens in the doing, so be it.[3]

From the beginning, Lincoln moved with vigor and promptness. Upon hearing the news that Confederates had fired on Fort Sumter, he declared a state of insurrection "too powerful to be suppressed by the ordinary course of judicial proceedings," and without consulting Congress, he called for seventy-five thousand three-month volunteers and enlarged the size of the regular army. Also without consulting Congress, he appropriated $2 million to personal agents in New York to pay for "military and naval measures necessary for the defense and support of the government." And he declared a blockade against the rebellious states, though under international law, blockades could be enforced only against sovereign powers.[4]

The need to amass troops to combat the rapidly mobilizing Confederate army was urgent, and the problem of disloyalty inside the Union was equally pressing. The border slave states—Maryland, Delaware, Kentucky, and Missouri—contained huge numbers of people who sympathized with and were eager to help the Confederacy. The southern portions of Ohio, Illinois, and Indiana were teeming with Confederate sympathizers. To bring these dangerous elements under control, on April 27, 1861, Lincoln ordered General Winfield Scott, who forwarded the order to subordinates, to arrest and detain all persons in the area between Washington and Philadelphia who were suspected of subversive deeds or utterances. The president specifically authorized the suspension of the writ of habeas corpus, the traditional and constitutional means of protecting the citizenry against arbitrary imprisonment, although article 1, section 9, restricting the powers of Congress, forbids the suspension of the writ except "when in Cases of Rebellion or Invasion the public safety may require it."[5]

The army began arresting suspected rebel sympathizers on a large scale, and the activity was immediately challenged in the courts. John

Merryman, a prominent Baltimorean who was a lieutenant in a secessionist drill company, was arrested and confined under military guard in Fort McHenry. He brought suit in circuit court, under Chief Justice Taney, who ordered his release, holding that only Congress could suspend the writ. General George Cadwallader, commander in the area, respectfully declined to obey the court order. Taney then issued a writ of attachment for contempt against Cadwallader, but the marshal who tried to serve this writ was forbidden to enter the fort. The chief justice had no further recourse.[6]

Thereafter, the disloyal were repressed with a vengeance. People taken by the military were, under Lincoln's order to Scott, placed in the custody of the secretary of state, and Secretary Seward acted ruthlessly. He erected a cadre of secret agents to scout out the disaffected, who were arrested on mere suspicion, were not told of the charges against them, and were detained without proof. After ten months, all political prisoners were released, and the internal security program was turned over to the secretary of war.[7]

A program of broader scope was instituted in September 1862. Lincoln proclaimed that during the insurrection, persons who resisted the draft, discouraged volunteers from enlisting, or were suspected of other disloyal acts were subject to martial law and trial by military commissions or courts-martial. In regard to these persons, the privilege of habeas corpus was suspended. Under the order, 13,535 citizens were arrested and confined in military prisons. A goodly number more were imprisoned under authority of the state and navy departments or confined in civilian prisons by state and local authorities.[8]

Lincoln extended presidential authority the furthest in his capacity as commander in chief. He appointed and removed generals and directed their campaigns. He occasionally, though not often, suppressed newspapers that he thought were hampering the war effort. As rebellious southern states were conquered—Louisiana, Arkansas, and Tennessee—he appointed military governors to rule them in accordance not with constitutional procedures but with the president's orders. He established provisional courts with unlimited power to determine "every question that could be the subject of judicial decision." This negation of the idea that the affected states had "rights" was accomplished without congressional authorization and in defiance of the Constitution, except as could be justified by the commander-in-chief clause.[9]

The same justification, or rationalization, underlay the Emancipation Proclamation. The early announcement that the war was being fought not to free the slaves but to save the Union had proved diplomatically and militarily embarrassing. Britain and France were strongly opposed to slavery, but the British sentimentally favored the underdog, and the French had designs on Mexico and perhaps Texas and Louisiana, so those powers were disposed to recognize the independence of the Confederacy and intervene to force mediation. Charles Francis Adams, the American minister to Britain, urged Lincoln to take an antislavery position to neutralize the threat, and in 1862, as the war was going badly for the Union, Lincoln reluctantly agreed. He drafted the proclamation but held back on issuing it, lest it be seen as an act of desperation, until the Union forces could claim a technical victory at the Battle of Antietam in September. The proclamation actually freed no slaves: it simply declared that all slaves in areas still in rebellion, and thus outside federal control, were liberated, on the ground that their labor contributed to the Confederate effort. But it served its purpose, for Britain and France ultimately abandoned the idea of intervening.[10]

Another aspect of the centralization of power by the Lincoln administration concerned the president's relations with the wartime governors. Lincoln needed to handle them with considerable skill, lest they constitute a fatally centrifugal force. They were accustomed to believing in states' rights, and they jealously protected their prerogatives, which included sole power to mobilize and command the militias, even when called into federal service. Moreover, they regarded Lincoln the president as being essentially their creation. The Republican party did not exist as a national entity in 1860 and 1861. It consisted instead of a coalition of local organizations, and in state after state, canvassers had turned out the voters to elect the governors and, as the governors viewed matters, coincidentally to elect a Republican president.[11]

This is not to suggest that the governors were dilatory in prosecuting the war or in going after rebel sympathizers in their states. Quite the contrary: they proceeded at a pace so fast as to discomfit Lincoln and to exceed the capacity of federal authorities to use their contributions. For example, John Andrew of Massachusetts started putting his state on a military footing in January 1861, and before the end of the month, he was offering troops to Lincoln (who would not take office for another six weeks) and asking General Scott what route the troops should take in marching to defend Washington. Most other governors, assuming that war was imminent, followed a similar course. Excluding the governors of the four border slave states that did not secede, all the northern governors but three took stances more vigorous than what Lincoln and Seward were as yet willing to adopt.[12]

When Lincoln issued his first call for troops on April 15, he assigned quotas for regiments of 37 officers and 743 men to the states in proportion to their populations, ranging from one apiece in Rhode Island and Vermont to seventeen in New York; every state raised more than its quota. The alacrity of the governors was not matched by the administration in Washington. The War Department had inadequate arms for the state regiments. Sometimes the governors interpreted War Department orders liberally and commandeered weapons: Governor Richard Yates of Illinois, instructed to protect the federal arsenal at St. Louis from rebel sympathizers, ordered Illinois troops to seize 21,000 stands of arms, 110,000 cartridges, and two field pieces and take them to Springfield. But direct action was not often possible, and the governors were soon disgusted by the army's inability to send officers to mobilize the militiamen they had raised and by the slowness of Washington in providing funds to support the troops.[13]

Moved by the governors' grumbling and by the chaos involved in having them assume authority, negotiate independently with other states, and instruct the commander in chief about policy, Lincoln started in May to bring the military under his exclusive authority. He called for forty regiments of volunteers to serve for three years in the capacity of soldiers "subject to the laws and regulations governing the army of the United States." The governors could continue to raise troops and commission officers, but the troops would be under the president's command. Two hundred eight regiments actually signed up, and when Congress convened in July, it authorized the expansion of the army to 500,000 men. As time went by, the governors realized that Lincoln had taken over an enormous military machine and that no military authority was left to them.[14]

Throughout the remainder of 1861 and much of 1862, however, several governors resisted what they regarded as usurpation. They especially resented the favoritism and erratic treatment they received from Secretary of War Simon Cameron (Lincoln eased Cameron out in January 1862 by appointing him minister to Russia; Edwin M. Stanton replaced him). Then Lincoln ordered generals to recruit troops directly, which provoked Governor Andrew to refuse to permit such recruitment, whereupon Lincoln declared that if quotas of volunteers were not met—enlistments declined in 1862—he would institute a draft. That set off minor riots in Wisconsin and threats of riots in Pennsylvania, and when a draft was instituted in 1863, major riots erupted in New York. In the meantime, the radical governors made Lincoln uncomfortable by demanding that he issue a proclamation declaring that emancipation was the aim of the war and by insisting that black troops be recruited. Some threatened to refuse further cooperation with the federal government unless the president remove General George B. McClellan, the politically conservative commander of the army in Virginia, and place the radical John C. Frémont in his stead.[15]

The electorate tipped the balance of power decisively from the governors to the president, though that was not at all what the electorate had in mind. Indeed, discontent with the Emancipation Proclamation, with the increasing radicalism of Republican officeholders, with high taxes, with military arrests, with the imminence of the draft, and with the ineffectualness of the Union army led in the fall of 1862 to a resurgence of the Democratic party. Democrats captured just two of the six contested governorships, but the congressional delegations went to Democrats in Ohio, Illinois, Wisconsin,

Pennsylvania, New York, and New Jersey, and in most of those states, Democrats also gained control of the state legislatures. In Indiana, seven of the eleven congressional seats were taken by Democrats, and the legislature was strongly opposed both to Lincoln and to radical Republican Governor Oliver P. Morton. Many of the newly elected Democrats were Copperheads or something close to it: Democrats in Ohio, Indiana, and Illinois, assuming that the rebellion could not be defeated, proposed to form a Northwest Confederacy to join the South.[16]

The two new Democratic governors were Joel Parker of New Jersey and Horatio Seymour of New York. Seymour was an articulate, able, and intelligent man who, as a champion of strict construction and states' rights, was outspoken in his opposition to Lincoln's unconstitutional actions. In his campaign, he had assailed the evils of arbitrary arrests and denounced the Emancipation Proclamation as "a proposal for the butchery of women and children," for "arson and murder," for "lust and rapine." In his inaugural address, he pointed out that he had sworn to uphold the constitution of New York as well as that of the United States, and he declared that the rights of the states must be held inviolate, for a consolidated central government would destroy "the essential home-rights and liberties of the people." He promised to support constitutional measures to restore the Union, but not the "bloody, barbarous, revolutionary, and unconstitutional scheme" of emancipation.[17]

Democrats throughout the North looked to Seymour as their champion, and Lincoln regarded him with genuine concern. Afterward, Thurlow Weed, the old-time New York Whig politico and alter ego of William H. Seward, claimed that Lincoln told him that Seymour had the greatest power for good of any man in the country and asked Weed to urge Seymour to unite the Democrats in support of the war. "Tell him for me," Lincoln reportedly said, "that if he'll render this service to his country, I shall cheerfully make way for him as my successor." Seymour did not reply to the purported offer, but he held to his course. Lincoln and the administration finessed him as well as they could, disingenuously treating him as nothing more than an ambitious schemer for power.[18]

Seymour's message and influence remained potent, and the administration determined to control the next elections, in which several legislatures and eight governors would be chosen, by using the technique that had been employed to keep the border states in line—namely, coercion. In July 1861, the president had appointed Frémont military governor of Missouri, a position he held until Lincoln removed him for corruption and for declaring the state's slaves emancipated. In November, Maryland soldiers were given leaves to go home and vote, and on election day they guarded the polls, arresting known Democrats, with the result that a unionist governor and legislature were elected. When, the next year, state judges instructed grand jurors to inquire into the election, the judges were summarily arrested and cast into federal military prisons. In Kentucky, the jails had been filled with Democrats and southern sympathizers, and unionist/Republican candidates were uniformly elected. In Delaware, after a peace convention had adopted resolutions opposing the war and declaring that the "war party" was erecting "a consolidated government on the ruins of the federal constitution," more than a thousand federal troops occupied Dover on election day, arresting Democrats or forcing them to cast Republican ballots. Even though a Republican was elected governor by a margin of 111 votes, Democrats won small majorities in both houses of the legislature.[19]

In the 1863 contests, the administration employed a policy of liberal grants of leaves to soldiers and civil servants, as well as intimidation. The cause was furthered by a mistake on Seymour's part: he vetoed a bill that would have allowed soldiers in the field to vote in absentia, and Republicans capitalized on the action, depicting him as an enemy of democracy. Throughout the North, Republicans were helped by renewed optimism in the wake of the Confederate defeats at Vicksburg and Gettysburg, once the import of those battles soaked in, and by the strong-arm tactics of a host of secret societies.[20]

The most blatant federal interference in a state election occurred in Ohio. Clement L. Vallandigham, a recently retired congressman with strong Copperhead tendencies, was nominated as the Democratic candidate for governor. Union General Ambrose Burnside ordered his men to arrest Vallandigham, and they carried him off to be court-martialed. He requested a writ of habeas corpus from the federal circuit court in Cincinnati, but it declined to act, and ultimately the Supreme Court refused the plea, holding that the Judiciary Act did not vest the Court with jurisdiction in appeals from military tribunals. President Lincoln, thinking that imprisoning Vallandigham was unnecessary, commuted his sentence to banishment to the Confederacy.[21]

Thus the unionists/Republicans won the contested gubernatorial seats, regained control of most legislatures, and retained control of Congress. The governors could no longer claim that Lincoln was their creature: now it was Lincoln who had elected the governors. They could offer only token resistance during the remainder of the war.[22]

The problems facing Jefferson Davis as president of the Confederacy were essentially those that Lincoln faced, except that the institutional barriers to centralization, in the form of constitutional protection of states' rights, were more formidable. The Confederate constitution, promulgated in Montgomery in February 1861, was the United States Constitution as the rebels interpreted it, but with certain features made explicit and with modifications added to correct what the Confederate framers regarded as flaws in the original.

The variations for the sake of explicitness were addressed to the nature of the compact and the locus of sovereignty. Whereas the preamble to the Constitution, beginning "We the People of the United States," had an ambiguity about it that could accommodate either Lincoln's or Calhoun's interpretation, that of the Confederacy permitted just one reading: "We, the People of the Confederate States, each State acting in its sovereign and independent character." The first stated purpose was "to form a permanent federal government," rather than "to form a more perfect Union." The ends of government in the two instruments were the same, except that "to provide for the common defense" and "promote the general Welfare" were omitted from the Confederate constitution. Those phrases, as experience had shown, could be read as justifying the exercise of powers beyond those that were enumerated. The general welfare clause was also deleted from the enumerated powers in article 1, section 8, of the Confederate constitution.[23]

Similar modifications were made with respect to the Ninth and Tenth Amendments of the Bill of Rights, which were incorporated into the body of the Confederate constitution at article 6. The Ninth Amendment provided that the enumeration of certain rights "shall not be construed to deny or disparage others retained by the people." The Confederate version was "by the people of the several states." The Confederate wording of the Tenth Amendment declared that powers not delegated to the central government nor prohibited to the states "are reserved to the States, respectively, or to the people thereof."[24]

Beyond these changes in the interest of clarifying the nature of the confederated compact, the document contained substantive prohibitions against various exercises of congressional power that southerners had long regarded as particularly onerous. The Confederacy was expressly forbidden to lay taxes on imports "to promote or foster any branch of industry" and to "appropriate money for any internal improvement intended to facilitate commerce," except for aids to navigation on the coasts or to grant bounties. The constitution required that "every law, or resolution having the force of law, shall relate to but one subject," the obvious intention of which was to prevent attaching unrelated riders to popular measures or appropriations bills.[25]

Other "corrections" were procedural or institutional and were designed to provide additional checks on the legislative power and to remove partisan politics as far as possible from governing. Such provisions included nonvoting executive branch representation in Congress, an executive line-item veto, a requirement of a two-thirds majority in both houses for most appropriations bills, and a six-year nonrenewable term for the president. Related was article 3, which provided for a court system in language almost identical to that in the corresponding article of the Constitution. Neither document actually required the creation of a court system, save for a chief justice to preside in impeachment trials of the president, and the Confederate Congress decided to make do without a supreme court, thus vesting the power of judicial review in the state supreme courts.[26]

A few miscellaneous points want notice. Property in slaves, including the right to carry them into any part of the Confederacy, was explicitly recognized, but the importation of slaves from the outside world was prohibited. All states reserved the right to abolish slavery in their domains, and new states could be admitted without slavery if two-thirds of the existing states agreed—the idea being that the tier of free states bordering the Ohio River might in time wish to join the Confederacy. No mention was made of the right of secession, for that was regarded as inherent in the Confederacy as it had been in the Union. Amending the Confederate constitution was easier than amending the United States Constitution. Impeachment of a Confederate official whose duties were performed in a single state could be brought by the state legislature, though as in other impeachments, trial was by the Confederate senate.[27]

Given the absence of a supreme court, the limitations on the powers delegated to the Confederacy, and the emphasis upon states' rights, the Confederacy's government might have been fatally handicapped in trying to fight the war. Actually, however, except for bungling and feuding in dealing with his generals and for lacking the common touch in making patriotic appeals, Jefferson Davis was quite as effective in bringing about the necessary centralization as Lincoln was, and he did so with less repression. In no small measure, his accomplishment was possible precisely because the institutional framework in which he operated made it imperative for him to plead with people for their cooperation rather than, as Lincoln did, attempt to ride roughshod over them.[28]

But in a larger sense, Davis was able to do what he did because of the political culture that pervaded the Confederacy from the outset, a culture that has been tellingly described as a "revolution against politics." In 1860–1861, secessionists and unionists alike were agreed that the troubles of recent years were attributable to the spread of democracy and its attendant system of party politics, and the founders of the new governments were determined to expel partisan politics and to return to the fancied pristine republicanism of the Revolutionary War era. Virtue, patriotism, simplicity, economy, and disinterested devotion to the weal of the public—and not partisanship—would be the guiding principles in government service. "No longer would selfish men make politics a profession; a glorious past of wise statesmanship would be restored."[29]

Almost astonishingly, the elections at all levels in 1861 and afterward were nonpartisan. Davis and Stephens were unopposed for the presidency and vice-presidency; the consensus was, as a Mississippi editor put it, that the two had been "touched by Providence" to lead the nation. Similarly, no one ran as a partisan in elections for the Confederate Congress or for state and local offices. Partisanship was taboo: anyone who had thrust himself forward as a former Whig or Democrat would have been rejected outright. And Davis, on assembling his cabinet, chose to name one member from each state, without special regard to past party affiliation, though most were former Democrats.[30]

The identification of the Confederate cause with that of the earlier cause of Independence was propagated endlessly. The "Confederate States of 1861 are acting over again the history of the American Revolution of 1776," opined the *New Orleans Picayune,* and the sentiment was echoed in newspapers and pulpits across the South. Jefferson Davis was cast as a latter-day George Washington combatting Lincoln as a latter-day George III, and Davis self-consciously acted the role. His inauguration as permanent president was held on Washington's birthday, 1862, on a speaker's platform erected next to a statue of Washington. He castigated the "tyranny of an unbridled majority, the most odious and least responsible form of despotism," called upon his countrymen "to renew such sacrifices as our fathers made to the holy cause of constitutional liberty," and urged that they prove themselves "worthy of the inheritance bequeathed to us by the patriots of the Revolution." Opposing Davis was as unfashionable as opposing Washington incarnate would have been—at least at first.[31]

No effort was made either to mobilize or to muzzle the press, even though some southern nationalists called for censorship in the interest of security and unity; there was no need. A few newspapers, notably the *Richmond Examiner* and the *Charleston Mercury,* were frequently critical of Davis's policies, and the *Savannah Republican* likened him to George III. But most supported Davis and the war ardently, sharing the view of the New Orleans editor who declared, "The man who strikes at [Davis] strikes at the heart and head of the Confederacy."[32]

The consensus was put to a test early in 1862. In February, McClellan's army being on the peninsula between the James and York Rivers, the Confederate Congress authorized the president to suspend the writ of habeas corpus in areas threatened by invasion, and Davis, despite having denounced Lincoln for his suspensions, did suspend the writ in Richmond, Petersburg, and several other Virginia communities. During the next few months, he also suspended it in counties in western Virginia and eastern Tennessee, where pro-Union sentiment was strong, and in the coastland of South Carolina. Protests were heard, but the steps taken had been moderate and the dangers so clear and present that nothing like the widespread northern discontent appeared in the South.[33]

The introduction of conscription severely strained the political culture. The Confederacy's gravest impending problem was manpower, for the twelve-month enlistments of the army's volunteers would shortly expire. Many thought that conscription was imperative, and Davis proposed to Congress that all white males between eighteen and thirty-five be held to military service and that a plan be adopted for their speedy induction and organization. By sizable votes in both houses, despite bitter debate, Congress complied in April. Many protested; in a typical outburst, R. C. Puryear of North Carolina denounced conscription as "unnecessary, unequal, unjust, and tyrannical," and he asked what had become of "that great paramount doctrine of states' rights which in fact was the prime cause of this revolution?" Most, however, acquiesced on the ground of necessity. Governor John Letcher of Virginia, who considered the draft the "most alarming stride towards consolidation that has ever occurred," went along anyway because "harmony, unity, and conciliation are indispensable to success now." Governor John Milton of Florida considered the matter a purely judicial question, and when the draft was contested in state supreme courts, most, led by Virginia and Georgia, upheld it. Only North Carolina's court demurred.[34]

One major public figure raised effective barriers against the draft. Governor Joe Brown of Georgia had already made waves by voicing strong opposition to Davis's appointment of officers to command Georgia volunteers, declaring that this "imperial power" could enable a popular future president "to trample underfoot all restraints and make his will the supreme law of the land." When conscription was put in place, he promised the secretary of war that he would "throw no obstacles" in the way of carrying out the policy, but he also ordered the arrest of enrolling officials who tried to conscript a militia officer, and he took the position that every male of draft age in the state was by definition a militiaman and thus not subject to the Confederate draft.[35]

Resistance like Brown's was rare, in the early going, for in the absence of political parties, opponents of particular policies had no means of rallying like-minded people without being called traitors, no way of criticizing the administration without seeming to criticize the government and the war. That was inherent in the political culture. But as time passed, dissenters began to evolve what might be called a counterculture, a cluster of positions around a politics of liberty. It may seem oxymoronic to refer to people who believed in slavery as libertarians, but libertarianism was the ideology that lent respectability to their dissent.[36]

Among the outspoken and, from the Confederacy's point of view, dangerous critics was the erstwhile unionist printer William W. Holden of North Carolina, who has been described as a "libertarian fanatic." In the aftermath of Vicksburg and Gettysburg, Holden printed and circulated petitions denouncing Confederate violations of civil liberties and calling for a convention to open peace negotiations or to secede from the Confederacy. Soon he was claiming that four-fifths of the people supported him. Governor Zebulon Vance, who is often depicted by historians as being in the same camp with Joe Brown, tried to hold his state to a moderate position between

Holden and extremists on the other side, but during the remainder of the war, North Carolina was plagued by division, and an internal civil war seemed possible.[37]

Another deserter, as it were, was Vice-President Alexander H. Stephens, who, like Holden, had been a unionist and remained committed to "an alternative political culture based . . . on a genuine, organic tradition of state, community, and individual liberties." Joining with Governor Brown in protesting Confederate encroachments, Stephens urged Georgians to remonstrate against Davis's arbitrary arrests and similar enormities. By the fall of 1864, he and his allies were issuing calls to Alabama and North Carolina to participate in seeking an armistice and a convention of southern and northern states to negotiate a settlement.[38]

Despite their mounting criticism, Stephens, Brown, and Holden received far more opposition than praise throughout the Confederacy, and Davis retained general public trust until the end. He did face resistance in the Confederate Congress, and indeed, he depended there on votes of representatives and senators from districts and states under Union control. Even so, legislature after legislature adopted resolutions, usually by large majorities, expressing unqualified confidence in him. The politics of unity triumphed over the politics of liberty. Curiously, after the war was lost, both political cultures would become enduring features of southern life.[39]

Southerners who complained of the "tyranny" of Jefferson Davis were, when the war ended, to learn what real tyranny was like—but not at the hands of the executive branch. President Lincoln took the position that secession had never happened, that the war had been fought to put down an insurrection, and that it was the chief executive's business to decide when legal governments had been resumed in the rebellious states. He was convinced that a large number of southerners had opposed the rebellion and devoutly desired a restoration of the Union. At least partly to hearten and encourage the peace movements that budded in 1864, he announced a reconstruction plan that accorded with the appeal he would make in his second inaugural address the next year: "With malice toward none; with charity for all; . . . let us . . . bind up the nation's wounds."[40]

He proposed to pardon all southerners, except high-ranking Confederate civil and military officials, who would take an oath of loyalty to the Union, and to grant recognition to the governments of each state in which 10 percent of the eligible voters took the oath, formed a government, and accepted emancipation of the slaves. On that basis, Lincoln recognized governments in Arkansas, Louisiana, Virginia, and Tennessee before the end of 1864, though by no means had the entire territory in those states been pacified or brought under Union control.

Lincoln's approach was not shared by Republicans in Congress, who for various reasons proposed to impose stricter terms upon the South. Some were driven by humanitarian concern that the slaves be freed and be granted equal status with whites, others saw opportunities for pillaging a prostrate region, and still others were moved by a political consideration—namely, that if southern whites were readmitted to full status, the area would be solidly Democratic for all futurity. Few of them, as yet, agreed with the radical position advanced by Senator Charles Sumner and Representative Thaddeus Stevens that the southern states had committed political suicide and that they were to be treated as conquered provinces, but the majority differed from Lincoln by holding that they had seceded and that it was up to Congress to determine when and on what terms they would be readmitted. Congress refused to seat senators and representatives elected by the states Lincoln had recognized, and it passed the Wade-Davis bill, designed to impose its own terms for readmitting the rebel states. A majority would be required to take loyalty oaths and draft a constitution that abolished slavery, disfranchised former Confederate officials, and repudiated state and Confederate war debts. Lincoln killed the bill with a pocket veto, but the Radicals issued a manifesto declaring that Reconstruction was the province of Congress and incorporated that principle into the Republicans' 1864 presidential platform. Lincoln was flexible in his approach, and he readily admitted that the Wade-Davis position was "one very proper plan" and signed into law in March 1865 an act creating the Freedman's Bureau, an agency designed to serve as guardian and educator for the freed southern blacks.[41]

When the war ended and Lincoln was assassinated in April, Andrew Johnson succeeded to the presidency and set out to effect his variation of presidential Reconstruction before Congress convened in December. He proclaimed a general amnesty to all oath-taking southerners except high-ranking Confederate officials and men having more than $20,000 estates. He appointed peace advocate William Holden as provisional governor of North Carolina with instructions to call a convention to adopt a republican constitution preparatory to readmission. Criticized for being excessively lenient, Johnson added further qualifications: that North Carolina repudiate its war debts, renounce secession, and ratify the Thirteenth Amendment, abolishing slavery, which had been passed by Congress in February. In the next few months, the same requirements were extended to the other states, except Texas, and though Mississippi refused to ratify the amendment, all but Texas were recognized by the president.[42]

A knotty constitutional problem inhered in this procedure. Either the southern states had legally left the Union or not. If they had not, no qualifications could have been imposed upon their "readmission," and their forced ratification of the Thirteenth Amendment was invalid. If they had left the Union and could not rejoin it until they met Johnson's requirements, they were not states and had no legal right to vote on the amendment. In the heat and confusion of the time, however, no one paid much attention to the constitutional niceties, and in December, having been ratified by the requisite three-quarters of the states (including the eleven rebellious southern states), the amendment was declared ratified.[43]

Meanwhile, southerners comported themselves almost as if they had won the war. Candidates for state offices boasted of having served in the Confederate army and were elected. Georgia sent Alexander Stephens to the Senate, and various states elected former generals and colonels to Congress, along with six Confederate cabinet officers and fifty-eight Confederate congressmen. The Carolinas and Georgia refused to repudiate their war debts or renounce secession, and Mississippi accepted abolition only after the Johnson administration exerted strong pressure. What also angered northerners, radical and conservative, were reports of violence against unionists and blacks and news that southern legislatures had begun to enact "black codes," convincing northerners that the blacks were being virtually re-enslaved.[44]

Thus, when Congress met in December, its members were prepared to undo Johnson's work of Reconstruction and start anew. The two houses appointed the Joint Committee of Fifteen, headed by Thaddeus Stevens and Charles Sumner, whose nominal purpose was to pass on the credentials of the newly elected southerners (all were denied seats) but whose real purpose was to develop and direct congressional Reconstruction. In short order, the committee drafted and Congress approved resolutions proclaiming that the former Confederate states had no legal existence and would have none until they provided civil rights for blacks and deprived rebels of such rights. In February 1866, Congress passed a bill, again drafted by the committee, effectually repealing the black codes, extending the scope of the Freedmen's Bureau, and authorizing the bureau to use military force against whites who obstructed its work. President Johnson vetoed the bill, saying that the federal courts could provide adequate protection for the rights of blacks, and Radical leaders fell short of mustering the votes to override him.[45]

But that was Johnson's last victory. The veto angered enough moderates to push them into the Radical camp. In early April, Congress passed the Civil Rights Act, declaring that all persons (except Indians) born in the United States were citizens with full civil and legal rights and authorizing the army to enforce those rights. Johnson vetoed again, but this time he was overridden. An expanded Freedmen's Bureau act followed the same course. For good measure, Congress amended the Judiciary Act so that Johnson could not fill vacancies that might occur on the Supreme Court. (Taney had died in 1864, and because of other deaths and resignations, Lincoln had appointed four associate justices along with Salmon P. Chase as chief justice.)[46]

This was beginning to amount to imposing upon the South constitutional deprivations tantamount to those Lincoln had imposed upon the wartime North—one of Johnson's declared reasons for vetoing the Civil Rights Act was that it embodied unprecedented intrusion of the federal government into the exclusive domain of the states—and now Congress proposed a complex amendment that would extend the intrusion. On June 13, 1866, largely to give sanction to the Civil Rights Act, Congress passed by the requisite two-thirds majority what became the Fourteenth Amendment. The first section of the amendment in effect overturned the *Dred Scott* decision by declaring all persons born or naturalized in the United States to be citizens thereof and "of the State wherein they reside." The section prohibited states from abridging the privileges or immunities of citizens of the United States, from depriving "any person of life, liberty, or property without due process of law," and from depriving "any person within its jurisdiction the equal protection of the laws." Section two repealed the original constitutional provision under which slaves counted as three-fifths of a person for apportioning representation, and it provided that if blacks were deprived of the suffrage, representation would be reduced proportionately. The third section disqualified various descriptions of former rebels from holding federal or state offices, and the fourth repudiated rebellion-incurred public debts. The fifth empowered Congress "to enforce, by appropriate legislation, the provisions of this article."[47]

Adoption of the amendment was accompanied by irregularities greater than those that attended the Thirteenth. Proponents fell one vote short of the necessary majority in the Senate, but they solved that problem underhandedly. An outspoken opponent, Senator John P. Stockton of New Jersey, had been formally seated when the Thirty-ninth Congress convened on December 5, 1865; now the Senate voted retroactively not to seat him, that device being used to avoid the constitutional requirement of a two-thirds vote for expelling a member. Then the amendment was sent to the governors for legislative approval by all thirty-six states, including the eleven southern nonstates, meaning that the approval of twenty-seven was necessary for ratification. The southern states except for Tennessee refused to ratify, and Tennessee ratified without a quorum in its legislature. Oregon ratified by an illegal process and promptly rescinded its ratification. Kentucky, Delaware, Maryland, and California rejected the proposal outright, and Ohio and New Jersey joined Oregon in rescinding. By the time the Thirty-ninth Congress adjourned in March 1867, seventeen of the thirty-six states had voted no or rescinded their earlier approval, and the Fourteenth Amendment appeared to be doomed.[48]

Two days before it went out of business, Congress passed, over Johnson's veto, a sweeping Reconstruction Act that was slightly amended by the Fortieth Congress later that month. The Radicals were emboldened to adopt this draconian measure by their whopping victory in the 1866 congressional elections, which Johnson had attempted to turn into a referendum on his policies, and also by news of bloody race riots that had left many blacks dead in Memphis and New Orleans. The Reconstruction Act, as amended, began by declaring that "no legal state governments" existed in the ten rebel states that had refused to ratify the Fourteenth Amendment. It divided the South into five military districts and replaced the existing non-governments by martial law. The act required the states to call elections in which black males could vote and whites who had taken part in the rebellion were disfranchised. The voters were to elect delegates to conventions that would draft constitutions providing for black suffrage; then, when these were ratified and approved by Congress, governments were organized under them, and the governments had ratified the Fourteenth Amendment, Congress would consider ending military rule. It would then recognize the legal existence of the states and readmit them to representation in Congress. By that means, the southern states were forced to ratify the amendment, though the same law that required them to do so declared that they were not legally states.[49]

Radicals interpreted the 1866 election returns as a mandate to punish the president as well as the South. In March, Congress passed the Military Appropriations Act, declaring that the president's military orders could be executed only with the approval of General of the Armies Ulysses S. Grant. It passed the Tenure of Office Act, stipulating that government officials whose appointments must be approved by the Senate could not be removed or replaced without the

Senate's approval. Johnson, convinced that the Tenure of Office Act was unconstitutional, decided to test it by suspending his most pestiferous cabinet member, Edwin Stanton. He hoped thereby to force Stanton to sue for the possession of the office, making it a dispute for the Supreme Court to adjudicate, but in January 1868, the Senate pointedly and formally refused to concur in the suspension. Then Johnson summarily dismissed Stanton, thus inviting impeachment, for the act expressly made removal a misdemeanor. The matter was not clear-cut, for a provision of the act limited the tenure of cabinet officers to "the term of the president by whom they may have been appointed and for one month thereafter," and Stanton had been appointed by Lincoln in 1862. Nevertheless, the removal of Stanton formed the basis for most of the articles of impeachment that were brought by the House and tried by the Senate from March 13 to May 26, 1868. Johnson was acquitted by a one-vote margin, but for practical purposes, his office was vacant for the rest of his term. Congress was, at just that time, also emasculating the Supreme Court by removing a controversial case from its jurisdiction. Congress had thus made itself the supreme law of the land.[50]

During the next few years, Radical Reconstruction gradually wound down. Civilian governments were restored in seven states during 1868, but coalitions of blacks, southern "scalawags," and northern "carpetbaggers" dominated them, and as military government ended in the other states, the same condition obtained. In 1869, to ensure that these arrangements would continue, Congress proposed the Fifteenth Amendment, providing for the protection of black voting rights against state interference, and it was ratified in 1870. Under its authority, Congress passed the Enforcement Act of 1870, imposing severe penalties on persons convicted of using force, intimidation, or bribery to prevent any citizen from voting. Nevertheless, southern "redeemers" step by step regained control, partly through terrorism (despite the antiterrorist legislation) and partly by other means—three states between 1869 and 1871, four more in 1874 and 1875, and the rest in 1876.[51]

Radicals continued to dominate the federal government, but after 1870, their eagerness to punish the South and protect the freedmen waned, giving way to corruption on a grand scale. The new president, Ulysses S. Grant, had no interest in expanding executive authority, and his administration too became infested with corruption. Thus the legislative and executive branches stopped exercising the greatly expanded powers they had assumed during and after the war. Into the ensuing vacuum rushed the Supreme Court, which would remain the single powerful branch of the federal government until the end of the century and beyond. And the states became more active than ever before.

After Lincoln had successfully defied Chief Justice Taney in the *Merryman* case, the Supreme Court was careful not to impede the war effort, and whenever possible it furthered the effort, as in upholding the legality of the blockade. As soon as it appeared safe, however, the Court began, cautiously at first, to undo the constitutional revolution that Lincoln and the Radicals, between them, had effected.[52]

Its opening venture in that direction was *Ex parte Milligan,* reversing and apologizing for the decision it had made in the *Vallandigham* case regarding trials by military commissions. Lambdin P. Milligan was an officer in a Copperhead paramilitary group that had operated in Indiana. In 1864 he was captured and tried by a military commission acting under the authority of the presidential suspension order of 1862 and the Habeas Corpus Act of 1863. He was sentenced to be hanged, but Lincoln stayed his execution for several months, during which period a civilian grand jury heard his case and declined to indict him. Shortly after Lincoln was assassinated, Johnson ordered Milligan's execution, but the Habeas Corpus Act provided that when a grand jury met after a prisoner had been taken and adjourned without indicting him, the federal courts were obliged to order his release. On that ground, Milligan appealed to the circuit court to be freed, and when the circuit judges were divided, they referred the question to the Supreme Court.[53]

The Court handed down its ruling in July 1866, assigning the writing of the opinion to Justice David Davis, whom Lincoln had appointed in 1862. "During the late wicked Rebellion," Davis wrote, "the temper of the times did not allow that calmness in deliberation and discussion so necessary to a correct conclusion of a purely judicial question." The public safety now having been assured, however, the subject could be considered "without passion." The power to suspend habeas corpus was sometimes necessary, but martial law could not be proclaimed for the whole country. "Martial law cannot arise from a threatened invasion," only from an actual one. "Martial rule can never exist where the courts are open, and in the proper and unobstructed exercise of their jurisdiction," which was the circumstance in Indiana. The Court unanimously ruled that Milligan's trial by a military commission had been unconstitutional and ordered his release.[54]

Despite howls from Radicals in Congress, the Court proceeded judiciously on its course. Early in 1867, it announced its rulings in the *Test Oath Cases, Ex parte Garland* and *Cummings v. Missouri*. A congressional statute forbade attorneys to practice law in federal courts unless they swore that they had never borne arms against the United States. A. H. Garland, a lawyer and Confederate veteran who had received a presidential pardon, sought to be admitted to practice before the Supreme Court and contended that the law preventing him from doing so was unconstitutional. Cummings, a Roman Catholic priest, was indicted and convicted of preaching and teaching in violation of a Missouri law requiring that to vote, hold office, or practice various professions, a person must take an oath attesting that he was and always had been loyal to the United States. In both cases, Justice Stephen J. Field abandoned the other four Lincoln appointees to join the four pre-Lincoln justices in holding the acts unconstitutional. Both acts were adjudged to be ex post facto laws, making something illegal retroactively, and bills of attainder, laws declaring individuals guilty without a trial; such laws are forbidden by article 1, sections 9 and 10. Again, Radicals in Congress denounced the decisions.[55]

Two decisions rendered in April 1867 met with Radical approval, but, taken together, they contained a strong hint that unfavorable rulings might be forthcoming. Immediately upon the passage of the

Reconstruction Act of 1867 and its modification, Mississippi sought an injunction against Andrew Johnson and the district military commander restraining them from enforcing the act. Despite objecting to the act, Johnson himself refused to support the challenge, and the Court refused to grant the order, saying that the president was beyond the Court's authority, even if the act was unconstitutional. But Mississippi was allowed to join Georgia in a similar suit addressed against the secretary of war and the commander of the third military district. The states argued that Congress had no power to annihilate a state and deprive its citizens of political rights. Again the Court refused to grant the injunction, though cabinet officials had been held subject to court orders since *Marbury* v. *Madison*. The Court declared that it had no jurisdiction because, for such a question to be judicially determined, "the rights in danger . . . must be rights of persons or property, not merely political rights, which do not belong to the jurisdiction of a court." The implication was that if a case were brought on the basis of an issue of personal or property rights, the Court would consider the constitutionality of the Reconstruction Act.[56]

Rumors that the Court was about to rule on the act circulated in 1868. William H. McCardle, a newspaper editor in Vicksburg, was arrested under the Reconstruction Act and held for trial by a military commission. He applied for a writ of habeas corpus in the federal circuit court in Mississippi, and his petition was denied. But a recent revision of the Judiciary Act, designed to protect federal officials and loyal citizens in the South, had defined the appellate jurisdiction of the Supreme Court so broadly that McCardle fell under its provisions, and the Court unanimously decided to hear the case.[57]

Substantive arguments were heard in March 1868, just before the impeachment trial of President Johnson began. Given the highly charged atmosphere, Congress was in no mood to brook interference from the judiciary, and after the arguments, but before a decision was reached, it exercised for the first time its authority to remove jurisdiction, amending the Judiciary Act accordingly. The Court, not wanting "to run a race with Congress," deferred its decision until the next term, for which it scheduled new arguments concerning jurisdiction.

When *Ex parte McCardle* was reheard in 1869, the Court had no recourse but to uphold Congress's power under article 3, section 2, to abolish its jurisdiction in the case.[58]

But on the very day that it bowed to the will of Congress in the *McCardle* case, the Court handed down a decision that undermined the Radical constitutional position as set forth in the opening of the 1867 Reconstruction Act. The state of Texas had, during the war, sold some bonds that had been held in the state treasury, and after the war, the state sued for their recovery. The Court, in *Texas* v. *White*, upheld the claim on the ground that, because secession was unconstitutional, the pretended government was itself illegal, being nothing more than a band of rebels. In a memorable passage, Chief Justice Chase declared that "the Constitution, in all its provisions, looks to an indestructible Union, composed of indestructible States." In that ringing declaration, Chase disposed of, once and for all time, the question that had vexed the Republic for more than six decades. Secession was not a constitutional possibility.[59]

In its fall term, 1869, the Supreme Court took steps that, while not explicitly declaring the Reconstruction Act unconstitutional, ran counter to it. A Mississippian named Edward Yerger had killed an army officer and had been tried and convicted in a military court. He appealed to the Supreme Court for a writ of habeas corpus, and the Court accepted jurisdiction by reasoning narrowly. The act that had removed jurisdiction in the *McCardle* case applied to cases arising under the Judiciary Act of 1867, but it was silent in regard to direct petitions, which had been provided for by the original Judiciary Act of 1789. On the basis of the 1789 act, the Court agreed to hear Yerger's case. That decision elicited the most outraged Radical response yet. Three drastic bills were introduced in Congress: to abolish the Court's jurisdiction in all habeas corpus cases; to abolish entirely judicial review of acts of Congress; and to deny the Court power to review "political questions," including cases arising under the Reconstruction Act. Loud protests against the measures were heard throughout the country, and none was passed. Had they been enacted, the Court would have been destroyed as an arbiter of the Constitution. The showdown was avoided when private negotiators arranged to remove the case from the military and turn it over to state courts.[60]

Thereafter, as Congress and the presidency consumed themselves with their own excesses, the Court had clear sailing, and it tacked in the direction of relaxing the restraints placed upon the states by the Fourteenth and Fifteenth Amendments. The most significant early Fourteenth Amendment decision was that in the *Slaughterhouse Cases,* rendered in 1873. The carpetbagger government of Louisiana had passed an act limiting the slaughtering of animals in New Orleans and a large surrounding area to a single location, the property of a monopoly corporation. The independent butchers in the area brought suits claiming that the act, by depriving them of their livelihoods, violated the Fourteenth Amendment's ban on state laws that "abridge the privileges or immunities of citizens of the United States."[61]

The Supreme Court, in a ruling written by Justice Samuel F. Miller, decided against the butchers by a five-to-four vote. Miller opined that the general aim of the three Civil War amendments was the same—namely, to free the slaves, to make that freedom secure, and to protect the freedmen from state oppression. The main purpose of the first section of the Fourteenth Amendment, which contains the privileges and immunities clause, was to establish Negro citizenship, contrary to the *Dred Scott* decision. But the section explicitly distinguished between citizens of the United States and citizens of a specific state. The privileges and immunities clause prohibited states from abridging rights arising from national citizenship, but not those arising from state citizenship. Those that derived from national citizenship and were common to all were few, including the right to travel to the seat of government, to transact business with it and seek its protection, to have access to seaports, and to be protected in one's life, liberty, and property on the high seas. The great mass of rights derived from state citizenship, including the right to engage in a particular occupation such as butchery, and those were not protected by the privileges and immunities clause of the Fourteenth Amendment. Miller also dismissed two other points that counsel for the butchers had raised, ruling that the Louisiana statute did not deprive plaintiffs of property without due process of law and that the equal protection clause referred only to blacks. (The dissenting justices held that the protected rights were of all citizens, not just blacks, and Justice Noah Swayne argued that the Fourteenth Amendment was intended to extend the Bill of Rights to the states. They were more than eighty years ahead of times.)[62]

In a number of decisions, the Court affirmed the powers of the states over their own citizens despite the Fourteenth Amendment. During the term in which it rendered the *Slaughterhouse* decision, for instance, it held that a state could prevent a female citizen from practicing law. The next year it ruled that a law depriving a man of the right to sell liquor did not violate the privileges and immunities clause. And in 1875 it held that the clause did not give female citizens of the United States the right to vote.[63]

Simultaneously, the Court curtailed the power of Congress to legislate to protect the rights of blacks. The Enforcement Act of 1870 (the "Ku Klux Klan Act") was aimed at enforcing the Fourteenth and Fifteenth Amendments by prescribing punishment for conspiracy to use force or intimidation to deprive any citizen of rights derived from the Constitution or federal laws. The act was based upon the last section of the Fourteenth Amendment, empowering Congress to pass appropriate enforcement legislation, but that justification was denied in a Louisiana case. A massacre of blacks at Colfax, Louisiana, led to the indictment and conviction of a number of whites under the Enforcement Act. When the case came before the Supreme Court in 1876, however, the Court held that the amendment authorized Congress to prevent the states from interfering with the rights in question, not to legislate against individual actions. The authorization, said the Court, "does not extend to the passage of laws for the suppression of ordinary crime within the states. This would be to clothe Congress with powers to pass laws for the general preservation of social order in every state. The enforcement of the guaranty does not require or authorize Congress to perform the duty which . . . it requires the state to perform."[64]

In the same term, the Court rendered a closely related decision regarding the Fifteenth Amendment. Election inspectors in Kentucky were indicted under the Enforcement Act for refusing to accept and count the vote of a black citizen. The Court ruled again that the Enforcement Act had gone too far. "The Fifteenth Amendment does not confer the right of suffrage on anyone," the Court declared. Instead, it prohibits states and the United States from discriminating, in matters of voting rights, "on account of race, color, or previous condition of servitude." The "appropriate legislation" authorized by the amendment could be directed against states, but not against the actions of individuals. Since Congress had gone beyond what was authorized, the Court had a duty to "annul its encroachments upon the reserved power of the States and the people."[65]

In basing its decision on the Tenth Amendment, the Supreme Court was reversing a long-term trend in American constitutionalism. Historically, the Court had rarely and reluctantly challenged Congress, for that branch was too dangerous to the Court's own well-being, and it had repeatedly checked the powers of the states, they being far more vulnerable. Now the Court had risen as the champion of the states against the authority of Congress. The doctrine of states' rights had found a powerful friend, albeit a fickle one.

Epilogue

THE DOCTRINE
TRANSFORMED

The powers that were reserved to the states or to the people comprehended the governance of property relations, family relations, morality (including sexual behavior), public health, public safety, criminal activity, education, and religion. Prospective limitations on the exercise of these police powers (in addition to the Supreme Court's scrutiny of state criminal proceedings under the due process clause of the Fourteenth Amendment) stemmed from three sources. The first was the people themselves, who in their state constitutions forbade their governments to do an assortment of things, such as interfering with the free exercise of religion. The second prospective source of interference in the states' exercise of the police powers was intrusion into that domain by the federal government. For six decades after the end of Reconstruction, however, such intrusion was, except during World War I, rare and ineffective; attempts to encroach upon the powers reserved to the states were struck down by the Supreme Court and were disapproved by the vast majority of Americans. Moreover, prior to the adoption of the Sixteenth Amendment (authorizing a federal income tax), the federal government lacked the wherewithal to take on police powers. Too, until the adoption of the Seventeenth Amendment (providing for direct popular election of senators), the states were represented as states in the upper house of Congress and, in that capacity, had a stake in restraining efforts to poach upon the states' turf. Until the adoption of the Eighteenth Amendment, the federal government had no occasion to attempt to enforce a police power on a major scale.

The third and most potent prospective check upon state power—and also upon federal power—was the Supreme Court. From a constitutional perspective, the truly revolutionary consequence of the Civil War and Reconstruction, one that was entirely unforeseen, was the general public's acceptance—over the objections of a number of "progressive" lawyers and academic reformers—of the idea that the Court was the sole and final arbiter of constitutional controversies. No longer could a Jefferson arise to insist that the other branches of the federal government had coequal authority to determine constitutionality. No more could a Calhoun arise to defend a doctrine of interposition or nullification. Charles Evans Hughes, who became chief justice in 1930, declared that "the Constitution is what the judges say it is," and though other justices were as yet too circumspect to voice that opinion, it was true.

For the most part, the Court left the states to do their bidding until after the turn of the century. In the South, the fruits of the hands-off policy were segregation and disfranchisement of blacks. Southern legislatures gradually enacted Jim Crow laws, separating whites and blacks in public accommodations. The landmark case testing Jim Crow legislation arose from a Louisiana act requiring the separation of the "colored race" from whites in railroad cars. In *Plessy* v. *Ferguson* (1896), the Court ruled that if public facilities were equal, they could constitutionally be separate. And the Court went a great deal further. In 1899, in a case involving a school district too poor to afford both white and black high schools, the Court denied the plea of a black to be allowed to attend the white school, even though it was a matter of separate and nonexistent rather than separate but equal. A decade later, the Court upheld a Kentucky statute prohibiting private schools from educating blacks and whites together. As for voting, states circumvented the Fifteenth Amendment through literacy tests and other devices, and the courts upheld the disfranchisement.

In the North and West, exercises of the police power were substantially immune to Court intervention, as was much of state economic regulatory activity. In the *Granger* cases, the Court ruled that fixing maximum rates charged by businesses "affected with a public interest" was not a violation of the due process clause of the Fourteenth Amendment, even though the statute involved amounted to taking private property without due process. The attitude of the Court varied until 1898, when the rate-setting power of the states was more or less reduced to a formula: rates must be sufficient to allow a "fair return" on the "fair value" of the investment. In the efforts of states to curtail gigantic industrial combinations, the Court scarcely intervened; hence Ohio's outlawing of "pools" in the 1870s and the outlawing of "trusts" by most states in the 1880s and 1890s held up.

At first, what the Court did instead was to keep a watchful eye on the federal government. Congress made a pair of futile and almost halfhearted stabs at getting into the regulatory action. In 1887, in response to a decision that states could not arbitrarily set interstate railroad rates, Congress created the Interstate Commerce Commission. The statute was poorly crafted, and though the Supreme Court never declared it unconstitutional, the justices whittled away the commission's powers during the next dozen years. Particularly, the Court denied it power to fix rates on the ground that rate making was a legislative function that could not be delegated, and it crippled the commission's investigatory authority by refusing to accept its findings as final and not subject to review by the courts. The Physical Valuations Act of 1913 at last provided a means of setting rates in accordance with the Court's "fair return" formula.

The other congressional venture into economic regulation was the passage in 1890 of the Sherman Antitrust Act. The act declared illegal and made punishable by fines and imprisonment "every contract, combination in the form of a trust or otherwise, or conspiracy in restraint of trade" and every effort "to monopolize any part of the trade or commerce of the several States." The statute contained no clues as to the meaning of its terms, and if its words were taken literally, it could apply to all economic activity. It was a blank check for the Court to fill in and thus to make national antitrust policy, but the Court's early decisions on the law could hardly have been what the legislators had in mind. It applied the statute to break a strike by unionized railroad workers, and it ruled that a firm that controlled 94 percent of the country's sugar production was not a monopoly under the act, the ground being that manufacturing was not commerce. At the time of the sugar monopoly case, a dozen or so significant industrial combinations existed, and their total capitalization was about half a billion dollars. Nine years later, in 1904, more than three hundred combinations had come into being, representing the merger of fifty-three hundred plants and a capitalization of $7 billion—some thirteen times the entire federal budget for that year.

During the next decade, the Court worked out a body of antitrust law, based on the concept of reasonableness ("unreasonable restraint of trade") that made convictions possible and gave the Sherman Act a semblance of meaning. The "trust-busting" activities of Theodore Roosevelt, though much publicized, brought limited results: two of the forty-four antitrust suits instituted by his administration ended in convictions and the breakup of combinations. William Howard Taft, however, instituted sixty-three antitrust suits in four years, many of which were prosecuted to convictions (sustained by the Supreme Court) that dissolved corporate giants, including the American Tobacco Company and Standard Oil. Then Congress amended the Sherman Act, augmenting it by the Clayton Act and the act creating the Federal Trade Commission, under whose aegis antitrust suits were essentially discontinued for a quarter of a century.

A more portentous kind of federal intervention was getting under way even as the Court was putting teeth into the Sherman Act. As recently as 1891, the Court had held that the police power "is a power originally and always belonging to the States, not surrendered by them to the general government nor directly restrained by the Constitution of the United States, and essentially exclusive"; within a dozen years, it reversed that judgment. In *Champion* v. *Ames* (*The Lottery Cases,* 1903), the Court upheld an act of Congress making it a crime to transport lottery tickets across state lines, which is to say, protecting morals by prohibiting gambling—clearly an exercise of a police power. A year later, the justices upheld a prohibitive tax on yellow margarine, enacted ostensibly as a public health measure. Soon Congress enacted and the Court approved the Pure Food and

Drug Act, outlawing impure or fraudulently labeled food and drugs (1906); the Meat Inspection Act, imposing inspection standards on meat shipped in interstate commerce (1906); and the Mann or "White Slave" Act (1910). These federal ventures into the area of police powers were tentative, and the Supreme Court's acceptance of them was limited as well. In 1918 the Court declared unconstitutional, in *Hammer* v. *Dagenhart,* a federal statute preventing the interstate shipment of goods manufactured by the labor of children, holding that regulating child labor was "a purely state authority"; the test of such laws, it added, was whether the goods being shipped were themselves harmful. In 1923, in *Adkins* v. *Children's Hospital,* it struck down a law setting a minimum wage for women in the District of Columbia as a violation of the freedom of contract (a right the Court had recently discovered) and a deprivation of employers' property without due process of law. And the general fear of establishing anything resembling a national police force—despite sometimes overzealous, sometimes comical efforts to enforce Prohibition—was so pervasive that Congress refused to permit the Justice Department to borrow Secret Service agents from the Treasury Department, and when it did create the Bureau of Investigations, it denied agents of that bureau the power to make arrests.

The Court did impose some restrictions on the states' regulation of working conditions, except in those circumstances when health or safety was involved. In *Lochner* v. *New York* (1906), the Court first promulgated the doctrine of freedom of contract to strike down a state statute limiting the hours that bakery employees could be required to work. Two years later, however, in *Muller* v. *Oregon,* it upheld a limitation on the workday of females, saying that a "woman's physical structure and the performance of maternal functions" made her well-being "an object of public interest and care in order to preserve the strength and vigor of the race." It upheld Wisconsin's pioneering Workmen's Compensation Act, requiring employers to compensate workers injured on the job. In the 1920s it tended to treat state regulation of hours, wages, and working conditions as valid only in regard to businesses affected with a public interest and to define public interest narrowly; by the early 1930s, it was holding that the states could define the public interest in any way they saw fit.

One additional line of constitutional reasoning was formulated by the Court during the 1920s, and it foretokened a large-scale limitation on the rights of the states. This was the so-called doctrine of incorporation: that certain "fundamental personal rights and 'liberties,'" as enumerated in the Bill of Rights, were "protected by the due-process clause of the Fourteenth Amendment from impairment by the states." The doctrine was announced in a freedom of speech case in 1925, and it was reiterated in cases during the next three decades. In none of the cases before the 1950s, however, was the right at issue deemed sufficiently "fundamental" to warrant protection of the individuals involved in the suits from state action.

The twilight of states' rights in America is conventionally but not entirely accurately dated as beginning in the 1930s with Franklin Roosevelt's New Deal. The era did witness an expansion of federal activity on a scale unprecedented in peacetime, as the administration mobilized the nation to combat the Great Depression, self-consciously likening its efforts to mobilization for war. The measures that were adopted, however, were primarily economic and did not represent encroachments on territory previously occupied by the states. Except for a half dozen crime control acts passed in 1934 in response to the kidnapping and murder of the son of aviation hero Charles A. Lindbergh and a rash of bank robberies by interstate gangs, none of the New Deal's doings impinged except tangentially upon the traditional police powers. Until 1939, when defense expenditures began to distort the figures, state and local spending exceeded that of the federal government by half again, and federal civilian employees (two-fifths of whom worked in the post office) were outnumbered by state and local employees by four to one.

The by-product of the New Deal that truly affected federal-state relations was the temporary eclipse of the Supreme Court. The Court incurred Roosevelt's wrath by declaring unconstitutional two of his major programs and threatening others with the same fate. After he had been reelected by a landslide, the president proposed a "Court packing" scheme that would have permitted him to appoint enough additional justices to change the Court's majority. The public outcry against the proposal demonstrated what a sacred cow the institution had become, and the plan was rejected. But two justices, unnerved by the threat, switched positions, and soon others died or retired, with the result that the Court was dominated by Roosevelt men and an age of "judicial restraint" set in. During the next generation, the Court let almost every federal action pass constitutional muster: in a twenty-year period, it declared one executive action and one act of Congress unconstitutional.

The timing of the Court's era of passivity was significant. The United States entered World War II in 1941, and the accompanying expansion of government dwarfed any that had taken place before. Scarcely had the war ended when the Cold War began, preventing the kind of retrenchment that had followed earlier wars. Too, both the New Deal and the war had taught Americans to expect the federal government to meet their needs, and Harry Truman's Fair Deal underscored the message. The growth, relative to the growth of state governments, can again be suggested by numbers. During Roosevelt's first year in office, the federal government spent $4.6 billion; during Truman's last year, the sum was $65 billion. When Roosevelt came in, state and local governments were outspending the federal government by a wide margin; when Truman went out, the federal government was spending more than twice as much as state and local governments.

Not long afterward, the idea of states' rights was to become all but defunct, in no small measure as a result of the activities of its most ardent supporters. In 1954 the Supreme Court rendered its decision in *Brown* v. *Board of Education,* overturning the separate-but-equal doctrine promulgated in *Plessy* v. *Ferguson.* A year later, it worked out rules whereby racially segregated school districts would be required to conform to the *Brown* decision: local school boards would draw up plans, subject to the approval of federal district judges, to implement desegregation "with all deliberate speed." But school boards dragged their feet, and in the doing they received powerful support from their governors, legislators, and congressmen.

States' rights theorists sprang up throughout the South to write law review articles and books, sometimes reasonable and sometimes hysterical, denouncing the Court for misinterpreting the Fourteenth Amendment's equal protection clause and for disregarding the history of the adoption of the amendment. Officials dodged court orders by closing public schools, and private white academies proliferated. Also, white citizens engaged in threats of violence against black parents who sought to enroll their children in school.

As of the school year 1957–1958, fewer than seven hundred of the three thousand white public schools in the southern and border states had allowed any blacks to be admitted. In 1964, a decade after the *Brown* decision, fewer than 2 percent of black children in the Deep South were attending integrated schools. A number of violent racial confrontations had taken place. Then, in the early and middle 1970s, the Supreme Court adopted a different strategy based upon a reversal of its original ruling. It had ruled that state and local authorities could not use race as a factor in assigning children to schools, and now it ordered that race be the principal factor, the goal being forced integration by busing if necessary instead of merely desegregation. Gradually, by the end of the 1970s, integration was practically completed, though vast numbers of white parents moved out of certain school districts to avoid racial mixing, and the number of private schools increased.

The South had discredited states' rights once again, and along the way, the Supreme Court gained an enormous fund of moral capital in the rest of the country, which it used to undermine the authority of the states still further. In a succession of cases, it ordered legislatures to reapportion their seats in accordance with the principle of "one person one vote," even though apportionment in the Senate and the electoral college defies that formula; it declared prayer in public schools to be unconstitutional, though the First Amendment says merely that "Congress shall make no law respecting an establishment of religion, or prohibiting the free exercise thereof"; it discovered previously nonexistent rights of criminals by applying the doctrine of incorporation; it declared that capital punishment was "cruel and unusual" and violated the Eighth Amendment, though the body of the Constitution clearly sanctions capital punishment; it declared unconstitutional state laws prohibiting abortions; and it sanctioned reverse racial discrimination by upholding "affirmative action" laws to compensate for past discrimination. These decisions were reached with minimal regard for the language of the Constitution, and Justice William Brennan proclaimed loudly that the Court was not bound by the letter of the Constitution.

Vestiges of states' rights that remained were obliterated by the Great Society of Lyndon Baines Johnson. Property relations, family relations, education, public health, public safety, crime—the whole panoply of police powers—were brought under the direct or indirect control of the federal government. States continued to function, but they were kept in line by threats that the federal government would cut off their funds if they strayed. Subsequent administrations, notably that of Richard Nixon, sought to revitalize the states through "revenue sharing," but that merely made the states more dependent on federal largesse.

The matter did not entirely end there, however. By the 1980s, it was becoming increasingly evident that the all-pervasive activities of the federal government were simply not working. The level of waste was mind-boggling; for instance, it was revealed that the armed forces had spent $400 to acquire a hammer. Boondoggling abounded: witness the payment of billions in subsidies for the production of synthetic fuels two decades after the energy crisis of the 1970s had passed. Special privileges were built into almost every program, mainly through a tax code so complicated that agents of the Internal Revenue Service were unable to fill out tax returns properly. Worst of all, the programs were counterproductive, aggravating the problems they were supposed to ameliorate. Peggy Noonan, erstwhile speechwriter for President Ronald Reagan, captured the essence of the mess when she quipped that if the Sahara Desert were turned over to the federal bureaucracy, there would be a shortage of sand within a week.

For a time, the state governments were almost as incompetent as the federal government, but that began to change rapidly in the 1990s. State after state devised innovative and successful programs to solve one problem or another. Michigan, Wisconsin, and Illinois were among the leaders, but governors throughout the country pooled their information about what measures worked and what did not, and the effectiveness of government on the state level improved dramatically. A return to "letting the states do it" became steadily more attractive.

And then, whether in response to these trends or for constitutional reasons, the Supreme Court began to discover anew that states' rights were an integral part of the constitutional order. It actually started to do so in 1976, when in *National League of Cities* v. *Usery* it declared unconstitutional the application of the Fair Labor Standards Act to state employees, on the ground that applying the act improperly interfered with the "integral governmental functions" of a state. The decision turned on a five-to-four vote, however, and Justice Harry Blackmun, who was in the majority, switched positions in the case of *Garcia* v. *San Antonio Metropolitan Transit Authority* nine years later, and the *Usery* verdict was expressly overruled. In dissent, Justice William Rehnquist expressed confidence that restricting congressional power over the states would "in time again command the support of a majority of this Court." Justice Sandra Day O'Connor, also in dissent, shared that belief.

They were right: in 1991 and 1992, a majority of the Court, declaring that the states "retain substantial sovereign powers under our constitutional scheme," struck down congressional enactments that coerced states to implement federal programs. Three years later, in *United States* v. *Lopez,* the Court stunned seasoned Court-watchers with its decision overruling a congressional act prohibiting the carrying of a firearm within "a distance of 1,000 feet from the grounds of a public, parochial or private school." Most of the reasoning in the opinions turned on Congress's power under the interstate commerce clause, which had long been used to justify whatever Congress chose to do, but Chief Justice Rehnquist went further. He wrote that one could spuriously argue that education affects commerce and that the act was therefore a regulation of commerce, but such reasoning, he declared, "would bid fair to convert congressional authority under the Commerce Clause to a general police power of the sort retained by the States." That, of course, was just what had been happening for decades, and Rehnquist's words hinted that the practice would have to be stopped.

If the *Lopez* decision and several similar rulings in 1996 and 1997 shocked Court-watchers, three decisions in 1999 arrested the attention of the entire nation. Reiterating a doctrine first promulgated in *Hans* v. *Louisiana* (1890), holding that the Eleventh Amendment gives states immunity not only from suits in federal courts by outsiders, as the amendment expressly says, but also from suits by the federal government and by citizens of the state itself, the Court ruled that state employees could not sue their states for violations of federal labor law, that patent owners could not sue state universities and agencies for infringement of their patents, and that people could not bring suits against states in federal or state courts for unfair competition by states in the marketplace. "Our federalism," wrote Justice Anthony M. Kennedy for the majority, "requires that Congress treat the states in a manner consistent with their status as residuary sovereigns and joint participants in the governance of the nation." The *New York Times* declared that the fault line in the Court was federalism. "Court Bolsters States' Rights," proclaimed headlines in newspapers the nation over.

Thus in the 1990s, as in the 1870s, states' rights had found a powerful friend but, given the five-to-four majority, still a fickle one.

NOTES

Prologue: The Problem of Divided Sovereignty

1. William Blackstone, *Commentaries on the Laws of England in Four Books,* 12th ed. (London, 1793), 1:44.

2. The idea of sovereignty and its indivisibility is usually credited to Jean Bodin. See Julian H. Franklin, *Jean Bodin and the Sixteenth-Century Revolution in the Methodology of Law and History* (New York, 1963).

3. On the question of the relationship between the Crown and the estates, see Michael Mendle, *Dangerous Positions: Mixed Government, the Estates of the Realm, and the Making of the* Answer to the xix propositions (Tuscaloosa, Ala., 1985).

4. Forrest McDonald, *The American Presidency: An Intellectual History* (Lawrence, Kans., 1994). 101, 103–121; Oliver Morton Dickerson, *American Colonial Government, 1696–1765; A Study of the British Board of Trade in Relation to the American Colonies, Political, Industrial, Administrative* (1912; repr., New York, 1962); James A. Henretta, *"Salutary Neglect": Colonial Administration under the Duke of Newcastle* (Princeton, N.J., 1972); Leonard Woods Labaree, *Royal Government in America: A Study of the British Colonial System before 1783* (1936; repr., New York, 1964).

5. Forrest McDonald, ed., *Empire and Nation: Letters from a Farmer in Pennsylvania, John Dickinson; Letters from the Federal Farmer, Richard Henry Lee,* 2d ed. (Indianapolis, 1999). Otis's argument in the 1761 Writs of Assistance Case was so inflammatory (and compelling) that John Adams said, "Then and there, the child of Independence was born" (C. Bradley Thompson, *John Adams and the Spirit of Liberty* [Lawrence, Kans., 1998], 35–36). Henry's argument in the Parson's Cause (1763) evoked from spectators cries of "Treason, Treason!"

6. John M. Head, *A Time to Rend: An Essay on the Decision for American*

Independence (Madison, Wis., 1968), 100, 105 n; Thompson, *John Adams,* 59–60, 67–72, 293 n. 57.

I. THE COMPACT

1. John Locke, *Two Treatises of Government,* 2d ed., ed. Peter Laslett (Cambridge, 1967); Marsilius of Padua, *Defensor pacis,* trans. Alan Gewirth (New York, 1956); Alan Gewirth, *Marsilius of Padua: The Defender of Peace* (New York, 1951); Forrest McDonald, *Novus Ordo Seclorum: The Intellectual Origins of the Constitution* (Lawrence, Kans., 1985), 1, 50–51, 60. See also Richard Ashcraft, *Revolutionary Politics & Locke's Two Treatises of Government* (Princeton, N.J., 1986); Steven M. Dworetz, *The Unvarnished Doctrine: Locke, Liberalism, and the American Revolution* (Durham, N.C., 1990); and Jerome Huyler, *Locke in America: The Moral Philosophy of the Founding Era* (Lawrence, Kans., 1995). Garry Wills, in *Inventing America: Jefferson's Declaration of Independence* (Garden City, N.Y., 1978), argued that Scottish Common Sense philosophy, not Locke, underlay the Declaration; he is devastatingly rebutted by Ronald Hamowy, "Jefferson and the Scottish Enlightenment: A Critique of Garry Wills's *Inventing America: Jefferson's Declaration of Independence,*" *William and Mary Quarterly* 36 (1979): 503–523. Donald Lutz, in *A Preface to American Political Theory* (Lawrence, Kans., 1992), demonstrates, accurately, that Locke's influence faded rapidly after 1781 but confirms Locke's powerful influence on the Declaration. The best reconstruction of the Declaration is Pauline Maier, *American Scripture: Making the Declaration of Independence* (New York, 1997). I have for many years required my undergraduate seminar students to read Locke and the Declaration; they invariably find the similarity unmistakable.

2. Locke, *Two Treatises,* 424 and passim; McDonald, *Novus Ordo Seclorum,* 145.

3. Oscar Handlin and Mary Handlin, eds., *The Popular Sources of Political Authority: Documents on the Massachusetts Constitution of 1780* (Cambridge, Mass., 1966), 90–91; Richard F. Upton, *Revolutionary New Hampshire* (Hanover, N.H., 1936), ch. 13. In Massachusetts and New Hampshire sovereignty reverted to the towns, and thus to the people of a town as citizens of that town rather than a state, and the constitutions of 1780 and 1784 were based on that principle. In Rhode Island and Connecticut the continuation of the corporate charters meant that sovereignty did not revert anywhere but remained in the existing political society.

4. McDonald, *Novus Ordo Seclorum*, 148–149; Handlin and Handlin, eds., *Documents on the Massachusetts Constitution;* Willi Paul Adams, *The First American Constitutions: Republican Ideology and the Making of the State Constitutions in the Revolutionary Era* (Chapel Hill, N.C., 1980), 86–93.

5. For an elaboration of this point, see McDonald, *Novus Ordo Seclorum*, 279–281.

6. Samuel H. Beer, *To Make a Nation: The Rediscovery of American Federalism* (Cambridge, Mass., 1993), 13; Head, *Time to Rend*, 113–114; Garry Wills, *A Necessary Evil: A History of American Distrust of Government* (New York, 1999).

7. Edmund Cody Burnett, *The Continental Congress* (New York, 1941), 154–169.

8. See, in addition to the Declaration itself, the analysis in James Jackson Kilpatrick, *The Sovereign States: Notes of a Citizen of Virginia* (Chicago, 1957), 4–6.

9. James D. Richardson, comp., *Messages and Papers of the Presidents, 1789–1897* (Washington, D.C., 1896), 1:9–18.

10. William M. Malloy, ed., *Treaties, Conventions, International Acts, Protocols and Agreements between the United States of America and Other Powers, 1776–1909*, 2 vols. (New York, 1968), 1:479–480.

11. Forrest McDonald, *E Pluribus Unum: The Formation of the American Republic, 1776–1790*, 2d ed. (Indianapolis, 1979), 38–39; Forrest McDonald and Ellen Shapiro McDonald, *Requiem: Variations on Eighteenth-Century Themes* (Lawrence, Kans., 1988), 28–32.

12. H. James Henderson, *Party Politics in the Continental Congress* (New York, 1874); McDonald, *American Presidency*, 136–138; Jack N. Rakove, *The Beginnings of National Politics: An Interpretive History of the Continental Congress* (New York, 1979); Merrill Jensen, *The Articles of Confederation: An Interpretation of the Social-Constitutional History of the American Revolution, 1774–1781* (Madison, Wis., 1940).

13. E. James Ferguson, *The Power of the Purse: A History of American Public Finance, 1776–1790* (Chapel Hill, N.C., 1961), 25–40, 70–105. For Washington's role, see Forrest McDonald, "George Washington: Today's Indispensable Man," *Intercollegiate Review* 30 (1995): 14–15; Richard Brookhiser, *Founding Father: Rediscovering George Washington* (New York, 1996); Forrest McDonald, "George Washington," in *American National Biography*, 24 vols., ed. John A. Garraty and Mark C. Carnes (New York, 1999), 22:760–762; McDonald, *American Presidency*, 138–141; Gary L. Gregg II and Matthew Spalding, eds., *Patriot Sage: George Washington and the American Political Tradition* (Wilmington, Del., 1999).

14. McDonald, *American Presidency*, 137–138; Burnett, *Continental Congress*, 490–493; Jackson Turner Main, *The Antifederalists: Critics of the Constitution, 1781–1788* (Chapel Hill, N.C., 1961), 72–102.

15. Clarence L. Ver Steeg, *Robert Morris: Revolutionary Financier* (New York, 1976); Ferguson, *Power of the Purse;* McDonald, *E Pluribus Unum,* 50–57.

16. McDonald, *American Presidency,* 141–143; McDonald, *E Pluribus Unum,* 57–67.

17. McDonald, *American Presidency,* 143–144; Burnett, *Continental Congress,* 575–580.

18. Burnett, *Continental Congress,* 580–648. See also Aaron Wildavsky, "What if the United States Were Still Governed under the Articles of Confederation? Noncentralized versus Federal Systems," in *Federalism & Political Culture* (New Brunswick, N.J., 1998), 83–134.

19. Edmund C. Burnett, ed., *Letters of Members of the Continental Congress,* 8 vols. (Washington, D.C., 1936), 8:208; McDonald, *Novus Ordo Seclorum,* 169; Burnett, *Continental Congress,* 655–659; Merrill Jensen, *The New Nation: A History of the United States, 1781–1789* (New York, 1950), 170–174.

20. McDonald, *Novus Ordo Seclorum,* 172, 178; McDonald, *E Pluribus Unum,* 239, 242, 247; Forrest McDonald, *Alexander Hamilton: A Biography* (New York, 1979), 90–91, 94; Burnett, *Continental Congress,* 654–658.

21. McDonald and McDonald, *Requiem,* 59–83; McDonald, *E Pluribus Unum,* 239–256; McDonald, *Novus Ordo Seclorum,* 176–177; David P. Szatmary, *Shays' Rebellion: The Making of an Agrarian Insurrection* (Amherst, Mass., 1980).

22. McDonald, *Novus Ordo Seclorum,* 185–224; McDonald, *American Presidency,* 160–162; M. E. Bradford, *Founding Fathers: Brief Lives of the Framers of the United States Constitution,* 2d ed. (Lawrence, Kans., 1994).

23. Max Farrand, ed., *The Records of the Federal Convention of 1787,* 4 vols. (New Haven, Conn., 1937), 1:10–11, Madison's notes for May 28 and May 30.

24. Ibid., 2:16, Madison's notes for July 16, and 1:510–516, Madison's notes for July 2.

25. Ibid., 1:468, Madison's notes for June 29, and 1:474, Yates's notes for June 29; Peter S. Onuf, "State Sovereignty and the Making of the Constitution," in *Conceptual Change and the Constitution,* ed. Terence Ball and J. G. A. Pocock (Lawrence, Kans., 1988), 81–82.

26. McDonald, *Novus Ordo Seclorum,* 262–268; *The Federalist,* intro. by Edward Mead Earle (New York, 1937), Nos. 41–43.

27. McDonald, *E Pluribus Unum,* chs. 2–4.

28. Farrand, ed., *Records,* 1:48 and 1:51, Madison's notes for May 31; George

Athan Billias, *Elbridge Gerry: Founding Father and Republican Statesman* (New York, 1976), 160.

29. Farrand, ed., *Records,* 1:164–168, Madison's notes for June 8; 2:27–28, Madison's notes for July 17; 2:390–391, Madison's notes for August 23; 3:132–133, letter to Thomas Jefferson, October 24, 1787. See also Lance Banning, "James Madison and the Dynamics of the Constitutional Convention," *Political Science Reviewer* 17 (1987): 19–22, 31, 46–47.

30. McDonald, *Novus Ordo Seclorum,* 268–276.

31. Forrest McDonald, "Original Unintentions: The Franchise and the Constitution," *Modern Age* 40 (1998): 344–351.

32. *Federalist,* 246; Gordon Lloyd, "Let Justice Be Our Guide: A Reconsideration of 'True Federalism' at the Constitutional Convention," *Political Science Reviewer* 17 (1987): 151–161, and Banning, "James Madison," 32–35, 47; Jack N. Rakove, *Original Meanings: Politics and Ideas in the Making of the Constitution* (New York, 1996), 161–202; Lance Banning, *The Sacred Fire of Liberty: James Madison and the Founding of the Federal Republic* (Ithaca, N.Y., 1995), 220–231, 476 n. 118, 532 n. 55.

33. *Federalist,* 248–249. On a later occasion, Madison commented upon "sovereignty, as divided between the Union and the members composing the Union" (Paul C. Nagel, *One Nation Indivisible: The Union in American Thought, 1776–1861* [New York, 1964], 33).

34. McDonald, *Novus Ordo Seclorum,* 279–281.

35. Farrand, ed., *Records,* 1:122, 123, 315; 2:96; 3:135, 257, 308, 351; McDonald, *Novus Ordo Seclorum,* 280–281.

36. Kilpatrick, *Sovereign States,* 16; for Patrick Henry in the ratifying convention, see also M. E. Bradford, *Against the Barbarians and Other Reflections on Familiar Themes* (Columbia, Mo., 1992), 83–99; Herbert J. Storing, ed., *The Complete Anti-Federalist,* 7 vols. (Chicago, 1981), 5:207–254; Kenneth M. Stampp, "The Concept of a Perpetual Union," *Journal of American History* 65 (1978): 11; *New Orleans Bee,* January 22, 1861, in Dwight L. Dumond, ed., *Southern Editorials on Secession* (New York, 1931), 410.

37. Farrand, ed., *Records,* 1:588, Madison's notes for September 12, 3:144, 162, 256; *Federalist,* 559; Forrest McDonald, "The Bill of Rights: Unnecessary and Pernicious," and Donald S. Lutz, "The Pedigree of the Bill of Rights," in *The Bill of Rights: Government Proscribed,* ed. Ronald Hoffman and Peter J. Albert (Charlottesville, Va., 1997); Leonard W. Levy, *Origins of the Bill of Rights* (New Haven, Conn., 1999), 1–43.

38. Forrest McDonald, *The Presidency of George Washington* (Lawrence, Kans., 1974), 32; Gary Rosen, *American Compact: James Madison and the*

Problem of Founding (Lawrence, Kans., 1999), 135; Jack N. Rakove, *James Madison and the Creation of the American Republic* (Glenview, Ill., 1990), 76, 77, 81, 83–84; Douglass Adair, *Fame and the Founding Fathers,* ed. Trevor Colbourn (New York, 1974), 136.

39. McDonald, *Presidency of Washington,* 34–36; McDonald, *E Pluribus Unum,* 366–369.

40. Marshall L. DeRosa, *The Ninth Amendment and the Politics of Creative Jurisprudence* (New Brunswick, N.J., 1996), 1–7. Jefferson, in his "Opinion on the Constitutionality of a National Bank," February 15, 1791, refers to it as the twelfth amendment, inasmuch as the ratification process was still ongoing; the quote can be found, among other places, in Peter S. Onuf, ed., *Thomas Jefferson: An Anthology* (New York, 1999), 135. See also Joseph Story, *Commentaries on the Constitution of the United States,* vol. 2 (Boston, 1833), sec. 1808; Eugene W. Hickok, Jr., "The Original Understanding of the Tenth Amendment," in *The Bill of Rights: Original Meaning and Current Understanding,* ed. Eugene W. Hickok, Jr. (Charlottesville, Va., 1991), 462; Jesse T. Carpenter, *The South as a Conscious Minority, 1789–1861: A Study in Political Thought* (New York, 1930), 41 and n. 23.

2. THE FEDERALIST ERA

1. McDonald, *Presidency of Washington,* 23–46; John C. Miller, *The Federalist Era, 1789–1801* (New York, 1960); McDonald, *American Presidency,* 209–232.

2. McDonald, *Hamilton,* 142, 163–188; McDonald, *Presidency of Washington,* 47–62; McDonald, *American Presidency,* 228–230.

3. McDonald, *Presidency of Washington,* 69–74; McDonald, *Hamilton,* 177–181; Whitney K. Bates, "Northern Speculators and Southern State Debts, 1790," *William and Mary Quarterly* 19 (1962): 32; Kenneth R. Bowling and Helen E. Veit, eds., *The Diary of William Maclay and Other Notes on Senate Debates* (Baltimore, 1988), 200–201, 206–207, 312.

4. McDonald, *Presidency of Washington,* 74–75; McDonald, *Hamilton,* 181–187; Jacob E. Cooke, "The Compromise of 1790," *William and Mary Quarterly* 27 (1970): 523–545; Kenneth R. Bowling, "Dinner at Jefferson's: A Note on Jacob E. Cooke's 'The Compromise of 1790,' " *William and Mary Quarterly* 28 (1971): 637; Kenneth R. Bowling, "Politics in the First Congress, 1789–1791" (Ph.D. diss., University of Wisconsin, 1968), 211–221; Ferguson, *Power of the Purse,* 300–310.

5. *The Papers of Alexander Hamilton,* 26 vols., ed. Harold C. Syrett et al. (New York, 1961–1979), 7:149–150; *Journal of the House of Delegates of Virginia . . . 1790* (Richmond, 1828), 35–36, 38.

6. McDonald, *Hamilton,* 200, 201; Winfred E. A. Bernhard, *Fisher Ames, Federalist and Statesman, 1758–1808* (Chapel Hill, N.C., 1965), 172–173; editorial note on locating the federal district, in *The Papers of Thomas Jefferson,* 24 vols. to date, ed. Julian Boyd et al. (Princeton, N.J., 1950–1990), 19:3–58; Kenneth R. Bowling, *The Creation of Washington, D.C.: The Idea and Location of the American Capital* (Fairfax, Va., 1991), 161–207.

7. McDonald, *Presidency of Washington,* 76–78; Rosen, *American Compact,* 144–155, 159, 172; Banning, *Sacred Fire of Liberty,* 158–164, 243–248, 332–334; Rakove, *James Madison,* 95–99; Benjamin B. Klubes, "The First Federal Congress and the First National Bank: A Case Study in Constitutional Interpretation," *Journal of the Early Republic* 10 (1990): 21–41.

8. Henry Steele Commager, ed., *Documents of American History,* 2 vols., 7th ed. (New York, 1963), 1:158–160; Onuf, ed., *Thomas Jefferson,* 135–138.

9. McDonald, *Hamilton,* 205, 206–210; Syrett, ed., *Papers of Hamilton,* 8:63–134. Hamilton's argument was substantially adopted by John Marshall in *M'Culloch* v. *Maryland.*

10. McDonald, *Hamilton,* 214–215; Franklin B. Sawvel, ed., *The ANAS of Thomas Jefferson* (New York, 1970), 36–37.

11. McDonald, *Hamilton,* 215–217; McDonald, *Presidency of Washington,* 80–81, 89–94; McDonald, *American Presidency,* 233–235; Lance Banning, *The Jefferson Persuasion: Evolution of a Party Ideology* (Ithaca, N.Y., 1978); Noble E. Cunningham, Jr., *The Jeffersonian Republicans: The Formation of Party Organization, 1789–1801* (Chapel Hill, N.C., 1957); William N. Chambers, *Political Parties in a New Nation: The American Experience, 1776–1809* (New York, 1963); Onuf, ed., *Thomas Jefferson,* 139–145.

12. McDonald, *Hamilton,* 256–257; Jefferson to Madison, October 1, 1792, in Syrett, ed., *Papers of Hamilton,* 12:85 n.

13. McDonald, *Presidency of Washington,* 127 n; William M. Wiecek, *The Sources of Antislavery Constitutionalism in America, 1760–1848* (Ithaca, N.Y., 1977), 98–100, 156–157, 192–193, 197–199.

14. Commager, ed., *Documents,* 1:163; McDonald, *Presidency of Washington,* 123–126, 128–129; Harry Ammon, *The Genet Mission* (New York, 1973), 25–53; McDonald, *Hamilton,* 272–278, 280–283, 287; Alexander DeConde, *Entangling Alliance: Politics & Diplomacy under George Washington* (Durham, N.C., 1958), 197–203, 217–222, 236–248; McDonald, *American Presidency,* 236–240.

15. McDonald, *Hamilton*, 276.

16. *Glass* v. *Sloop Betsy,* 3 Dallas 6 (1794); Charles Warren, *The Supreme Court in United States History,* 2 vols. (Boston, 1922, 1926), 1:105, 115–117.

17. *Vanstophorst* v. *Maryland,* 2 Dallas 401 (1791); *Oswald* v. *New York,* ibid.; *Indiana Company* v. *Virginia* is mentioned in a letter from William R. Davie to Judge Iredell, June 12, 1793.

18. Warren, *Supreme Court,* 1:92–93, 97.

19. *Chisholm* v. *Georgia,* 2 Dallas 419 (1793); Julius Goebel, Jr., *The Oliver Wendell Holmes Devise History of the Supreme Court of the United States,* vol. 1, *Antecedents and Beginnings to 1801* (New York, 1971), 726–734, 740; Warren, *Supreme Court,* 1:100; Louis Fisher, *American Constitutional Law* (New York, 1990), 375.

20. *Boston Independent Chronicle,* September 16, 1793; Warren, *Supreme Court,* 1:99 n, 101; James E. Pfander, "History and State Suability: An 'Explanatory' Account of the Eleventh Amendment," *Cornell Law Review* 83 (1998): 1270–1382; John J. Gibbons, "The Eleventh Amendment and State Sovereign Immunity: A Reinterpretation," *Columbia Law Review* 83 (1983): 1895–1938; John V. Orth, *The Judicial Power of the United States: The Eleventh Amendment* (New York, 1987), 3–29; *John H. Alden* v. *Maine,* 13 Supreme Court Reporter 488–491, 506–509 (1999).

21. *Ware* v. *Hilton,* 3 Dallas 199 (1796); *The Papers of John Marshall,* 9 vols., ed. William C. Stinchcombe (vol. 3), Charles F. Hobson (vol. 5) (Chapel Hill, N.C., 1974–1998), 3:4–14, 5:295–329; Goebel, *Antecedents and Beginnings to 1801,* 748–756; Charles R. Ritcheson, *Aftermath of Revolution: British Policy toward the United States, 1783–1795* (Dallas, 1969), 332 ff.; Charles F. Hobson, "The Recovery of British Debts in the Federal Circuit Court of Virginia, 1790 to 1797," *Virginia Magazine of History and Biography* 92 (1984): 176–200.

22. McDonald, *Hamilton,* 255–256, 297; Commager, *Documents,* 1:163–164.

23. Washington and Jefferson College, W. Thomas Mainwaring, ed., "The Whiskey Rebellion and the Trans-Appalachian Frontier," *Topic: A Journal of the Liberal Arts* 45 (1994), especially Jeffrey A. Davis, "The Whiskey Rebellion and the Demise of the Democratic-Republican Societies of Pennsylvania," 22–38; Jacob E. Cooke, "The Whiskey Insurrection: A Re-evaluation," *Pennsylvania History* 30 (1963): 316–346.

24. McDonald, *Hamilton,* 297–299; McDonald, *Presidency of Washington,* 129–131, 145–147; Leland D. Baldwin, *Whisky Rebels: The Story of a Frontier Uprising* (Pittsburgh, 1939), 10, 25–28, 73, 92–95, 108–109, 113–115.

25. McDonald, *Hamilton,* 299–301; Richard H. Kohn, "The Washington

Administration's Decision to Crush the Whiskey Rebellion," *Journal of American History* 59 (1972): 570–571, 582–583, 584.

26. McDonald, *Hamilton,* 301–302; McDonald, *Presidency of Washington,* 147; Eugene Perry Link, *Democratic-Republican Societies, 1790–1800* (New York, 1942), 200–203. Equally skillful was Washington's handling of an episode in North Carolina; Jeffrey J. Crow, "The Whiskey Rebellion in North Carolina," *North Carolina Historical Review* 66 (1989): 1–28, presents the evidence with a different emphasis.

27. McDonald, *Presidency of Washington,* 159–160, 162–164, 169–175; Joseph Charles, *The Origins of the American Party System: Three Essays* (New York, 1961). According to the extreme states' rights theorist John Taylor of Caroline, as the Jay negotiations were pending, Taylor was approached by arch-Federalist senators Oliver Ellsworth and Rufus King with a suggestion that the Union be dissolved and new unions be formed, one each in the North and the South. Such was the intensity of feelings in regard to England and France. Gaillard Hunt, ed., *Disunion Sentiment in Congress in 1794* (Washington, D.C., 1905).

28. McDonald, *Hamilton,* 325–326; *American State Papers, Documents, Legislative and Executive, of the Congress of the United States* (Washington, D.C., 1832–1861), 1:576, 577; Pierre Auguste Adet to Timothy Pickering, October 27, 1796, published in the *Philadelphia Aurora.*

29. Concerning the Adams presidency, see Ralph A. Brown, *The Presidency of John Adams* (Lawrence, Kans., 1975); Manning J. Dauer, *The Adams Federalists* (Baltimore, 1968); Stephen G. Kurtz, *The Presidency of John Adams: The Collapse of Federalism, 1795–1800* (Philadelphia, 1957).

30. William Stinchcombe, "The Diplomacy of the WXYZ Affair," *William and Mary Quarterly* 34 (1977): 590–617; William Stinchcombe, *The XYZ Affair* (Westport, Conn., 1980); Alexander DeConde, *The Quasi-War: The Politics and Diplomacy of the Undeclared War with France, 1797–1801* (New York, 1966), 66–108; Page Smith, *John Adams,* 2 vols. (New York, 1962), 2:952–965.

31. McDonald, *Hamilton,* 345; Dice Robins Anderson, *William Branch Giles: A Study in the Politics of Virginia and the Nation from 1790 to 1830* (Gloucester, Mass., 1965), 69–70; Kurtz, *Presidency of Adams,* 354; Henry Adams, *John Randolph* (Boston, 1883), 28.

32. Thomas Jefferson to John Taylor, June 4, 1798, in *Thomas Jefferson: Writings* (New York, 1984), 1050.

33. Commager, *Documents,* 1:175–178; James Morton Smith, *Freedom's Fetters: The Alien and Sedition Laws and American Civil Liberties* (Ithaca, N.Y., 1956).

34. Commager, *Documents,* 1:178–182; William J. Watkins, Jr., "The Kentucky and Virginia Resolutions: Guideposts of Limited Government," *Independent Review: A Journal of Political Economy* 3 (1999): 385–405; James Morton Smith, "The Grass Roots Origins of the Kentucky Resolutions," *William and Mary Quarterly* 28 (1970): 221–245; K. R. Constantine Gutzman, " 'Oh, What a Tangled Web We Weave . . . ': James Madison and the Compound Republic," *Continuity* 22 (1998): 21–22; Dumas Malone, *Jefferson and the Ordeal of Liberty* (Boston, 1962), 396; Adrienne Koch and Harry Ammon, "The Virginia and Kentucky Resolutions: An Episode in Jefferson's and Madison's Defense of Civil Liberties," *William and Mary Quarterly* 5 (1948): 145–176; Leonard W. Levy, *Jefferson & Civil Liberties: The Darker Side* (New York, 1968), 56; David N. Mayer, *The Constitutional Thought of Thomas Jefferson* (Charlottesville, Va., 1994), 201–208.

35. Commager, *Documents,* 1:182; Madison also refers to the Tenth Amendment and in doing so used the word "expressly"; Rosen, *American Compact,* 140–141; James Morton Smith, "Virginia and Kentucky Resolutions," in *James Madison and the American Nation, 1751–1836: An Encyclopedia* (New York, 1994); Banning, *Sacred Fire of Liberty,* 387–395; Drew R. McCoy, *The Last of the Fathers: James Madison and the Republican Legacy* (Cambridge, 1989), 139–147.

36. Watkins, "The Kentucky and Virginia Resolutions," 404; Kilpatrick, *Sovereign States,* 81; McCoy, *Last of the Fathers,* 119–170.

37. Commager, *Documents,* 1:184–185; Donald Stewart, *The Opposition Press of the Federalist Period* (Albany, N.Y., 1969), 473–474.

38. Kilpatrick, *Sovereign States,* 86; Banning, *Sacred Fire of Liberty,* 390–391, 393; Kevin R. Gutzman, "A Troublesome Legacy: James Madison and 'The Principles of '98,' " *Journal of the Early Republic* 15 (1995): 569–590.

39. Bureau of the Census, *Historical Statistics of the United States, Colonial Times to 1957* (Washington, D.C., 1960), 692; Saul Cornell, "Mere Parchment Barriers?" in Hoffman and Albert, eds., *Bill of Rights,* 182.

40. McDonald, *Hamilton,* 348; Syrett, ed., *Papers of Hamilton,* 24:445.

41. Kurtz, *Presidency of Adams,* 389–402; Syrett, ed., *Papers of Hamilton,* 24:446–452.

42. Cunningham, *Jeffersonian Republicans, 1789–1801,* 176–185; Morton Borden, "The Election of 1800: Charge and Countercharge," *Delaware History* 5 (1952): 42–62; Milton Lomask, *Aaron Burr: The Years from Princeton to Vice President, 1756–1805* (New York, 1979); Herbert S. Parmet and Marie B. Hecht, *Aaron Burr: Portrait of an Ambitious Man* (New York, 1967).

43. McDonald, *Hamilton,* 349; Beatrice G. Reubens, "Burr, Hamilton, and

the Manhattan Company," *Political Science Quarterly* 72 (1957): 578–607 and 73 (1958): 100–125.

44. Cunningham, *Jeffersonian Republicans, 1789–1801,* 239–244; Andrew A. Lipscomb and Albert Ellery Bergh, eds., *The Writings of Thomas Jefferson,* 20 vols. (Washington, D.C., 1903–1904), 10:198.

45. McDonald, *American Presidency,* 249–250; Warren, *Supreme Court,* 1:182–183; Lipscomb and Bergh, eds., *Writings of Jefferson,* 10:201–204; Merrill D. Peterson, *Thomas Jefferson and the New Nation: A Biography* (New York, 1970), 643–651.

46. Richardson, comp., *Messages and Papers,* 1:323; *Thomas Jefferson: Writings,* 493, 494. In his first annual message, December 8, 1801, Jefferson again defined the position of state governments vis-à-vis the general government: "this Government is charged with the external and mutual relations only of these States; that the States themselves have principal care of our persons, our property, and our reputation, constituting the great field of human concerns" (*Messages and Papers,* 1:328).

3. The Jeffersonians

1. Syrett, ed., *Papers of Hamilton,* 25:311, 320; Forrest McDonald, *The Presidency of Thomas Jefferson* (Lawrence, Kans., 1976), 21–22, 29–39; McDonald, *American Presidency,* 246–248, 250–253; Robert M. Johnstone, Jr., *Jefferson and the Presidency: Leadership in the Young Republic* (Ithaca, N.Y., 1978), 32 ff. and passim.

2. McDonald, *Presidency of Jefferson,* 41; Noble E. Cunningham, Jr., *The Jeffersonian Republicans in Power: Party Operations, 1801–1809* (Chapel Hill, N.C., 1963); Levy, *Jefferson and Civil Liberties,* 56–60; McDonald, *American Presidency,* 268.

3. Dumas Malone, *Jefferson the President: First Term, 1801–1805* (Boston, 1970), 206–220; Harry Ammon, *James Monroe: The Quest for National Identity* (New York, 1971), 197–198.

4. *Thomas Jefferson: Writings,* 497–500, 1100–1101; Henry Adams, *History of the United States during the Presidencies of Thomas Jefferson and James Madison,* 9 vols. (New York, 1889–1891), 1:226–237.

5. McDonald, *Presidency of Jefferson,* 34–38; Cunningham, *Jeffersonian Republicans, 1801–1809,* 18–29, 60–63; McDonald, *American Presidency,* 254–255; Leonard D. White, *The Jeffersonians: A Study in Administrative History, 1801–1829* (New York, 1951), 379–380.

6. *Thomas Jefferson: Writings,* 495; Robert W. Tucker and David C. Hendrickson, *Empire of Liberty: The Statecraft of Thomas Jefferson* (New York, 1990), 41–42, 123; McDonald, *Presidency of Jefferson,* 43; Samuel P. Huntington, *The Soldier and the State: The Theory and Politics of Civil-Military Relations* (Cambridge, Mass., 1957). The wording that standing armies were "dangerous to liberty" appeared commonly in the early state constitutions: see Massachusetts, 1780; New Hampshire, 1784 and 1792; North Carolina, 1776; Pennsylvania, 1776; Tennessee, 1796; and Vermont, 1793, in Francis Newton Thorpe, ed., *The Federal and State Constitutions,* 7 vols. (Washington, D.C., 1909), 3:1892, 4:2456, 2474, 5:2788, 3083, 6:3424, 3764. The prohibition on standing armies in peacetime continued, and the precise phrase "dangerous to liberty" also continued to be used: see Ohio, 1851; Tennessee, 1834; Virginia, 1850; and Maryland, 1851, in Thorpe, ed., *Federal and State Constitutions,* 5:2914, 6:3428, 7:3830, 3:1715.

7. McDonald, *Presidency of Jefferson,* 43–44; *Thomas Jefferson: Writings,* 506–507, 539–542; Tucker and Hendrickson, *Empire of Liberty,* 40–41; Craig L. Symonds, *Navalists and Antinavalists: The Naval Policy Debate in the United States, 1785–1827* (Newark, N.J., 1980); Alexander Balinky, *Albert Gallatin: Fiscal Theories and Policies* (New Brunswick, N.J., 1958), 72–78.

8. McDonald, *Presidency of Jefferson,* 44, 61–62, 76–80; McDonald, *American Presidency,* 263–265; David A. Carson, "Jefferson, Congress, and the Question of Leadership in the Tripolitan War," *Virginia Magazine of History and Biography* 94 (1986): 409–424; Gardner W. Allen, *Our Navy and the Barbary Corsairs* (Boston, 1905).

9. McDonald, *Presidency of Jefferson,* 42–44; Raymond Walters, Jr., *Albert Gallatin: Jeffersonian Financier and Diplomat* (New York, 1957); Balinky, *Albert Gallatin,* 39–48, 89–127.

10. Henry Adams (*History,* 2:135) said that despite the cost of Louisiana, Gallatin projected retiring the debt in 1818. Balinky, *Albert Gallatin,* 39–48, reports the same projection.

11. McDonald, *American Presidency,* 257–258; Bray Hammond, *Banks and Politics in America from the Revolution to the Civil War* (Princeton, N.J., 1957), 209–226, 230–243; Balinky, *Albert Gallatin,* 100, 101, 171.

12. George Lee Haskins and Herbert A. Johnson, *Foundations of Power: John Marshall, 1801–1815,* The Oliver Wendell Holmes Devise History (New York, 1981), 126–181; Paul Douglas Newman, "Fries's Rebellion and American Political Culture, 1798–1800," *Pennsylvania Magazine of History and Biography* 119 (1995): 37–74.

13. Syrett, ed., *Papers of Hamilton,* 25:274 n; Kathryn Turner, "Federalist Pol-

icy and the Judiciary Act of 1801," *William and Mary Quarterly* 22 (1965): 3–32; McDonald, *American Presidency,* 268–269; Warren, *Supreme Court,* 1:192–193.

14. McDonald, *Presidency of Jefferson,* 35–36, 49–50; Kathryn Turner, "The Midnight Judges," *University of Pennsylvania Law Review* 109 (1960–1961): 494–523; Mayer, *Constitutional Thought of Jefferson,* 265–294.

15. Charles F. Hobson, *The Great Chief Justice: John Marshall and the Rule of Law* (Lawrence, Kans., 1996), 47–49, 50; Warren, *Supreme Court,* 186–208; Richard E. Ellis, *The Jeffersonian Crisis: Courts and Politics in the Young Republic* (New York, 1974), 36–52; Jerry W. Knudson, "The Jeffersonian Assault on the Federalist Judiciary, 1802–1805: Political Forces and Press Reaction," *American Journal of Legal History* 14 (1970): 55–75.

16. Warren, *Supreme Court,* 1:279; Adams, *History,* 1:274–298; Forrest McDonald, "The Political Thought of Gouverneur Morris," *Continuity* 22 (1998): 39–54; *Connecticut Courant,* February 22, 1802; *The Diary and Letters of Gouverneur Morris,* 2 vols., ed. Anne Cary Morris (New York, 1888), 1:411.

17. Adams, *History,* 1:298; Warren, *Supreme Court,* 1:222–224.

18. *Stuart* v. *Laird,* 1 Cranch 299 (1803); Warren, *Supreme Court,* 1:200–206; Malone, *Jefferson: First Term,* 117 ff., 145–146; Haskins and Johnson, *Foundations of Power,* 180–181, 209, 383–384.

19. *Marbury* v. *Madison,* 1 Cranch 137 (1803); Warren, *Supreme Court,* 1:231–268; Robert Lowry Clinton, *Marbury v. Madison and Judicial Review* (Lawrence, Kans., 1989); Haskins and Johnson, *Foundations of Power,* 182–204.

20. Hobson, *Great Chief Justice,* 51–58, 64–71; see also Herbert A. Johnson, *The Chief Justiceship of John Marshall, 1801–1835* (Columbia, S.C., 1997).

21. In 1792, Congress enacted a law requiring circuit judges to review and pass on the claims of certain invalid pensioners. Protesting that such activity was not a proper judicial function, the Supreme Court justices in their capacity as circuit judges refused. Warren, *Supreme Court,* 1:69–71.

22. McDonald, *Presidency of Jefferson,* 80; Lynn W. Turner, "The Impeachment of John Pickering," *American Historical Review* 54 (1949): 485–507; Haskins and Johnson, *Foundations of Power,* 211–215.

23. Warren, *Supreme Court,* 1:277; McDonald, *Presidency of Jefferson,* 80–82; McDonald, *American Presidency,* 270; William H. Rehnquist, *Grand Inquests: The Historic Impeachments of Justice Samuel Chase and President Andrew Johnson* (New York, 1992), 11–132; Bradford, *Against the Barbarians,* 100–113. Chase believed the charges of "partisanship" were unfair; he thought that his accusers were the partisans. For an understanding of loyal opposition

and partisanship, see Richard Hofstadter, *The Idea of a Party System: The Rise of Legitimate Opposition in the United States, 1780–1840* (Berkeley, Calif., 1969). For a detailed study of Chase's jurisprudence and his conflict with the Jeffersonians in Virginia, see Stephen B. Presser, *The Original Misunderstanding: The English, the Americans and the Dialectic of Federalist Jurisprudence* (Durham, N.C., 1991), 131–169.

24. Adams, *History,* 2:222; Warren, *Supreme Court,* 1:294; Haskins and Johnson, *Foundations of Power,* 211.

25. Adams, *History,* 2:220, 227; McDonald, *Presidency of Jefferson,* 91–94.

26. *Thomas Jefferson: Writings,* 1105; McDonald, *Presidency of Jefferson,* 64; Malone, *Jefferson: First Term,* 254 ff., quote at 256; Tucker and Hendrickson, *Empire of Liberty,* 88–93; Ammon, *James Monroe,* 203–224.

27. McDonald, *Presidency of Jefferson,* 70–71; Tucker and Hendrickson, *Empire of Liberty,* 94; Paine to Jefferson, September 23, 1803, in *The Complete Writings of Thomas Paine,* 2 vols., ed. Philip S. Foner (New York, 1945), 2:1447–1448; *Thomas Jefferson: Writings,* 1137–1141, 1142.

28. Gerald H. Clarfield, *Timothy Pickering and the American Republic* (Pittsburgh, 1980); for reaction to the purchase, see Henry Adams, ed., *Documents Relating to New England Federalism, 1800–1815* (Boston, 1877); David Hackett Fischer, *The Revolution of American Conservatism: The Federalist Party in the Era of Jeffersonian Democracy* (New York, 1965); Hervey Putnam Prentiss, *Timothy Pickering as the Leader of New England Federalism, 1800–1815* (New York, 1972).

29. As Pickering wrote to George Cabot on January 29, 1804, "The people of the East cannot reconcile their habits, views, and interests with those of the South and West" (Adams, *Documents Relating to New England Federalism,* 338).

30. Adams, *History,* 2:122.

31. *Salem (Mass.) Gazette,* November 15, 1803; Helen R. Pinkney, *Christopher Gore: Federalist of Massachusetts, 1758–1827* (Waltham, Mass., 1969), 100, 124; Prentiss, *Timothy Pickering,* 24–25.

32. Prentiss, *Timothy Pickering,* 25–32; Claude G. Bowers, *Jefferson in Power: The Death Struggle of the Federalists* (Boston, 1936), 243; Thomas J. DiLorenzo, "Yankee Confederates: New England Secession Movements Prior to the War between the States," in *Secession, State & Liberty,* ed. David Gordon (New Brunswick, N.J., 1998), 136–142.

33. In Maryland, Jefferson received nine of the eleven electoral votes. For Jefferson's perspective on the Burr trial, see the letter to William Branch Giles, April 20, 1807, in *Thomas Jefferson: Writings,* 1173–1176; for the lessons of

the conspiracy, see the Letter to Governor William C. C. Clairborne, February 3, 1807, ibid., 1172.

34. McDonald, *Presidency of Jefferson,* 143–144, 145, 147; Tucker and Hendrickson, *Empire of Liberty,* 204–213, 222–228; Dumas Malone, *Jefferson the President: Second Term, 1805–1809* (Boston, 1974), 469–490; Pinkney, *Christopher Gore,* 104–108.

35. Adams, *History,* 5:257; McDonald, *Presidency of Jefferson,* 148–150; Walter W. Jennings, *The American Embargo, 1807–1809* (Iowa City, Iowa, 1921); Louis M. Sears, *Jefferson and the Embargo* (Durham, N.C., 1927); Douglas Lamar Jones, " 'The Caprice of Juries': The Enforcement of the Jeffersonian Embargo in Massachusetts," *American Journal of Legal History* 24 (1980): 307–330.

36. McDonald, *Presidency of Jefferson,* 149; Levy, *Jefferson and Civil Liberties,* 122–123, 130–131; Irving Brant, *James Madison: Secretary of State, 1800–1809* (Indianapolis, 1953), 402–403; Malone, *Jefferson: Second Term,* 561–582.

37. Adams, *History,* 4:271.

38. Warren, *Supreme Court,* 1:363, 364, 365; James M. Banner, Jr., *To the Hartford Convention: The Federalists and the Origins of Party Politics in Massachusetts* (New York, 1970), 300–305; Arthur A. Ekirch, Jr., *The Decline of American Liberalism* (New York, 1969), 55–72; Pinkney, *Christopher Gore,* 110–112.

39. *Richmond Enquirer,* February 4 and March 24, 1809.

40. *United States* v. *Peters,* 5 Cranch 115 (1809); *Papers of John Marshall,* ed. Hobson, 7:190–196; Haskins and Johnson, *Foundations of Power,* 322–331; Hobson, *Great Chief Justice,* 9. The *Aurora,* April 11, 1803, warned, "The people ought ever to be aware that the grand object of modern Federalism is to lessen and encroach upon the authority of individual States, and that the movements of the Federal Courts having this tendency ought to be regarded with a very jealous eye."

41. Warren, *Supreme Court,* 1:376–387; Kilpatrick, *Sovereign States,* 102–118.

42. Adams, *History,* 4:418, 432–453, 5:14–20; Malone, *Jefferson: Second Term,* 653–655; Pinkney, *Christopher Gore,* 111–115.

43. Robert Allen Rutland, *The Presidency of James Madison* (Lawrence, Kans., 1990), 102. The vote in the House was on June 4; the vote in the Senate was on June 18.

44. Adams, *History,* 6:207, 400; Banner, *To The Hartford Convention,* 301; DiLorenzo, "Yankee Confederates," 144; Pinkney, *Christopher Gore,* 128–133, 136–137.

45. Adams, *History,* 6:405, 8:15–16; Donald R. Hickey, "American Trade Restrictions during the War of 1812," *Journal of American History* 68 (1981): 517–538.

46. Rakove, *James Madison,* 160–169; Banning, *Sacred Fire of Liberty,* 188, 230, 249, 386, 396–398; Lawrence Delbert Cress, *Citizens in Arms: The Army and Militia in American Society to the War of 1812* (Chapel Hill, N.C., 1982); J. C. A. Stagg, *Mr. Madison's War: Politics, Diplomacy, and Warfare in the Early Republic, 1783–1830* (Princeton, N.J., 1983); Donald R. Hickey, *The War of 1812: A Forgotten Conflict* (Urbana, Ill., 1989).

47. Adams, *History,* 7:262 ff., 367, 386–389.

48. Ibid., 8:17, 220–221; Hickey, *War of 1812,* 259–268; John K. Mahon, *The War of 1812* (Gainesville, Fla., 1972), 100–101, 219, 332.

49. Joseph R. Stromberg, "Republicanism, Federalism, and Secession in the South, 1790 to 1865," in Gordon, ed., *Secession, State and Liberty,* 105–106; Ekirch, *Decline of American Liberalism,* 65–69; Banner, *To The Hartford Convention,* 322 ff.; Pinkney, *Christopher Gore,* 134–135.

50. Robert V. Remini, *Daniel Webster: A Conservative in a Democratic Age* (New York, 1997), 88, 119. According to Carpenter (*South as Conscious Minority,* 211), Webster said in 1851 that southern secession would be warranted if the federal government failed to live up to its constitutional obligations regarding fugitive slaves.

51. Frank Maloy Anderson, "A Forgotten Phase of the New England Opposition to the War of 1812," *Proceedings of the Mississippi Valley Historical Association* 6 (1913): 176–188.

52. Ibid., 179; *Boston Gazette,* October 31, 1814.

4. An Era of Mixed Feelings, 1815–1828

1. Richardson, comp., *Messages and Papers,* 1:578.

2. Robert E. Shalhope, *John Taylor of Caroline: Pastoral Republican* (Columbia, S.C., 1980); Adam Tate, "John Taylor and the Formation of an American Ideology," *Continuity* 22 (1998): 55–76. The words *capitalist* and *capitalism* had only recently entered the language, and they were often employed in a derogatory way; the idea that money could be used to make money, without being mixed with land or labor, seemed unnatural and unsavory. John Taylor, *Arator,* ed. M. E. Bradford (Indianapolis, 1977), 87, 102, 108; McDonald, *Novus Ordo Seclorum,* 128–131; Forrest McDonald, "The Constitution and Hamiltonian Capitalism," in *How Capitalistic Is the Consti-*

tution? ed. Robert A. Goldwin and William A. Schambra (Washington, D.C., 1982), 49–71.

3. Richardson, comp., *Messages and Papers,* 1:562–568; Philip Coolidge Brooks, *Diplomacy and the Borderlands: The Adams-Onis Treaty of 1819* (Berkeley, Calif., 1939); George Dangerfield, *The Awakening of American Nationalism, 1815–1828* (New York, 1965), 46–51; Charles C. Griffin, *The United States and the Disruption of the Spanish Empire, 1810–1822* (New York, 1937). On the postwar navy, see Forrest McDonald, *The Boys Were Men: The American Navy in the Age of Fighting Sail* (New York, 1971), 142–151.

4. Richardson, comp., *Messages and Papers,* 1:567–568; Frank W. Taussig, *Tariff History of the United States* (New York, 1931), 18 ff.; McCoy, *Last of the Fathers,* 81; Rakove, *James Madison,* 171.

5. Shaw Livermore, Jr., *The Twilight of Federalism: The Disintegration of the Federalist Party, 1815–1830* (Princeton, N.J., 1962), 16; McDonald, "Political Thought of Gouverneur Morris," 51–52.

6. McCoy, *Last of the Fathers,* 94–95; Taussig, *Tariff History,* 17–20; Edward Stanwood, *American Tariff Controversies in the Nineteenth Century,* 2 vols. (Boston, 1903), 1:160–175.

7. *Abridgement of the Debates in Congress from 1789 to 1856,* from Gales and Seaton's Annals, 16 vols. (New York, 1857–1861), 5:477, 627 (March 14, April 3, 1816); Herman E. Krooss and Martin R. Blyn, *A History of Financial Intermediaries* (New York, 1971), 34, 41, 44, 45; Hammond, *Banks and Politics in America;* Merrill D. Peterson, *The Great Triumvirate: Webster, Clay, and Calhoun* (New York, 1987), 48–49, 66–67.

8. *The Works of John C. Calhoun,* 6 vols., ed. Richard K. Crallé (New York, 1851–1857), 2:186–196; Dangerfield, *Awakening of American Nationalism,* 18, 19; Peterson, *Great Triumvirate,* 79, 89–90.

9. Rosen, *American Compact,* 176; McCoy, *Last of the Fathers,* 92–99, 101–103, 104, 105, 116, 131, 152; Richardson, comp., *Messages and Papers,* 1:584–585.

10. Story, though a Republican Jefferson appointee, ruled as a Marshall Federalist; the best study of Story is James McClellan, *Joseph Story and the American Constitution* (Norman, Okla., 1971). For Story as a constitutional nationalist, see R. Kent Newmyer, *Supreme Court Justice Joseph Story: Statesman of the Old Republic* (Chapel Hill, N.C., 1985), 181–195. For the definitive study of the matter, see F. Thornton Miller, *Juries and Judges Versus the Law: Virginia's Provincial Legal Perspective, 1783–1828* (Charlottesville, Va., 1994). For a study of Roane, see Clyde C. Gelbach, "Spencer Roane of

Virginia, 1762–1822: A Judicial Advocate of State Rights" (Ph.D. diss., University of Pittsburgh, 1955).

11. *Fairfax's Devisee* v. *Hunter's Lessee,* 7 Cranch 602 (1813); *Papers of John Marshall,* ed. Hobson, 5:228–256; Newmyer, *Joseph Story,* 106, 107, 110, 113; F. Thornton Miller, "John Marshall Versus Spencer Roane: A Reevaluation of *Martin* v. *Hunter's Lessee,*" *Virginia Magazine of History and Biography* 96 (1988): 307–312.

12. Miller, *Juries and Judges;* Warren, *Supreme Court,* 1:447–448; Timothy S. Huebner, "The Consolidation of State Judicial Power: Spencer Roane, Virginia Legal Culture, and the Southern Legal Tradition," *Virginia Magazine of History and Biography* 102 (1994): 47–72.

13. *Martin* v. *Hunter's Lessee,* 1 Wheaton 304 (1816); Miller, *Juries and Judges,* 84–86, 90; Hobson, *Great Chief Justice,* 124–125, 130; *Papers of John Marshall,* ed. Hobson, 8:108–125; Newmyer, *Joseph Story,* 106–114.

14. Shalhope, *John Taylor,* 188–193, 197, 199; Eugene Tenbroeck Mudge, *The Social Philosophy of John Taylor of Caroline: A Study in Jeffersonian Democracy* (New York, 1939), 137–144; Miller, *Juries and Judges,* 135 n. 6; Harry Ammon, "The Richmond Junto, 1800–1824," *Virginia Magazine of History and Biography* 61 (1953): 407–409. Jefferson wrote to Spencer Roane on June 27, 1821, about Taylor's book that "It is the most logical retraction of our government to the original and true principles of the Constitution. . . . it contains the true political faith, to which every catholic republican should steadfastly hold" (Onuf, ed., *Thomas Jefferson,* 246). See also Jefferson to Giles, December 26, 1825, concerning the government's "usurpation of all the rights reserved to the States, and the consolidation in itself of all powers" (Onuf, ed., *Thomas Jefferson,* 253–254).

15. John Taylor, *Tyranny Unmasked,* ed. F. Thornton Miller (Indianapolis, 1992), 204; Shalhope, *John Taylor.*

16. *Cohens* v. *Virginia,* 6 Wheaton 264 (1821); W. Ray Luce, *Cohens v. Virginia (1821): The Supreme Court and State Rights, A Reevaluation of Influences and Impacts* (New York, 1990); G. Edward White, *The Marshall Court and Cultural Change, 1815–1835,* The Oliver Wendell Holmes Devise History (New York, 1991), 504–524; Hobson, *Great Chief Justice,* 127–130; Newmyer, *Joseph Story,* 113, 115, 160.

17. *Papers of John Marshall,* ed. Hobson, 9:167–168, 178–179. In his July 13 letter to Story, Marshall wrote, "In Virginia the tendency of things verges rapidly to the destruction of the government & the reestablishment of a league of Sove[reign] States. I look elsewhere for safety."

18. *Green* v. *Biddle*, 8 Wheaton 1 (1823); White, *Marshall Court and Cultural Change*, 567–568, 641–648; Newmyer, *Joseph Story*, 200, 204.

19. Henry Clay to Francis T. Brooke, August 28, 1823, in *The Papers of Henry Clay*, vol. 3, ed. James F. Hopkins (Lexington, Ky., 1963), 478–479; Peterson, *Great Triumvirate*, 67.

20. Warren, *Supreme Court*, 1:505–506; Thorpe, ed., *Federal and State Constitutions*, 2:983, 1069; Herman V. Ames, ed., *State Documents on Federal Relations: The States and the United States* (New York, 1970), 89–91.

21. *M'Culloch* v. *Maryland*, 4 Wheaton 316 (1819); Hobson, *Great Chief Justice*, 111–124; *Papers of John Marshall*, ed. Hobson, 8:254–279; White, *Marshall Court and Cultural Change*, 541–567; Raoul Berger, *Federalism: The Founders' Design* (Norman, Okla., 1987), 89–90, 94–95, 97, 147, 151, 183.

22. Fisher, *American Constitutional Law*, 403; Peterson, *Great Triumvirate*, 102.

23. Fisher, *American Constitutional Law*, 397–398; Hobson, *Great Chief Justice*, 111–113, 118–119.

24. Newmyer, *Joseph Story*, 200–207; Hobson, *Great Chief Justice*, 132.

25. *Osborn* v. *Bank of the United States*, 9 Wheaton 738 (1824); Hobson, *Great Chief Justice*, 133–139; White, *Marshall Court and Cultural Change*, 524–535.

26. Warren, *Supreme Court*, 1:643–645; Peter J. Coleman, *Debtors and Creditors in America: Insolvency, Imprisonment for Debt, and Bankruptcy, 1607–1900* (Madison, Wis., 1974); Dangerfield, *Awakening of American Nationalism*, 208–210.

27. Warren, *Supreme Court*, 1:646; Dangerfield, *Awakening of American Nationalism*, 208–210.

28. Warren, *Supreme Court*, 1:647–650.

29. Ibid., 650.

30. *Dartmouth College* v. *Woodward*, 4 Wheaton 518 (1819); Newmyer, *Joseph Story*, 127–137; Hobson, *Great Chief Justice*, 88–95; *Papers of John Marshall*, ed. Hobson, 8:217–239; White, *Marshall Court and Cultural Change*, 612–628; Daniel Webster, *The Works of Daniel Webster*, 6 vols. (Boston, 1851–1853), 5:462–501; Francis N. Stites, *Private Interest & Public Gain: The Dartmouth College Case, 1819* (Amherst, Mass., 1972); Bruce Campbell, "John Marshall, the Virginia Political Economy, and the *Dartmouth College* Decision," *American Journal of Legal History* 19 (1975): 40–65.

31. *Gibbons* v. *Ogden*, 9 Wheaton 1 (1824); Hobson, *Great Chief Justice*, 139–147; White, *Marshall Court and Cultural Change*, 468–469, 568–584;

Berger, *Federalism,* 60–61, 67, 77, 97, 99, 114, 122, 124, 126–127, 131, 133–137, 147; Webster, *Works,* 6:3–23; Maurice G. Baxter, *The Steamboat Monopoly: Gibbons v. Ogden, 1824* (New York, 1972).

32. Warren, *Supreme Court,* 597–627; Felix Frankfurter, *The Commerce Clause* (Chapel Hill, N.C., 1937), 27, says, "In *Gibbons* v. *Ogden* there begins to emerge a source of authority for state legislation characterized as designed 'to act directly on its system of police.'" He notes that despite counsel's urging that the Tenth Amendment be regarded "as a generating principle of restriction upon the affirmative *grants* of national power," the Court refused to regard the Tenth "as an active principal of limitation" (40).

33. Hobson, *Great Chief Justice,* 143–146. The Court found it necessary to retreat from its broad commerce clause ruling in *Brown* v. *Maryland,* 12 Wheaton 419 (1827), and *Willson* v. *Black Bird Creek Marsh Company,* 2 Peters 245 (1829); White, *Marshall Court and Cultural Change,* 582–583, 181–182, 583–585; Newmyer, *Joseph Story,* 204.

34. Warren, *Supreme Court,* 1:653; Richard Brookhiser, *Alexander Hamilton: American* (New York, 1999); McDonald, *Hamilton,* 4, 117–122, 231–236, 303–305.

35. George Rogers Taylor, *Transportation Revolution, 1815–1860,* vol. 4 of *The Economic History of the United States* (New York, 1951).

36. Robert Greenhalgh Albion, *The Rise of New York Port [1815–1860]* (New York, 1939); Ronald W. Filante, "A Note on the Economic Viability of the Erie Canal, 1825–1860," *Business History Review* 48 (1974): 95–102; Ralph D. Gray, *The National Waterway: A History of the Chesapeake and Delaware Canal, 1769–1965* (Urbana, Ill., 1967); Julius Rubin, *Canal or Railroad? Imitation and Innovation in the Response to the Erie Canal in Philadelphia, Baltimore, and Boston* (Philadelphia, 1961); Russel Blaine Nye, *The Cultural Life of the New Nation* (New York, 1960), 118–123.

37. Jefferson to Benjamin Austin, January 9, 1816, in Onuf, ed., *Thomas Jefferson,* 232–235; Hammond, *Banks and Politics in America,* 274; James Neal Primm, *Economic Policy in the Development of a Western State Missouri, 1820–1860* (Cambridge, Mass., 1954).

38. Thomas Payne Govan, *Nicholas Biddle: Nationalist and Public Banker, 1786–1844* (Chicago, 1959), 88–99; Gary Lawson Browne, *Baltimore in the Nation, 1789–1861* (Chapel Hill, N.C., 1980); Keith L. Bryant, Jr., and Henry C. Dethloff, *A History of American Business* (Englewood Cliffs, N.J., 1990), 56–72; Douglass C. North, *The Economic Growth of the United States, 1790–1860* (Englewood Cliffs, N.J., 1961).

39. Lewis Cecil Gray, *History of Agriculture in the Southern United States to*

1860, 2 vols. (Gloucester, Mass., 1958), 1:453–458, 462–464, 473–475, 2:656, 663–668, 932–936, 941–942; Dangerfield, *Awakening of American Nationalism*, 104–106.

40. Caroline F. Ware, *The Early New England Cotton Manufacture* (Boston, 1931); Barbara M. Tucker, *Samuel Slater and the Origins of the American Textile Industry, 1790–1862* (Ithaca, N.Y., 1984); Robert K. Lamb, "The Entrepreneur and the Community," in *Men in Business: Essays on the Historical Role of the Entrepreneur*, ed. William Miller (Cambridge, Mass., 1952), 106–107; Henry A. Miles, *Lowell: As It Was, and As It Is* (1972; repr., Lowell, Mass., 1845), 69–70, 101, 112–134.

41. Frank Luther Mott, *American Journalism: A History of Newspapers in the United States through 260 Years: 1690 to 1950* (New York, 1950), 202.

42. Chilton Williamson, *American Suffrage from Property to Democracy, 1760–1860* (Princeton, N.J., 1960); Edward Pessen, *Jacksonian America: Society, Personality, and Politics* (Homewood, Ill., 1969), 156–162, 166–169.

43. Jefferson to John Taylor, May 28, 1816, in *Thomas Jefferson: Writings*, 1393; Dangerfield, *Awakening of American Nationalism*, 102; Charles R. Sydnor, *The Development of Southern Sectionalism* (Baton Rouge, La., 1948), ch. 2.

44. Thorpe, ed., *Federal and State Constitutions*, 1:544–545, 5:2639–2651, 3:1911–1913, 7:3819–3828; Pessen, *Jacksonian America*, 159–165; William W. Freehling, *The Road to Disunion: Secessionists at Bay, 1776–1854* (New York, 1990), 162–177.

45. Francis S. Philbrick, *The Rise of the West, 1754–1830* (New York, 1965), 331.

46. Richardson, comp., *Messages and Papers*, 2:144–183; Dangerfield, *Awakening of American Nationalism*, 200; Peterson, *Great Triumvirate*, 78–79, 89–90; Archer Butler Hulbert, *The Old National Road: A Chapter of American Expansion* (Columbus, Ohio, 1901); Philip D. Jordan, *The National Road* (Indianapolis, 1948); *United States Statutes at Large* 3 (1846): 206, 426.

47. Govan, *Nicholas Biddle*, 101–103.

48. Ibid., 102; Philbrick, *Rise of the West*, 331–334.

49. First Message to Congress, 1825, in Richardson comp., *Messages and Papers*, 2:296–297.

50. Ames, ed., *State Documents on Federal Relations*, 136–137.

51. Ibid., 138, 139–140, 148; Kevin R. Gutzman, "Preserving the Patrimony: William Branch Giles and Virginia versus the Federal Tariff," *Virginia Magazine of History and Biography* 104 (1996): 341–372; Giles thought that the states were being "stripped of every atom of sovereignty" (360).

52. It is to be observed that each of the powers enumerated in article 1, section 8, begins with the word "To," capitalized, but that in the introduction of the common defense and general welfare clause, the introductory word is "to" in lower case, indicating that it was not an additional power but a qualifier.

53. Govan, *Nicholas Biddle*, 70; Taussig, *Tariff History;* Dangerfield, *Awakening of American Nationalism*, 13–15, 73, 155, 204–207, 211; *American State Papers: Finance* 3:15.

54. Dangerfield, *Awakening of American Nationalism*, 279–283, 299–300; Taussig, *Tariff History*, 44, 90–91, 93, 100; Robert V. Remini, "Martin Van Buren and the Tariff of Abominations," *American Historical Review* 63 (1958): 903–917; Robert V. Remini, *Martin Van Buren and the Making of the Democratic Party* (New York, 1959), ch. 12; Peterson, *Great Triumvirate*, 159–161; Stanwood, *American Tariff Controversies*, 1:270–289.

55. Dangerfield, *Awakening of American Nationalism*, ch. 12; Livermore, *Twilight of Federalism*, 162–164; Robert V. Remini, *The Election of Andrew Jackson* (Philadelphia, 1963); Pessen, *Jacksonian America*, 173–175, 212; Michael Wallace, "Changing Concepts of Party in the United States: New York, 1815–1828," in *After the Constitution: Party Conflict in the New Republic,* ed. Lance Banning (Belmont, Calif., 1989), 455–459.

5. States' Rights Triumphant

1. Richardson, comp., *Messages and Papers,* 2:436–438, 442–462; Francis Newton Thorpe, ed., *The Statesmanship of Andrew Jackson* (New York, 1909), 35–65.

2. Richardson, comp., *Messages and Papers,* 2:462; Donald B. Cole, *The Presidency of Andrew Jackson* (Lawrence, Kans., 1993), 55–57; Peter Temin, *The Jacksonian Economy* (New York, 1969), 28–58.

3. Ulrich Bonnell Phillips, *Georgia and State Rights: A Study of the Political History of Georgia from the Revolution to the Civil War, with Particular Regard to Federal Relations* (Washington, D.C., 1902).

4. Ibid., 60–64; William G. McLoughlin, "Georgia's Role in Instigating Compulsory Indian Removal," *Georgia Historical Quarterly* 70 (1986): 605–632; Michael D. Green, *The Politics of Indian Removal: Creek Government and Society in Crisis* (Lincoln, Nebr., 1982).

5. Phillips, *Georgia and State Rights,* 72; William G. McLoughlin, *Cherokees and Missionaries, 1789–1839* (New Haven, Conn., 1984); David Williams, "The North Georgia Gold Rush" (Ph.D. diss., Auburn University, 1988).

6. Warren, *Supreme Court*, 1:731; Mary Elizabeth Young, *Redskins, Ruffleshirts, and Rednecks: Indian Allotments in Alabama and Mississippi, 1830–1860* (Norman, Okla., 1961), 9–10; Robert V. Remini, *Andrew Jackson and the Course of American Freedom, 1822–1832* (New York, 1981), 258; Peterson, *Great Triumvirate*, 90–92; Anthony F. C. Wallace, *The Long, Bitter Trail: Andrew Jackson and the Indians* (New York, 1993), 50–72.

7. Remini, *Andrew Jackson, 1822–1832*, 260, 261.

8. Young, *Redskins, Ruffleshirts, and Rednecks*, 17, 48; Warren, *Supreme Court*, 1:731.

9. Warren, *Supreme Court*, 1:731 n, 732; Jill Norgren, "Lawyers and the Legal Business of the Cherokee Republic in the Courts of the United States, 1829–1835," *Law and History Review* 10 (1992): 253–314.

10. Phillips, *Georgia and State Rights*, 75–76; Warren, *Supreme Court*, 1:733–734.

11. John Spencer Bassett, ed., *Correspondence of Andrew Jackson*, vol. 4, *1829–1832* (Washington, D.C., 1929), 219–220; *United States Telegraph*, January 3 and 7, 1831; Warren, *Supreme Court*, 1:736–742.

12. *Cherokee Nation v. Georgia*, 5 Peters 1 (1831); Joseph Burke, "The Cherokee Cases: A Study in Law, Politics, and Morality," *Stanford Law Review* 21 (1969): 500–531; Robert V. Remini, "The Jackson Era," in *The Constitution and the American Presidency*, ed. Martin L. Fausold and Alan Shank (Albany, N.Y., 1991), 39.

13. *Worcester v. Georgia*, 6 Peters 515 (1832); Remini, *Andrew Jackson, 1822–1832*, 276; Johnson, *Chief Justiceship of Marshall*, 82; White, *Marshall Court and Cultural Change*, 730–740.

14. Remini, *Andrew Jackson, 1822–1832*, 376; Warren, *Supreme Court*, 1:753–759; Phillips, *Georgia and State Rights*, 78–83. Jackson wrote, "The decision of the supreme court has fell still born, and they find that it cannot coerce Georgia to yield to its mandate" (Remini, "Jackson Era," 40). See also Edwin A. Miles, "After John Marshall's Decision: *Worcester v. Georgia* and the Nullification Crisis," *Journal of Southern History* 39 (1973): 519–544.

15. Phillips, *Georgia and State Rights*, 83–84.

16. Charles M. Wiltse, *John C. Calhoun: Nationalist, 1782–1828* (Indianapolis, 1944), 372–381; Bureau of Census, *Historical Statistics*, 120, 124. Robert Barnwell Rhett's name was orginally Robert Barnwell Smith. On the nullification controversy in general, see Richard E. Ellis, *The Union at Risk: Jacksonian Democracy, States' Rights, and the Nullification Crisis* (New York, 1987), and William H. Freehling, *Prelude to Civil War: The Nullification Crisis in South Carolina, 1816–1836* (New York, 1966). Freehling's contention

that fears concerning slavery underlay the nullificationists' position has been challenged, I believe successfully, by David Schroeder, "Nullification in South Carolina: A Revisitation" (Ph.D. diss., University of Alabama, 1999).

17. Wiltse, *Calhoun: Nationalist,* 379–381, 389–390; Freehling, *Road to Disunion,* 1:253–270.

18. Clyde N. Wilson and W. Edwin Hamphill, eds., *The Papers of John C. Calhoun,* vol. 10, *1825–1829* (Columbia, S.C., 1977), 445–469, quote at 456; David F. Ericson, *The Shaping of American Liberalism: The Debates over Ratification, Nullification and Slavery* (Chicago, 1993), 76–78.

19. Calhoun to Bolling Hall, February 13, 1832: "We are certainly more United against the Tariff, than we ever have been; and, I think, better disposed to enhance the old Republican doctrines of 98, which can save the Constitution" (Clyde N. Wilson, ed., *The Papers of John C. Calhoun,* vol. 11, *1829–1832* [Columbia, S.C., 1978], 553). Calhoun "always considered himself to be, a Jeffersonian Republican" (Clyde N. Wilson, ed., *The Essential Calhoun* [New Brunswick, N.J., 1992], xix). See also Major L. Wilson, " 'Liberty and Union': An Analysis of Three Concepts Involved in the Nullification Controversy," *Journal of Southern History* 33 (1967): 331–335.

20. John C. Van Deusen, *Economic Bases of Disunion in South Carolina* (New York, 1928); Freehling, *Prelude to Civil War,* 49–52, 85–86, 257–259; Peterson, *Great Triumvirate,* 169–173; Raynor G. Wellington, *The Political and Sectional Influence of the Public Lands* (n.p., 1914).

21. Remini, *Daniel Webster,* 289–304; Charles M. Wiltse, *John C. Calhoun: Nullifier, 1829–1839* (Indianapolis, 1949), 54–66, quote at 62; Peterson, *Great Triumvirate,* 170–180.

22. John F. Marszalek, *The Petticoat Affair: Manners, Sex, and Mutiny in Andrew Jackson's White House* (New York, 1998), passim, quote at 102; Wiltse, *Calhoun: Nullifier,* 26–38, 76–85, quote at 83; Jackson to Mrs. Andrew J. Donelson, November 28, 1830, in Bassett, ed., *Correspondence of Andrew Jackson, 1829–1832,* 207–209; Peterson, *Great Triumvirate,* 183–190.

23. Wilson, ed., *Papers of Calhoun, 1829–1832,* 417, 418–419. For an analysis of "concurrent majority" doctrine, see Calhoun to Governor James Hamilton, Jr., August 28, 1832, ibid., 640–648; this long letter was further development of Calhoun's theory of nullification. See also Ericson, *Shaping of American Liberalism,* 78–79, 81–89; Peterson, *Great Triumvirate,* 190–194; Kilpatrick, *Sovereign States,* 186–199; Lacy K. Ford, Jr., "Inventing the Concurrent Majority: Madison, Calhoun, and the Problem of Majoritarianism in American Political Thought," *Journal of Southern History* 60 (1994): 19–58.

24. Wilson, ed., *Papers of Calhoun, 1829–1832,* xxxiii–xxxix.

25. Wiltse, *Calhoun: Nullifier,* 150; Commager, ed., *Documents,* 1:261–262.

26. Jackson to Joel R. Poinsett, December 9, 1832; to Martin Van Buren, December 15, 1832; and to Secretary of War Lewis Cass, December 17, 1832, in Bassett, ed., *Correspondence of Andrew Jackson, 1829–1832,* 498, 500, 502; Wiltse, *Calhoun: Nullifier,* 171–172; Commager, ed., *Documents,* 1:262–268.

27. Wiltse, *Calhoun: Nullifier,* 179–194; Commager, ed., *Documents,* 1:268–269; Freehling, *Road to Disunion,* 1:271–286; Claude Bowers, *The Party Battles of the Jackson Period* (New York, 1922), ch. 10; Lawrence F. Kohl, *The Politics of Individualism: Parties and the American Character in the Jacksonian Era* (New York, 1989).

28. Peterson, *Great Triumvirate,* 217–233; David F. Ericson, "The Nullification Crisis, American Republicanism, and the Force Bill Debate," *Journal of Southern History* 61 (1995): 693–724.

29. Young, *Redskins, Ruffleshirts, and Rednecks,* 76–77 and ch. 4.

30. Remini, *Andrew Jackson, 1822–1832,* 369; Richardson, comp., *Messages and Papers,* 2:1153.

31. Jackson's veto was May 27, 1830; Commager, ed., *Documents,* 1:253–254; Remini, *Andrew Jackson, 1822–1832,* 251–256, quote at 252. Before Jackson, the veto had been used nine times; he expanded the veto power by wielding it for a variety of purposes, not solely constitutional. Remini, *"Jackson Era,"* 32–33; Carlton Jackson, *Presidential Vetoes, 1792–1940* (Athens, Ga., 1967), 15–27; Bowers, *Party Battles of the Jackson Period,* 171, 175–176; Edward S. Corwin, *The President, 1789–1957* (New York, 1957), 23.

32. Govan, *Nicholas Biddle,* 169–200; Thomas P. Govan, "Fundamental Issues of the Bank War," *Pennsylvania Magazine of History* 82 (1958): 305–315; Reginald Charles McGrane, *The Panic of 1837: Some Financial Problems of the Jacksonian Era* (Chicago, 1924), 70–90.

33. Richardson, comp., *Messages and Papers,* 2:576 ff., 1139–1154; Commager, ed., *Documents,* 1:272, 274. For a defense of Jackson's veto and a contrary perspective of his attitude toward the Bank, see Edwin J. Perkins, "Lost Opportunities for Compromise in the Bank War: A Reassessment of Jackson's Veto Message," *Business History Review* 61 (1987): 531–550.

34. Govan, *Nicholas Biddle,* 207–228, quote at 213; McDonald, *American Presidency,* 318; Robert V. Remini, *Andrew Jackson and the Bank War: A Study in the Growth of Presidential Power* (New York, 1967), 63, 72, 82, 118–119.

35. Richardson, comp., *Messages and Papers,* 3:5 ff.; Govan, *Nicholas Biddle,* 207–228; Hammond, *Banks and Politics in America;* James Roger Sharp, "Andrew Jackson and the Limits of Presidential Power," *Congressional Studies* 7 (1980): 63–80; Carl Brent Swisher, *Roger B. Taney* (New York, 1935), 232.

36. Charles W. Smith, *Roger B. Taney: Jacksonian Jurist* (Chapel Hill, N.C., 1936); Kenneth Bernard Umbreit, *Our Eleven Chief Justices* (New York, 1938), 221–226.

37. William MacDonald, *Jacksonian Democracy, 1829–1837* (New York, 1906), chs. 13 and 16; Commager, ed., *Documents,* 1:283–284; James Roger Sharp, *The Jacksonians* versus *the Banks: Politics in the States after the Panic of 1837* (New York, 1970); Peterson, *Great Triumvirate,* 265, 274; John Bach McMaster, *History of the People of the United States,* vol. 6 (New York, 1885), 389–415; Temin, *Jacksonian Economy,* 113–136; McGrane, *Panic of 1837,* 91–144.

38. Hobson, *Great Chief Justice,* 11–12; Warren, *Supreme Court,* 1:652–685, 721–723, 727–728, 742–743; Richard P. Longaker, "Andrew Jackson and the Judiciary," *Political Science Quarterly* 71 (1956): 341–364; Irving Dillard, "Gabriel Duvall," in *The Justices of the United States Supreme Court, 1789–1969, Their Lives and Major Opinions,* 5 vols., ed. Leon Friedman and Fred L. Israel (New York, 1969–1978), 1:419–429.

39. *Willson* v. *Black Bird Creek Marsh Company,* 2 Peters 245 (1829); Johnson, *Chief Justiceship of Marshall,* 171; Warren, *Supreme Court,* 1:610, 708–709; White, *Marshall Court and Cultural Change,* 181–182, 583–585; Hobson, *Great Chief Justice,* 147–149.

40. *Brown* v. *Maryland,* 12 Wheaton 419 (1827); Warren, *Supreme Court,* 1:695 n; Johnson, *Chief Justiceship of Marshall,* 169–170; White, *Marshall Court and Cultural Change,* 582–583; Berger, *Federalism,* 63, 136.

41. *Fairfax's Devisee* v. *Hunter's Lessee,* 7 Cranch 602 (1813); *New York* v. *Miln,* 8 Peters 120 (1834), 11 Peters 102 (1837); Umbreit, *Our Eleven Chief Justices,* 232–233; Berger, *Federalism,* 70 n, 98 n, 141.

42. *Sturges* v. *Crowninshield,* 4 Wheaton 122 (1819); *Ogden* v. *Saunders,* 12 Wheaton 213 (1827); Johnson, *Chief Justiceship of Marshall,* 210; *Papers of John Marshall,* ed. Hobson, 8:239–253; White, *Marshall Court and Cultural Change,* 633–641, 648–657, 666–668; Albert P. Blaustein and Roy M. Mersky, "Bushrod Washington," in Friedman and Israel, eds., *Justices of the United States Supreme Court,* 1:243–257, 258–266; Hobson, *Great Chief Justice,* 95–100; Coleman, *Debtors and Creditors,* 6–15, 31–36; Webster, *Works,* 6:24–40; Newmyer, *Joseph Story,* 126, 127, 191, 198, 203, 209.

43. *Providence Bank* v. *Billings,* 4 Peters 514 (1830); White, *Marshall Court and Cultural Change,* 661–662, 667; Newmyer, *Joseph Story,* 205, 210, 225.

44. *Baron* v. *Baltimore,* 7 Peters 243 (1833); White, *Marshall Court and Cultural Change,* 585, 589–593; Hobson, *Great Chief Justice,* 107–110.

45. Warren, *Supreme Court,* 1:704–707, 711–712, 795–796.

46. Carl B. Swisher, *The Taney Period, 1836–64,* The Oliver Wendell Holmes Devise History (New York, 1974), 15–38; Umbreit, *Our Eleven Chief Justices,* 225–228.

47. Warren, *Supreme Court,* 2:7–19, quotes at 19 and 10; Frank Otto Gatell, "Philip Barbour," in Friedman and Israel, eds., *Justices of the United States Supreme Court,* 1:717–727.

48. *United States* v. *Peters,* 5 Cranch 115 (1809); *Hagan* v. *Lucas,* 10 Peters 400 (1836); Warren, *Supreme Court,* 2:19.

6. GOVERNMENT IN LIMBO, 1837–1845

1. Major L. Wilson, *The Presidency of Martin Van Buren* (Lawrence, Kans., 1984), 73–74.

2. Ibid., 67–68, 73, 83, 137.

3. Ibid., 73, 75–76, 102–103, 123, 126–127; McGrane, *Panic of 1837,* 209–236.

4. Norma Lois Peterson, *The Presidencies of William Henry Harrison & John Tyler* (Lawrence, Kans., 1989), 34; Robert Seager II, *and Tyler too: A Biography of John & Julia Gardiner Tyler* (New York, 1963); Peterson, *Great Triumvirate,* 297–301.

5. Peterson, *Presidencies of Harrison and Tyler,* 19–20; Seager, *and Tyler too,* 73–101; Peterson, *Great Triumvirate,* 301–303, 308, 312–313.

6. Peterson, *Presidencies of Harrison and Tyler,* 60–71; Peterson, *Great Triumvirate,* 304–308.

7. Peterson, *Presidencies of Harrison and Tyler,* 77–93; Peterson, *Great Triumvirate,* 310–313; Robert J. Morgan, *A Whig Embattled: The Presidency under John Tyler* (Lincoln, Nebr., 1954), 43–45.

8. Michael F. Holt, *The Rise and Fall of the American Whig Party: Jacksonian Politics and the Onset of the Civil War* (New York, 1999), 122–161; Peterson, *Presidencies of Harrison and Tyler,* 169–170 and passim; Peterson, *Great Triumvirate,* 317–334. During this period, the federal government did make some grants of land from the public domain to the states for internal improvements.

9. Stanley I. Kutler, *Privilege and Creative Destruction: The Charles River Bridge Case* (Baltimore, 1990); Swisher, *Roger B. Taney;* Umbreit, *Our Eleven Chief Justices;* Warren, *Supreme Court,* vol. 2, chs. 22–24; Newmyer, *Joseph Story,* 310–316; Frank Otto Gatell, "Roger Taney," in Friedman and Israel, eds., *Justices of the United States Supreme Court,* 1:635–655.

10. Kutler, *Privilege and Creative Destruction*, 60–61, 90, 93, 161.

11. *Proprietors of the Charles River Bridge* v. *Proprietors of the Warren Bridge*, 11 Peters 420 (1837); Kutler, *Privilege and Creative Destruction*, 1–2; Swisher, *Taney Period*, 74–98.

12. Kutler, *Privilege and Creative Destruction*, 54–73; Warren, *Supreme Court*, 1:746.

13. Kutler, *Privilege and Creative Destruction*, 90; Warren, *Supreme Court*, 2:25; R. Kent Newmyer, "Justice Joseph Story, the Charles River Bridge Case, and the Crisis of Republicanism," *American Journal of Legal History* 17 (1973): 232–245; James McClellan, "Comments on Kent Newmyer's Paper, 'Justice Joseph Story, the Charles River Bridge Case, and the Crisis of Republicanism,'" *American Journal of Legal History* 17 (1973): 271–273.

14. *Mayor of the City of New York* v. *Miln*, 11 Peters 102 (1837); Kutler, *Privilege and Creative Destruction*, 125; Swisher, *Taney Period*, 360–365, 368, 370; Newmyer, *Joseph Story*, 221–223, 234; Friedmen and Israel, eds., *Justices of the United States Supreme Court*, 1:728–734.

15. *Briscoe* v. *Bank of Kentucky*, 11 Peters 257 (1837), and *Craig* v. *Missouri*, 4 Peters 410 (1830); White, *Marshall Court and Cultural Change*, 585–588; Swisher, *Taney Period*, 94, 105–109; Newmyer, *Joseph Story*, 210, 218, 219, 221–222.

16. Swisher, *Taney Period*, 106, 108; Kutler, *Privilege and Creative Destruction*, 126–127.

17. *Bank of Augusta* v. *Earle*, 13 Peters 519 (1839); Warren, *Supreme Court*, 2:50–61; Swisher, *Taney Period*, 115–121, 464, 472; Friedman and Israel, eds., *Justices of the United States Supreme Court*, 1:705–713; Tony Freyer and Timothy Dixon, *Democracy and Judicial Independence: A History of the Federal Courts of Alabama, 1820–1994* (New York, 1995), 42–44, 53; Tony Freyer, *Forums of Order: The Federal Courts and Business in American History* (Greenwich, Conn., 1979), 28–30.

18. Morton J. Horwitz, *The Transformation of American Law, 1780–1860* (Cambridge, Mass., 1977), 1–30, 141 ff., 160–181.

19. Louis Hartz, *Economic Policy and Democratic Thought: Pennsylvania, 1776–1860* (Cambridge, Mass., 1948), 122, 200, 204–205, 206–207; Milton Sydney Heath, *Constructive Liberalism: The Role of the State in Economic Development in Georgia to 1860* (Cambridge, Mass., 1954); Stephen Salsbury, *The State, the Investor, and the Railroad: The Boston & Albany, 1825–1867* (New York, 1967); Carter Goodrich, *Governmental Promotion of American Canals and Railroads, 1800–1890* (New York, 1960); Ronald E. Shaw, *Erie*

Water West: A History of the Erie Canal, 1792–1854 (Lexington, Ky., 1990). 20. Holt, *Rise and Fall of the Whig Party*, 53–54; Tony A. Freyer, *Producers versus Capitalists: Constitutional Conflict in Antebellum America* (Charlottesville, Va., 1994), 3–8 and passim; Thorpe, ed., *Federal and State Constitutions*, 5:3107; J. Willard Hurst, *Legitimacy of the Business Corporation in the Law of the United States, 1780–1970* (Charlottesville, Va., 1970).

21. Hartz, *Economic Policy*, 40–41; Thorpe, ed., *Federal and State Constitutions*, Delaware (1831), 1:586; Louisiana (1845), 3:1405; Arkansas (1846), 1:287; Maine (1819), 3:1656; Iowa (1846), 2:1132; Tony A. Freyer, "Law and the Antebellum Southern Economy: An Interpretation," in *Ambivalent Legacy: A Legal History of the South*, ed. David J. Bodenheimer and James W. Ely, Jr. (Jackson, Miss., 1984).

22. Hartz, *Economic Policy*, 38, 57–60; Thorpe, ed., *Federal and State Constitutions*, 2:1006 (1818). See, for example, in Thorpe: Maryland (1776 and 1851), 3:1690, 1716; North Carolina (1776), 5:2788; Massachusetts (1780), 3:1890; Tennessee (1796 and 1834), 6:3423, 3428; Indiana (1851), 2:1074.

23. Holt, *Rise and Fall of the Whig Party*, 77, 78; Forrest McDonald, *The Phaeton Ride: The Crisis of American Success* (Garden City, N.Y., 1974), 23; Hartz, *Economic Policy*, 49–57, 316–320; Thorpe, ed., *Federal and State Constitutions*, Illinois (1848), 2:1006; Indiana (1851), 2:1088.

24. McDonald, *Phaeton Ride*, 21–22; Thorpe, ed., *Federal and State Constitutions*, Alabama (1819), 1:111; Mississippi (1817), 4:2044; Missouri (1820), 4:2161.

25. Glover Moore, *The Missouri Controversy, 1819–1821* (Lexington, Ky., 1953); David C. Frederick, "John Quincy Adams, Slavery, and the Disappearance of the Right of Petition," *Law and History Review* 9 (1991): 113–115. On the early antislavery movement, see Gilbert H. Barnes, *The Anti-Slavery Impulse, 1830–1844* (New York, 1933); John L. Thomas, *The Liberator: William Lloyd Garrison, A Biography* (Boston, 1963); Dwight L. Dumond, *Antislavery: The Crusade for Freedom in America* (Ann Arbor, Mich., 1961); Louis Filler, *The Crusade against Slavery: Friends, Foes, and Reforms, 1820–1860* (Algonac, Mich., 1986).

26. Swisher, *Taney Period*, 158–168; Peterson, *Great Triumvirate*, 257–259, 261; Leonard D. White, *The Jacksonians: A Study in Administrative History* (New York, 1954), 251–283; *The Autobiography of Amos Kendall*, ed. William Stickney (Boston, 1872), 333–366.

27. Thorpe, ed., *Federal and State Constitutions*, 2:1009, 1089; the new gag rule was adopted on December 21, 1837; Paul Finkelman, *An Imperfect Union:*

Slavery, Federalism, and Comity (Chapel Hill, N.C., 1981), 146–155; *Abridgement of the Debates in Congress,* 13:567; Freehling, *Road to Disunion,* 1:308–345.

28. Crallé, ed., *Works of Calhoun,* 3:140–202; Holt, *Rise and Fall of the Whig Party,* 95–96; Wilson, *Presidency of Van Buren,* 103; Peterson, *Great Triumvirate,* 274–276.

29. Wilson, *Presidency of Van Buren,* 103–104.

30. Russell B. Nye, *Fettered Freedoms: Civil Liberties and the Slavery Controversy* (East Lansing, Mich., 1949); Warren, *Supreme Court,* 2:87 n. 3; Thomas D. Morris, *Free Men All: The Personal Liberty Laws of the North, 1780–1861* (Baltimore, 1974).

31. *Prigg* v. *Pennsylvania,* 16 Peters 539 (1842); R. Kent Newmyer, *Supreme Court Justice Story* (Chapel Hill, N.C., 1985), 370–374; Paul Finkelman, "*Prigg* v. *Pennsylvania* and Northern State Courts: Anti-Slavery Use of a Pro-Slavery Decision," *Civil War History* 25 (1979): 5–35; Paul Finkelman, "Story Telling on the Supreme Court: *Prigg* v. *Pennsylvania* and Justice Joseph Story's Judicial Nationalism," in *1994: The Supreme Court Review,* ed. Dennis J. Hutchinson, David A. Strauss, and Geoffrey R. Stone (Chicago, 1995), 247–294; Richard S. Arnold, "The Power of State Courts to Enjoin Federal Officers," *Yale Law Journal* 73 (1964): 1385–1406.

32. Warren, *Supreme Court,* 2:84–85, 87; Swisher, *Taney Period,* 535–547; Peterson, *Great Triumvirate,* 458.

33. Frederick Merk, *Slavery and the Annexation of Texas* (New York, 1972); Holt, *Rise and Fall of the Whig Party,* 178–181, 224–228; Michael A. Morrison, "Martin Van Buren, The Democracy, and the Partisan Politics of Texas Annexation," *Journal of Southern History* 61 (1995): 695–724.

34. Peterson, *Presidencies of Harrison and Tyler,* 228, 251–252, 254–258; Peterson, *Great Triumvirate,* 344–348; Calhoun letter to Sir Richard Pakenham, in Crallé, ed., *Works of Calhoun,* 5:333–347; Freehling, *Road to Disunion,* 388–439.

35. Peterson, *Presidencies of Harrison and Tyler,* 259.

36. Van Deusen, *Economic Bases of Disunion,* 83–90; Peterson, *Great Triumvirate,* 348–349; Chauncey S. Boucher, "The Annexation of Texas and the Bluffton Movement in South Carolina," *Mississippi Valley Historical Review* 6 (1919): 3–33; Laura A. White, *Robert Barnwell Rhett: Father of Secession* (New York, 1931), 68–84; Eric H. Walther, *The Fire-Eaters* (Baton Rouge, La., 1992), 121–159.

37. *Bronson* v. *Kinzie,* 1 Howard 311 (1843); *McCracken* v. *Hayward,* 2

Howard 608 (1844); Newmyer, *Joseph Story,* 308, 309; Swisher, *Taney Period,* 137, 148–151.

38. George M. Dennison, *The Dorr War: Republicanism on Trial, 1831–1861* (Lexington, Ky., 1976), 25; Newmyer, *Joseph Story,* 358–365.

39. Dennison, *Dorr War,* 13–14.

40. Ibid., 27; Swisher, *Taney Period,* 515–518; C. Peter Magrath, "Optimistic Democrat: Thomas W. Dorr and the Case of *Luther* v. *Borden,*" *Rhode Island History* 29 (1970): 94–112.

41. Dennison, *Dorr War,* 14–26; Arthur May Mowry, "Tammany Hall and the Door Rebellion," *American Historical Review* 3 (1898): 292; Arthur M. Mowry, *The Dorr War, or the Constitutional Struggle in Rhode Island* (Providence, 1901).

42. Dennison, *Dorr War,* 32–33.

43. Ibid., 34–37, chs. 2–4.

44. Ibid., 77–83, 65–66, 71.

45. Peterson, *Presidencies of Harrison and Tyler,* 110–111; Dennison, *Dorr War,* 72, 216 n. 29; John S. Schuchman, "The Political Background of the Political Question Doctrine: The Judges and the Dorr War," *American Journal of Legal History* 16 (1972): 111–125.

46. *Luther* v. *Borden,* 7 Howard 1 (1849); Swisher, *Taney Period,* 522–527, 851–852; Peterson, *Great Triumvirate,* 338, 396; Dennison, *Dorr War,* ch. 8 and epilogue; Notes, "Political Rights as Political Questions: The Paradox of *Luther* v. *Borden,*" *Harvard Law Review* 100 (1987): 1125–1145.

7. A CHANGED DYNAMIC, 1845–1852

1. *Swift* v. *Tyson,* 16 Peters 1 (1842); Tony Freyer, *Harmony and Dissonance: The* Swift *and* Erie *Cases in American Federalism* (New York, 1981); Charles A. Heckman, "The Relationship of *Swift* v. *Tyson* to the Status of Commercial Law in the Nineteenth Century and the Federal System," *American Journal of Legal History* 17 (1973): 246–255; Newmyer, *Joseph Story,* 334–343; William M. Wiecek, *Liberty under Law: The Supreme Court in American Life* (Baltimore, 1988), 56–81.

2. *Passenger Cases,* 7 Howard 283 (1849); *Propeller Genesee Chief* v. *Fitzhugh,* 12 Howard 443 (1851); Swisher, *Taney Period,* 382–391, 444–445, 446, 449.

3. *License Cases,* 5 Howard 504 (1847); Warren, *Supreme Court,* 2:152;

Swisher, *Taney Period,* 370–377; Friedman and Israel, eds., *Justices of the United States Supreme Court,* 1:696–705, 750–759.

4. *Cooley* v. *Board of Wardens of the Port of Philadelphia,* 12 Howard 299 (1852); Swisher, *Taney Period,* 404–406, 407, 411, 422.

5. *Rhode Island* v. *Massachusetts,* 4 Howard 591 (1846), 12 Peters 657 (1838), 13 Peters 23 (1839), 14 Peters 210 (1840), 15 Peters 233 (1841); Warren, *Supreme Court,* 2:159 n, 76, 148–149; McMaster, *History of the People,* 6:243, 249, 303, 307; Swisher, *Taney Period,* 320, 513, 514–515.

6. *Missouri* v. *Iowa,* 7 Howard 660 (1849); Warren, *Supreme Court,* 2:150–151; "National Politics and the Admission of Iowa into the Union," *American Historical Association Annual Report* (1897).

7. Paul H, Bergeron, *The Presidency of James K. Polk* (Lawrence, Kans., 1987); Charles Grier Sellers, Jr., *James K. Polk: Jacksonian, 1795–1843* (Princeton, N.J., 1957).

8. Bureau of Census, *Historical Statistics,* 691; Bergeron, *Presidency of Polk,* 186–191; Peterson, *Great Triumvirate,* 421–422; James P. Shenton, *Robert John Walker: A Politician from Jackson to Lincoln* (New York, 1961), 87–98.

9. Bergeron, *Presidency of Polk,* 191–193; Charles Setts, *James K. Polk: Continentalist, 1843–1846* (Princeton, N.J., 1966), 468–470; Eugene Irving McCormac, *James K. Polk: A Political Biography* (Berkeley, Calif., 1922), 659–670.

10. Wilson, ed., *Papers of Calhoun,* 23:228–229, 327, 372, 398; Don E. Fehrenbacher, *Chicago Giant: A Biography of "Long John" Wentworth* (Madison, Wis., 1959), 65–68.

11. Bergeron, *Presidency of Polk,* 196–200.

12. Allan Nevins, *Ordeal of the Union,* 2 vols. (New York, 1947), 2:194–200, 203; Arthur B. Darling, *Political Changes in Massachusetts, 1824–1848: A Study of Liberal Movements in Politics* (New Haven, Conn., 1925), 236, 255–257.

13. Nevins, *Ordeal of the Union,* 2:202, 238; George Fort Milton, *The Eve of Conflict: Stephen A. Douglas and the Needless War* (New York, 1969), 9–11; Paul Wallace Gates, *The Illinois Central Railroad and Its Colonization Work* (Cambridge, Mass., 1934), 3–65; Benjamin Horace Hibbard, *A History of the Public Land Policies* (New York, 1939), 241–242.

14. Milton, *Eve of Conflict,* 10–11; Fred Albert Shannon, *America's Economic Growth* (New York, 1940), 162–165; Harold F. Williamson, *The Growth of the American Economy* (New York, 1951), 354–357; Hibbard, *History of Public Land Policies,* 244–249.

15. Samuel Eliot Morison, Frederick Merk, and Frank Freidel, *Dissent in Three American Wars* (Cambridge, Mass., 1970), 37–40; John H. Schroeder,

Mr. Polk's War: American Opposition and Dissent, 1846–1848 (Madison, Wis., 1973), 10–17; Bergeron, *Presidency of Polk,* 74–77; Merk, *Slavery and the Annexation of Texas.*

16. Schroeder, *Mr. Polk's War,* 23–24; Morison, Merk, and Freidel, *Dissent in Three Wars,* 39; Peterson, *Great Triumvirate,* 422–428, 436–437; Wilson, ed., *Essential Calhoun,* 160.

17. Holt, *Rise and Fall of the Whig Party,* 224; Ames, ed., *State Documents on Federal Relations,* 230–231 (resolves of March 15, 1844, and March 25, 1845); Seymour V. Connor and Odie B. Faulk, *North America Divided: The Mexican War, 1846–1848* (New York, 1971).

18. Morison, Merk, and Freidel, *Dissent in Three Wars,* 49; Darling, *Political Changes,* 335; Schroeder, *Mr. Polk's War,* 35–39; Eric Foner, "Radical Individualism in America: Revolution to Civil War," *Literature of Liberty* 1 (1978): 5–31.

19. Bergeron, *Presidency of Polk,* 42, 87, 89, 104, 105–106; Schroeder, *Mr. Polk's War,* 120–141; Frederick Merk, *Manifest Destiny and Mission in American History* (New York, 1963).

20. Schroeder, *Mr. Polk's War,* 76, 151, 155; Holt, *Rise and Fall of the Whig Party,* 250, 311.

21. Morison, Merk, and Freidel, *Dissent in Three Wars,* 51; Schroeder, *Mr. Polk's War,* 46–48; Peterson, *Great Triumvirate,* 424, 426, 428, 431, 447, 454; Chaplain W. Morrison, *Democratic Politics and Sectionalism: The Wilmot Proviso Controversy* (Chapel Hill, N.C., 1967), 26–33; Charles Buxton Going, *David Wilmot, Free-Soiler: A Biography of the Great Advocate of the Wilmot Proviso* (Gloucester, Mass., 1966); Ernest M. Lander, Jr., *Reluctant Imperialists: Calhoun, the South Carolinians, and the Mexican War* (Baton Rouge, La., 1980), 159 ff.; Don E. Fehrenbacher, *Sectional Crisis and Southern Constitutionalism* (Baton Rouge, La., 1995), 25–26, 29, 34–36, 37–39, 43–44, 132.

22. Avery O. Craven, *A History of the South,* vol. 6, *The Growth of Southern Nationalism, 1848–1861* (Baton Rouge, La., 1953), 33–34, 39, 40, 65; Stephen E. Maizlish, *The Triumph of Sectionalism: The Transformation of Ohio Politics, 1844–1856* (Kent, Ohio, 1983), 69, 88.

23. *Abridgement of the Debates in Congress,* 16:82–86; Wilson, ed., *Essential Calhoun,* 382–389.

24. Craven, *History of the South,* 6:40–41; Freehling, *Road to Disunion,* 475–479; Norman Graebner, "1848: Southern Politics at the Crossroads," *The Historian* 25 (1962): 14–35.

25. Holt, *Rise and Fall of the Whig Party,* 368–382; Joseph G. Rayback, *Free Soil: The Election of 1848* (Lexington, Ky., 1970).

26. Craven, *History of the South*, 6:44; John C. Inscoe, *Mountain Masters, Slavery, and the Sectional Crisis in North Carolina* (Knoxville, Tenn., 1989); Marc W. Kruman, "Thomas L. Clingman and the Whig Party: A Reconsideration," *North Carolina Historical Review* 64 (1987): 1–18.

27. Craven, *History of the South*, 6:66–69.

28. Holt, *Rise and Fall of the Whig Party*, 476–482; Peterson, *Great Triumvirate*, 455–462, 468–475; Robert W. Johanssen, *Stephen Douglas* (Urbana, Ill., 1997), 190, 270–275, 277–282, 285, 294–295.

29. Webster, *Works*, 5:325–367, quote at 325; Crallé, ed., *Works of Calhoun*, 4:542–573, quote at 573; Peterson, *Great Triumvirate*, 460–461, 462–463; Craven, *History of the South*, 6:70–77; Holt, *Rise and Fall of the Whig Party*, 484, 488–489.

30. Milton, *Eve of Conflict*, 54–78; Craven, *History of the South*, 6:77–82, 94–98; Marshall L. DeRosa, *The Confederate Constitution of 1861: An Inquiry into American Constitutionalism* (Columbia, Mo., 1991), 11–12; Holt, *Rise and Fall of the Whig Party*, 532–543; Peterson, *Great Triumvirate*, 467, 472, 475, 477–478, 486–487; Thelma Jennings, *The Nashville Convention: Southern Movement for Unity, 1848–1851* (Memphis, 1980).

31. Craven, *History of the South*, 6:60, 83–115, 120; Bureau of Census, *Historical Statistics*, 124; E. Merton Coulter, *Georgia: A Short History* (Chapel Hill, N.C., 1960), 308–310.

32. Craven, *History of the South*, 6:77; Holt, *Rise and Fall of the Whig Party*, 489; Peterson, *Great Triumvirate*, 464–466; Wiecek, *Sources of Antislavery Constitutionalism;* Larry Gara, "The Fugitive Slave Law: A Double Paradox," *Civil War History* 10 (1964): 229–240.

33. *Strader* v. *Graham*, 10 Howard 82 (1850); Finkelman, *Imperfect Union*, 271–274; Newmyer, *Joseph Story*, 354; Warren, *Supreme Court*, 2:224–225.

34. *Abridgement of the Debates in Congress*, 16:593–594; Nevins, *Ordeal of the Union*, 1:381–382; Peterson, *Great Triumvirate*, 470, 480–483; Swisher, *Taney Period*, 570–573, 596–598.

35. Craven, *History of the South*, 6:146–149, quotes at 147; Milton, *Eve of Conflict*, 165; Norman L. Rosenberg, "Personal Liberty Laws and the Sectional Crisis: 1850–1861," *Civil War History* 17 (1971): 25–44.

36. Milton, *Eve of Conflict*, 165; Craven, *History of the South*, 6:149.

37. Nevins, *Ordeal of the Union*, 1:385–388; Stanley W. Campbell, *The Slave Catchers: Enforcement of the Fugitive Slave Law, 1850–1860* (Chapel Hill, N.C., 1970); Larry Gara, *The Liberty Line: The Legend of the Underground Railroad* (Lexington, Ky., 1961).

38. Nevins, *Ordeal of the Union*, 1:385–389; W. Freeman Galpin, "The Jerry Rescue," *New York History* 43 (1945): 19–34.

39. Nevins, *Ordeal of the Union*, 1:383–390; Freehling, *Road to Disunion*, 536–537.

40. Milton, *Eve of Conflict*, 165–166; Craven, *History of the South*, 6:151–152; Nevins, *Ordeal of the Union*, 1:405–407; Joan D. Hedrick, *Harriet Beecher Stowe: A Life* (New York, 1994).

41. Milton, *Eve of Conflict*, 78–94; Holt, *Rise and Fall of the Whig Party*, 596–597, 664–669, 671–672, 680–684, 711–712, 723–725, 730, 756–763; William E. Gienapp, *The Origins of the Republican Party, 1852–1856* (New York, 1987).

8. DISSOLVING THE UNION

1. The nationalist school of Civil War historiography was fully articulated in James Ford Rhodes, *History of the United States from the Compromise of 1850*, 7 vols. (New York, 1893–1906), and in McMaster, *History of the People*, and culminated in Arthur C. Cole, *The Irrepressible Conflict* (New York, 1934). The revisionist or repressible conflict school is represented by Milton, *Eve of Conflict;* James G. Randall, "The Blundering Generation," *Mississippi Valley Historical Review* 27 (1940): 3–28; James G. Randall, *Lincoln the President*, vol. 1 (New York, 1945); and Avery O. Craven, *The Repressible Conflict, 1830–1861* (Baton Rouge, La., 1939).

2. Milton, *Eve of Conflict*, 116–117; Freehling, *Road to Disunion*, 152–155, 550–565.

3. Milton, *Eve of Conflict*, 118–119; the original Nebraska bill was introduced on January 4, 1854, and came up for consideration on January 30; Nevins, *Ordeal of the Union*, 2:94–96; Johanssen, *Stephen Douglas*, 206–234

4. Milton, *Eve of Conflict*, 120–121; Nevins, *Ordeal of the Union*, 2:112, 114; Gerald W. Wolf, *The Kansas-Nebraska Bill: Party, Section, and the Coming of the Civil War* (New York, 1977); James C. Malin, *The Nebraska Question, 1852–1854* (Ann Arbor, Mich., 1963), 288–345.

5. Nevins, *Ordeal of the Union*, 2:127–132, 153.

6. Votes calculated from Bureau of Census, *Historical Statistics;* Nevins, *Ordeal of the Union*, 2:132–135.

7. Nevins, *Ordeal of the Union*, 2:116–117, 380 ff.; Larry Gara, *The Presidency of Franklin Pierce* (Lawrence, Kans., 1991).

8. Nevins, *Ordeal of the Union*, 2:356–363, 368–374; Ivor Debenham Spencer, *The Victor and the Spoils: A Life of William L. Marcy* (Providence, 1959), 330–334, 337–338; Henry H. Simms, *A Decade of Sectional Controversy, 1851–1861* (Chapel Hill, N.C., 1942), 188–193.

9. Milton, *Eve of Conflict*, 159, 171–174, 176–177; Holt, *Rise and Fall of the Whig Party*, 836–985; Frederick J. Blue, *The Free Soilers: Third Party Politics, 1848–54* (Urbana, Ill., 1973).

10. Nevins, *Ordeal of the Union*, 2:341–345, 414; Francis Curtis, *The Republican Party*, 2 vols. (New York, 1904), 1:172–201; John P. Mulkern, *The Know-Nothing Party in Massachusetts: The Rise and Fall of a People's Movement* (Boston, 1990).

11. Milton, *Eve of Conflict*, 187–200; David Grimsted, *American Mobbing: 1828–1861: Toward Civil War* (New York, 1998), 246–265.

12. Nevins, *Ordeal of the Union*, 2:437–443, quotes at 439, 440; Charles Sumner, *The Crime Against Kansas. Speech of Hon. Charles Sumner in the Senate of the United States, 19th and 20th of May, 1856* (Boston, 1856); David Herbert Donald, *Charles Sumner*, 2 parts (New York, 1996), 1:278–311.

13. Harold S. Schultz, *Nationalism and Sectionalism in South Carolina, 1852–1860* (Durham, N.C., 1950), 114–120; Craven, *History of the South*, 6:225–228; Milton, *Eve of Conflict*, 232–237.

14. Nevins, *Ordeal of the Union*, 2:447, 448; William E. Gienapp, "The Crime against Sumner: The Caning of Charles Sumner and the Rise of the Republican Party," *Civil War History* 25 (1979): 218–245.

15. Warren, *Supreme Court*, 2:221, 224, 327.

16. *Piqua Branch of the State Bank of Ohio* v. *Knoop*, 16 Howard 369 (1854); Warren, *Supreme Court*, 2:250–253; Swisher, *Taney Period*, 475–480; Friedman and Israel, eds., *Justices of the United States Supreme Court*, 1:759–766.

17. Warren, *Supreme Court*, 2:256.

18. Ibid., 257–258.

19. Ibid., 258–259.

20. Ibid., 259–261, 332–333. In *Ableman* v. *Booth*, 21 Howard 506 (1859), the Taney Court unanimously ruled against Wisconsin, but to no avail (ibid., 343, 343 n); Earl M. Maltz, "Slavery, Federalism, and the Structure of the Constitution," *American Journal of Legal History* 36 (1992): 494–496; Swisher, *Taney Period*, 661–672; Morris, *Free Men All*, 173–178.

21. Warren, *Supreme Court*, 2:265–266; Hans Louis Trefousse, *Benjamin Franklin Wade: Radical Republican from Ohio* (New York, 1963), 104–106.

22. Warren, *Supreme Court*, 2:290, 333–334.

23. Ibid., 268, 274, 278.

24. Nevins, *Ordeal of the Union*, 2:452–471; Malcolm Moos, *The Republicans: A History of Their Party* (New York, 1956), 53–63; Craven, *History of the South*, 6:238–245; Allan Nevins, *Frémont: Pathmaker of the West* (New York, 1939), 439–458; Andrew Rolle, *John Charles Frémont: Character as Destiny* (Norman, Okla., 1991), 162–177; Robert J. Zalimas, Jr., " 'Contest MY seat sir!': Lewis D. Campbell, Clement L. Vallandigham, and the Election of 1856," *Ohio History* 106 (1997): 5–30.

25. Craven, *History of the South*, 6:243–244; Nevins, *Ordeal of the Union*, 2:497–499; Browne, *Baltimore in the Nation*, 213; Craig M. Simpson, *A Good Southerner: The Life of Henry A. Wise of Virginia* (Chapel Hill, N.C., 1985).

26. Bureau of Census, *Historical Statistics*, 682, 691; Dale Brown and Dale T. Knobel, "Anatomy of a Realignment: New York Presidential Politics, 1848–1860," *New York History* 65 (1984): 61–81; Jeter A. Isely, *Horace Greeley and the Republican Party, 1853–1861* (Princeton, N.J., 1947); Paul Kleppner, *The Third Electoral System, 1853–1892: Parties, Voters, and Political Cultures* (Chapel Hill, N.C., 1979), 48–96; Curtis, *Republican Party*, 1:249–267.

27. *Dred Scott* v. *Sandford*, 19 Howard 393 (1857); the defendant's name was Sanford but was misspelled in the official report. The definitive work is Don E. Fehrenbacher, *The Dred Scott Case: Its Significance in American Law and Politics* (New York, 1978). See also Milton, *Eve of Conflict*, 247–254; John S. Vishnecki III, "What the Court Decided in *Dred Scott* v. *Sandford*," *American Journal of Legal History* 32 (1988): 373–390; Swisher, *Taney Period*, 611–636, 638–648, 650–653.

28. Warren, *Supreme Court*, 2:280, 281, 296–297; Finkelman, *Imperfect Union*, 274–276.

29. Warren, *Supreme Court*, 2:293, 294, 296–297, 302; Fehrenbacher, *Dred Scott*, 306–308; Swisher, *Taney Period*, 556–558.

30. Milton, *Eve of Conflict*, 252; Fisher, *American Constitutional Law*, 970, 971; Finkelman, *Imperfect Union*, 279–280.

31. Swisher, *Taney Period*, 600, 605, 608, 610, 616, 617, 624–628; Finkelman, *Imperfect Union*, 278.

32. Finkelman, *Imperfect Union*, 282–284; Milton, *Eve of Conflict*, 248–249.

33. *Federalist* 78, 504. As the *New York Independent* said, "The moment the supreme Judicial Court becomes a court of injustice, that moment its claim to obedience ceases" (Milton, *Eve of Conflict*, 254).

34. Allan Nevins, *The Emergence of Lincoln*, 2 vols. (New York, 1950), 1:176, 190–192; Roy F. Nichols, *The Stakes of Power, 1845–1877* (New York, 1961), 64–65; Browne, *Baltimore in the Nation*, 171–172; Elbert B. Smith, *The Pres-*

idency of James Buchanan (Lawrence, Kans., 1980), 55; George W. Van Vleck, *The Panic of 1857: An Analytical Study* (New York, 1943), 60–79.

35. Nevins, *Emergence of Lincoln*, 1:193–194; James L. Huston, *The Panic of 1857 and the Coming of the Civil War* (Baton Rouge, La., 1987).

36. Nevins, *Emergence of Lincoln*, 1:192–193, 215–217.

37. Ibid., 195; Nichols, *Stakes of Power*, 65–66.

38. Nevins, *Emergence of Lincoln*, 1:220–227; Stanwood, *American Tariff Controversies*, 1:98–108.

39. Nichols, *Stakes of Power*, 66; Nevins, *Emergence of Lincoln*, 1:195–197; Gavin Wright, *The Political Economy of the Cotton South: Households, Markets and Wealth in the Nineteenth Century* (New York, 1978); Taussig, *Tariff History*, 140–143; Harold D. Woodman, *King Cotton & His Retainers: Financing & Marketing the Cotton Crop of the South, 1800–1925* (Lexington, Ky., 1968); Gray, *History of Agriculture*, 1:709, 720, 1026, 1027.

40. Smith, *Presidency of Buchanan*, 43–44; Nevins, *Emergence of Lincoln*, 1:217–220, quote at 220; Nichols, *Stakes of Power*, 66; Walther, *Fire-Eaters*, 228–269; Gray, *History of Agriculture*, 2:930–932; Van Deusen, *Economic Bases of Disunion*, ch. 3, 334–339; Bruce W. Collins, "Governor Joseph E. Brown, Economic Issues, and Georgia's Road to Secession, 1857–59," *Georgia Historical Quarterly* 71 (1987): 189–225.

41. George Fitzhugh, *Cannibals All! or, Slaves without Masters*, ed. C. Vann Woodward (Cambridge, Mass., 1960).

42. Smith, *Presidency of Buchanan*, 31–46; Nichols, *Stakes of Power*, 68–69; Nevins, *Emergence of Lincoln*, 1:173–175, 229–279; Milton, *Eve of Conflict*, 273 ff.

43. Nevins, *Emergence of Lincoln*, 1:254 ff.; Smith, *Presidency of Buchanan*, 81; Milton, *Eve of Conflict*, 315 ff.

44. Milton, *Eve of Conflict*, 312–352; Harry Jaffa, *Crisis of the House Divided: An Interpretation of the Issues in the Lincoln-Douglas Debates* (Garden City, N.Y., 1959); Bradford, *Against the Barbarians*, 229–245; Ericson, *Shaping of American Liberalism*, 117–174; Johanssen, *Stephen Douglas*, 664–666, 668–677.

45. Nevins, *Emergence of Lincoln*, 1:361; Finkelman, *Imperfect Union*, 317–318.

46. Eugene D. Genovese, *A Consuming Fire: The Fall of the Confederacy in the Mind of the Christian South* (Athens, Ga., 1998), 82; Nevins, *Emergence of Lincoln*, 1:382; Milton, *Eve of Conflict*, 344; Smith, *Presidency of Buchanan*, 52–53.

47. Bureau of Census, *Historical Statistics*, 691; Nevins, *Emergence of Lin-*

coln, 1:396–403; George H. Mayer, *The Republican Party, 1854–1964* (New York, 1964), 48–60.

48. Nevins, *Emergence of Lincoln*, 1:400–459, 2:68–69; Milton, *Eve of Conflict*, 391–393.

49. Nevins, *Emergence of Lincoln*, 2:79–84; Milton, *Eve of Conflict*, 393–396; Nichols, *Stakes of Power*, 74–75; J. C. Furnas, *The Road to Harpers Ferry* (New York, 1959).

50. Smith, *Presidency of Buchanan*, 94; Nevins, *Emergence of Lincoln*, 2:86–93, quote at 99; Paul Finkelman, ed., *His Soul Goes Marching On: Responses to John Brown and the Harpers Ferry Raid* (Charlottesville, Va., 1995).

51. Nevins, *Emergence of Lincoln*, 2:102–105.

52. Smith, *Presidency of Buchanan*, 95–96; Schultz, *Nationalism and Sectionalism*, 205; Nevins, *Emergence of Lincoln*, 2:110–131, quote at 121; Milton, *Eve of Conflict*, 400–401.

53. Nevins, *Emergence of Lincoln*, 2:188–193; Shannon, *America's Economic Growth*, 242–243, 325, 358–359, 368–370; Louis M. Hacker, *The Triumph of American Capitalism* (New York, 1947), 332–335; Williamson, *Growth of the American Economy*, 359, 362–364; Paul Wallace Gates, "The Homestead Law in an Incongruous Land System," *American Historical Review* 41 (1936): 652–681.

54. Milton, *Eve of Conflict*, 425–449; Nevins, *Emergence of Lincoln*, 2:204, 207; Frederick McKee Beatty, "William Lowndes Yancey and Alabama Secession" (master's thesis, University of Alabama, 1990), 96–99; John Witherspoon DuBose, *The Life and Times of William Lowndes Yancey* (New York, 1942); Austin L. Venable, "The Role of William L. Yancey in the Secession Movement" (Ph.D. diss., Vanderbilt University, 1937); Alto L. Garner and Nathan Stott, "William Lowndes Yancey: Statesman of Secession," *Alabama Review* 15 (1962): 190–202.

55. Nevins, *Emergence of Lincoln*, 2:223–228, 261–272; Milton, *Eve of Conflict*, 470–477; Joseph Howard Parks, *John Bell of Tennessee* (Baton Rouge, La., 1950), 348–360.

56. Milton, *Eve of Conflict*, 483; Nichols, *Stakes of Power*, 77–82.

57. David M. Potter, *Lincoln and His Party in the Secession Crisis* (New Haven, Conn., 1942), 6; Nevins, *Emergence of Lincoln*, 2:287–290, 305–306; Milton, *Eve of Conflict*, 484–500.

58. Potter, *Lincoln and His Party*, 10–12, 45–46; Howard Cecil Perkins, ed., *Northern Editorials on Secession*, 2 vols. (New York, 1942), 1:65, 91, 97, 107; Kenneth M. Stampp, *And the War Came: The North and the Secession Crisis, 1860–1861* (Baton Rouge, La., 1950), 14–15.

59. Potter, *Lincoln and His Party,* 45–46; Commager, ed., *Documents,* 1:372; Rhodes, *History of the United States,* 3:114–125; Dwight L. Dumond, *The Secession Movement, 1860–1861* (New York, 1931); Beatty, "William Lowndes Yancey," 99–112; Walther, *Fire-Eaters,* 48–82; Ralph A. Wooster, *The Secession Conventions of the South* (Princeton, N.J., 1962), 11–25.

60. Potter, *Lincoln and His Party,* 208–218; Commager, ed., *Documents,* 1:372–374; Stampp, *And the War Came,* 32–33, 34, 68, 69–75; Steven A. Channing, *Crisis of Fear: Secession in South Carolina* (New York, 1970), 269–285; Judah P. Benjamin, "Right of Secession," December 31, 1860, speech on the floor of the Senate, in *Southern Pamphlets on Secession: November 1860–April 1861,* ed. Jon L. Wakelyn (Chapel Hill, N.C., 1996), 101–142.

61. Nevins, *Emergence of Lincoln,* 2:390–405; Potter, *Lincoln and His Party,* 107–111, 157, 188–267; Stampp, *And the War Came,* 129–158; Herman Belz, *Reconstructing the Union: Theory and Policy during the Civil War* (Ithaca, N.Y., 1969), 1–3; Tyler G. Anbinder, "Fernando Wood and New York City's Secession from the Union: A Political Reappraisal," *New York History* 68 (1987): 67–92; Albert Kirwan, *John J. Crittenden: The Struggle for Union* (Lexington, Ky., 1962).

9. CIVIL WAR AND RECONSTRUCTION

1. Alexander H. Stephens, *A Constitutional View of the Late War between the States,* 2 vols. (Philadelphia, 1868–1870), 1:532–534, 538–539, 542, 2:357, 426–427; Henry Cleveland, *Alexander H. Stephens in Public and Private* (Philadelphia, 1866), 721–723. As will be seen later, Stephens was more ardently committed to states' rights than were most of his fellow Confederates.

2. David Donald, *Lincoln Reconsidered* (New York, 1966), 191–201; Allan Nevins, *The War for the Union,* vol. 1, *The Improvised War, 1861–1862* (New York, 1959), 387, 405, 412.

3. The most thorough account of Lincoln's wartime policies is J. G. Randall, *Constitutional Problems under Lincoln* (Urbana, Ill., 1951). For a good brief defense of the policies, see Michael Les Benedict, "The Constitution of the Lincoln Presidency and the Republican Era," in Fausold and Shank, eds., *The Constitution and the American Presidency,* 45–61. See also David Donald, *Lincoln* (New York, 1995), 299–304; Mark E. Neely, Jr., *The Fate of Liberty: Abraham Lincoln and Civil Liberties* (New York, 1991); Philip Shaw Paludan, *The Presidency of Abraham Lincoln* (Lawrence, Kans., 1994). On the "dictator-

ship" question, see Herman Belz, *Abraham Lincoln, Constitutionalism, and Equal Rights in the Civil War Era* (New York, 1998), 18–43, and Swisher, *Taney Period*, 901–930.

4. Donald, *Lincoln Reconsidered*, 188; *Prize Cases*, 2 Black 635 (1863); Proclamations of April 19 and 27, 1861, in Roy P. Basler et al., eds., *The Collected Works of Abraham Lincoln* (New Brunswick, N.J., 1953), 4:338–339, 346–347; Swisher, *Taney Period*, 877–900; Neely, *Fate of Liberty*, 139–147.

5. Randall, *Constitutional Problems under Lincoln*, 149; Donald, *Lincoln Reconsidered*, 188–189; Benedict, "Constitution of the Lincoln Presidency," 49–50; Richard O. Curry, "The Union as It Was: A Critique of Recent Interpretations of the 'Copperheads,'" *Civil War History* 13 (1967): 25–39; Frank L. Klement, *Copperheads in the Middle West* (Chicago, 1960); Kellee Green Blake, "Aiding and Abetting: Disloyalty Prosecutions in the Federal Civil Courts of Southern Illinois, 1861–1866," *Illinois Historical Journal* 87 (1994): 95–108; Wood Gray, *The Hidden Civil War: The Story of the Copperheads* (New York, 1942).

6. Randall, *Constitutional Problems under Lincoln*, 161–162; Warren, *Supreme Court*, 2:368–374; *Ex parte Merryman*, 17 Federal Cases 144 (1861); Wiecek, *Liberty under Law, 83–84*.

7. Randall, *Constitutional Problems under Lincoln*, 149–151. Neely, *Fate of Liberty*, 19–31, 75–77, maintains that Seward's arrests were not nearly so extensive or harsh as they have been depicted by historians. See also Frank A. Flower, *Edwin McMasters Stanton: The Autocrat of Rebellion, Emancipation and Reconstruction* (New York, 1905), 133–137.

8. Sydney George Fisher, "The Suspension of Habeas Corpus during the War of the Rebellion," *Political Science Quarterly* 3 (1888): 454–485; Randall, *Constitutional Problems under Lincoln*, 151–152, 152 n.

9. Randall, *Constitutional Problems under Lincoln*, 218–219, 225–233; Donald, *Lincoln Reconsidered*, 191.

10. Howard Jones, *Union in Peril: The Crisis over British Intervention in the Civil War* (Chapel Hill, N.C., 1992); Howard Jones, *Abraham Lincoln and a New Birth of Freedom: The Union and Slavery in the Diplomacy of the Civil War* (Lincoln, Nebr., 1999), 14–17, 112–127; William B. Hesseltine, *Lincoln and the War Governors* (New York, 1948), 247–261, which focuses upon domestic pressure for emancipation.

11. Hesseltine, *Lincoln and the War Governors*, 74–91; Mayer, *Republican Party*, 1, 69–75, 88; Curtis, *Republican Party*, 1:346–365.

12. Hesseltine, *Lincoln and the War Governors*, 113–115; Nevins, *The War*

for the Union, 1:79–80; Randall, *Constitutional Problems under Lincoln*, 413–414; Henry Greenleaf Pearson, *The Life of John A. Andrew, Governor of Massachusetts, 1861–1865* (Boston, 1904).

13. Hesseltine, *Lincoln and the War Governors*, 146–155; Randall, *Constitutional Problems under Lincoln*, 414–416; Phillip Shaw Paludin, *A People's Contest: The Union and the Civil War, 1861–1865*, 2d ed. (Lawrence, Kans., 1996), 15–20; Victor Hicken, *Illinois in the Civil War* (Urbana, Ill., 1966), 1–5, 13–15; Jack Nortrup, Jr., "Richard Yates, Civil War Governor of Illniois" (Ph.D. diss., University of Illinois at Urbana-Champaign, 1960).

14. Hesseltine, *Lincoln and the War Governors*, 165, 178–179; Eugene C. Murdock, *One Million Men: The Civil War Draft in the North* (Madison, Wis., 1971), 3–24.

15. Benjamin P. Thomas and Harold M. Hyman, *Stanton: The Life and Times of Lincoln's Secretary of War* (New York, 1962), 131–168; Hesseltine, *Lincoln and the War Governors*, chs. 9, 10, and 297–302; Lawrence H. Larsen, "Draft Riot in Wisconsin, 1862," *Civil War History* 7 (1961): 421–427; Arnold M. Shankman, *The Pennsylvania Antiwar Movement, 1861–1865* (Rutherford, N.J., 1980), 141–159; Murdock, *One Million Men*, 19, 83–90; Adrian Cook, *Armies of the Street: The New York City Draft Riots of 1863* (Lexington, Ky., 1974).

16. Hesseltine, *Lincoln and the War Governors*, 265–272, 312; Kenneth M. Stampp, *Indiana Politics during the Civil War* (Indianapolis, 1949); William Dudley Foulke, *The Life of Oliver P. Morton*, 2 vols. (Indianapolis, 1899).

17. Hesseltine, *Lincoln and the War Governors*, 269, 283, 284; Maurice Tandler, "The Political Front in Civil War New Jersey," *Proceedings of the New Jersey Historical Society* 83 (1965): 223–233; Eugene C. Murdock, "Horatio Seymour and the 1863 Draft," *Civil War History* 11 (1965): 117–141; Neely, *Fate of Liberty*, 192–199.

18. Glyndon G. Van Deusen, *Thurlow Weed: Wizard of the Lobby* (Boston, 1947), 274–275; Thurlow Weed, *Autobiography of Thurlow Weed*, ed. Harriet A. Weed (Boston, 1883), 615–619.

19. Hesseltine, *Lincoln and the War Governors*, 215, 220–221, 245, 269–271; Harold Bell Hancock, *Delaware During the Civil War: A Political History* (Wilmington, Del., 1961), 147–153.

20. Hesseltine, *Lincoln and the War Governors*, 333–339.

21. Ibid., 329 ff.; *Ex parte Vallandigham*, 1 Wallace 243 (1864); Warren, *Supreme Court*, 2:388; George H. Porter, *Ohio Politics During the Civil War Period* (New York, 1911), 155–199; Whitelaw Reid, *Ohio in War* (Cincinnati, 1868), 1:23, 99–124; Craig D. Tenney, "To Suppress or Not to Suppress: Abra-

ham Lincoln and the *Chicago Times,*" *Civil War History* 27 (1981): 248–259; Frank L. Klement, *The Limits of Dissent: Clement L. Vallandigham and the Civil War* (Lexington, Ky., 1970).

22. Hesseltine, *Lincoln and the War Governors,* ch. 15; William Frank Zornow, *Lincoln and the Party Divided* (Norman, Okla., 1954).

23. DeRosa, *Confederate Constitution,* 135, 139–140; William C. Davis, "*A Government of Our Own" : The Making of the Confederacy* (New York, 1994).

24. DeRosa, *Confederate Constitution,* 39–40.

25. Confederate constitution, article 1, section 8, clauses 1 and 3, section 9, clause 20; DeRosa, *Confederate Constitution,* 86, 94, 139, 142.

26. DeRosa, *Confederate Constitution,* 79–99, 108, 147–148. Section 2 of article 3 added that "no State shall be sued by a citizen or subject of any foreign state," thus incorporating the Eleventh Amendment of the U.S. Constitution.

27. Confederate constitution, article 1, section 9; DeRosa, *Confederate Constitution,* 42, 43, 52, 71–72; Don E. Fehrenbacher, *Constitutions and Constitutionalism in the Slaveholding South* (Athens, Ga., 1989).

28. See Ludwell H. Johnson, "Jefferson Davis and Abraham Lincoln as War Presidents: Nothing Succeeds Like Success," *Civil War History* 27 (1981): 49–63. For a fuller comparison of Union and Confederate governments during the war, see Richard Franklin Bensel, *Yankee Leviathan: The Origins of Central State Authority in America, 1859–1877* (Cambridge, 1990), 94–237.

29. Here and in the remainder of this section, I follow closely the analysis in George C. Rable, *The Confederate Republic: A Revolution against Politics* (Chapel Hill, N.C., 1994), quote at 29. Frank Lawrence Owsley, in *State Rights in the Confederacy* (Gloucester, Mass., 1961), argues that states' rights extremism severely hampered the Confederacy. Curtis Arthur Amlund, in *Federalism in the Southern Confederacy* (Washington, D.C., 1966), challenges that view in an interpretation that is compatible with, though far less sophisticated than, that of Rable. See also Paul D. Escott, *After Secession: Jefferson Davis and the Failure of Confederate Nationalism* (Baton Rough, La., 1978).

30. Rable, *Confederate Republic,* 71–74, 95–110, quote at 91; Frank E. Vandiver, *Their Tattered Flags: The Epic of the Confederacy* (New York, 1970), 25; Rembert W. Patrick, *Jefferson Davis and His Cabinet* (Baton Rouge, La., 1944), 49–50.

31. Rable, *Confederate Republic,* 46, 64–67, 121–124, quotes at 46 and 122.

32. Ibid., 113–114, 133–135, quote at 134; Harrison A. Trexler, "The Davis Administration and the Richmond press, 1861–1865," *Journal of Southern History* 16 (1950): 177–195.

33. Rable, *Confederate Republic,* 145–146; John B. Robbins, "The Confed-

eracy and the Writ of Habeas Corpus," *Georgia Historical Quarterly* 55 (1971): 83–101.

34. Rable, *Confederate Republic*, 138–145, 156, 200, quotes at 141; Thomas B. Alexander and Richard E. Beringer, *The Anatomy of the Confederate Congress: A Study of the Influence of Member Characteristics on Legislative Voting Behavior, 1861–1865* (Nashville, 1972), 114–115; Albert Burton Moore, *Conscription and Conflict in the Confederacy* (New York, 1924), 21–23; F. N. Boney, *John Letcher of Virginia: The Story of Virginia's Civil War Governor* (Tuscloosa, Ala., 1966), 162.

35. Rable, *Confederate Republic*, 115, 141–142; Owsley, *State Rights in the Confederacy*, 15–17, 35–36; Louise Biles Hill, *Joseph E. Brown and the Confederacy* (Chapel Hill, N.C., 1939); Joseph H. Parks, *Joseph E. Brown of Georgia* (Baton Rouge, La., 1977).

36. Rable, *Confederate Republic*, 157–158, 160, 251–252, and passim thereafter.

37. Ibid., 187, 200–205; Horace W. Raper, *William W. Holden: North Carolina's Political Enigma* (Chapel Hill, N.C., 1985); Glen Tucker, *Zeb Vance: Champion of Personal Freedom* (Indianapolis, 1965). Owsley, *State Rights in the Confederacy*, 38–40, 173–174, depicts Vance as being extremely opposed to Davis; he does not mention Holden.

38. Rable, *Confederate Republic*, 256–259, 272, quote at 257; Owsley, *State Rights in the Confederacy*, 183–190; Thomas E. Schott, *Alexander H. Stephens of Georgia: A Biography* (Baton Rouge, La., 1988); John R. Brumgardt, "Alexander Stephens and the State Convention Movement in Georgia: A Reappraisal," *Georgia Historical Quarterly* 59 (1975): 38–49; Mark Hall, "Alexander Stephens and Joseph E. Brown and the Georgia Resolutions for Peace," *Georgia Historical Quarterly* 64 (1980): 50–63.

39. Rable, *Confederate Republic*, 232, 240, 259, 299–302; John R. Brumgardt, "The Confederate Career of Alexander H. Stephens: The Case Reopened," *Civil War History* 27 (1981): 64–100.

40. Richardson, comp., *Messages and Papers*, 6:276 ff.

41. William A. Dunning, *Reconstruction: Political & Economic, 1865–1877* (New York, 1962; repr. of 1907 original), 14–15; John Hope Franklin, *Reconstruction after the Civil War* (Chicago, 1994; repr. of 1961 original), 16–20. These two works are written from perspectives poles apart, but they are in substantial agreement as to the bare facts. For a compendium of revisions of the original Dunning school, see Kenneth M. Stampp and Leon F. Litwak, eds., *Reconstruction: An Anthology of Revisionist Writings* (Baton Rouge, La., 1969). For perhaps the best single revisionist work, see Eric Foner, *Recon-*

struction: America's Unfinished Revolution, 1863–1877 (New York, 1988). See also Earl M. Maltz, *Civil Rights, the Constitution, and Congress, 1863–1869* (Lawrence, Kans., 1990), which argues persuasively that much of "Radical" Reconstruction actually reflected the attitudes of the more conservative Republicans, and Belz, *Reconstructing the Union,* 198–243. For an exposition of state-based federalism, see Harold M. Hyman, *A More Perfect Union: The Impact of the Civil War and Reconstruction on the Constitution* (New York, 1973); 438–439.

42. Dunning, *Reconstruction,* 35–41; Franklin, *Reconstruction,* 30–31; David Donald, *The Politics of Reconstruction, 1863–1867* (Baton Rouge, La., 1965); Eric McKitrick, *Andrew Johnson and Reconstruction* (Chicago, 1960).

43. Randall, *Constitutional Problems under Lincoln,* 398–401.

44. Franklin, *Reconstruction,* ch. 3; Dunning, *Reconstruction,* 54–58.

45. Dunning, *Reconstruction,* 58–62; Donald, *Charles Sumner,* 2:414–454; Franklin, *Reconstruction,* 57–60; John W. Burgess, *Reconstruction and the Constitution, 1866–1876* (New York, 1902); C. E. Chadsey, *The Struggle between President Johnson and Congress over Reconstruction* (Baltimore, 1897); John Hope Franklin, *From Slavery to Freedom: A History of American Negroes* (New York, 1956), 298–311.

46. Franklin, *Reconstruction,* 61–62; Dunning, *Reconstruction,* 61–67; William M. Wiecek, "The Reconstruction of Federal Judicial Power, 1863–1876," *American Journal of Legal History* 13 (1969): 333–359; Stanley Kutler, *Judicial Power and Reconstruction Politics* (Chicago, 1968).

47. Franklin, *Reconstruction,* 61–63; Dean James E. Bond, "The Original Understanding of the Fourteenth Amendment in Illinois, Ohio, and Pennsylvania," *Akron Law Review* 18 (1985): 435–463; Joseph B. James, *The Framing of the Fourteenth Amendment* (Urbana, Ill., 1965); William E. Nelson, *The Fourteenth Amendment: From Political Principle to Judicial Doctrine* (Cambridge, Mass., 1988), 40–63, 140–155.

48. Forrest McDonald, "Was the Fourteenth Amendment Legally Adopted?" *Georgia Journal of Southern Legal History* 1 (1991): 5–11.

49. Dunning, *Reconstruction,* 79–83, 93–94; *Statutes at Large* 14 (1868): 428, 15 (1869): 12, 14; Franklin, *Reconstruction,* 63–65, 70–71.

50. Hodding Carter, *The Angry Scar: The Story of Reconstruction* (Garden City, N.Y., 1959); 129–145; Rehnquist, *Grand Inquests,* 209–248; Dunning, *Reconstruction,* 99–108; *Ex parte McCardle,* 7 Wallace 506 (1869); Leonard G. Ratner, "Congressional Power over the Appellate Jurisdiction of the Supreme Court," *University of Pennsylvania Law Review* 109 (1960): 178–180; Charles Fairman, *Reconstruction and Reunion, 1864–88,* The Oliver Wendell

Holmes Devise History, vol. 6 (New York, 1971), 415–417, 421, 426, 437–440; Michael Les Benedict, *The Impeachment and Trial of Andrew Johnson* (New York, 1973); Hans L. Trefousse, "The Acquittal of Andrew Johnson and the Decline of the Radicals," *Civil War History* 14 (1968): 148–161.

51. Dunning, *Reconstruction,* 109–123, 174, 189, 266–280; William Gillette, *Retreat from Reconstruction, 1869–1879* (Baton Rouge, La., 1979).

52. *Prize Cases,* 2 Black 635 (1863); Fairman, *Reconstruction and Reunion,* 21, 42, 544; Ludwell H. Johnson III, "Abraham Lincoln and the Development of Presidential War-Making Powers: *Prize Cases* (1863) Revisited," *Civil War History* 35 (1989): 208–224.

53. *Ex parte Milligan,* 4 Wallace 2 (1866); Warren, *Supreme Court,* 2:425; Fairman, *Reconstruction and Reunion,* 199–229, 236–238; Neely, *Fate of Liberty,* 160–184; Samuel Klaus, ed., *The Milligan Case* (New York, 1905).

54. Joseph G. Gambone, *"Ex Parte Milligan:* The Restoration of Judicial Prestige?" *Civil War History* 16 (1970): 246–292.

55. *Ex parte Garland,* 4 Wallace 333 (1867); *Cummings* v. *Missouri,* 4 Wallace 277 (1867); Warren, *Supreme Court,* 2:449–452; Fairman, *Reconstruction and Reunion,* 240–246, 271.

56. *Mississippi* v. *Johnson,* 4 Wallace 475 (1867); *Georgia* v. *Stanton,* 6 Wallace 50 (1867); Fairman, *Reconstruction and Reunion,* 381–383, 384–398.

57. *Ex parte McCardle,* 6 Wallace 318 (1868); Fairman, *Reconstruction and Reunion,* 57, 58; Warren, *Supreme Court,* 2:464–465, 473.

58. *Ex parte McCardle,* 7 Wallace 506 (1869); Warren, *Supreme Court,* 2:487–488; Fairman, *Reconstruction and Reunion,* 449–456.

59. *Texas* v. *White,* 7 Wallace 700 (1869); Warren, *Supreme Court,* 2:488–490; Fairman, *Reconstruction and Reunion,* 628–672; Harold M. Hyman, *The Reconstruction of Justice Salmon P. Chase:* In Re Turner *and* Texas *v.* White (Lawrence, Kans., 1997), 140–150. Chase's position is reminiscent of Lincoln's position at the start of the war.

60. *Ex parte Yerger,* 8 Wallace 85 (1869); Warren, *Supreme Court,* 2:491–497; Fairman, *Reconstruction and Reunion,* 445, 447, 449, 477, 495–496, 565–590.

61. *Slaughterhouse Cases,* 16 Wallace 36 (1873); Fairman, *Reconstruction and Reunion,* 1324–1363; Nelson, *Fourteenth Amendment,* 155–169.

62. Warren, *Supreme Court,* 2:531–549; Michael Les Benedict, "Preserving Freedom: Reconstruction and the Waite Court," in *Supreme Court Review 1978,* ed. Philip B. Kurland and Gerhard Casper (Chicago, 1979), 39–79.

63. *Bradwell* v. *Illinois,* 16 Wallace 130 (1873); *Bartemeyer* v. *Iowa,* 18 Wallace 129 (1874); *Minor* v. *Happersett,* 21 Wallace 162 (1875); Fairman, *Recon-*

struction and Reunion, 1364–1366, 1418–1419; Nelson, *Fourteenth Amendment*, 165–168.

64. *United States* v. *Cruikshank*, 92 U.S. 542 (1876); Fairman, *Reconstruction and Reunion*, 1120, 1373, 1379; Gillette, *Retreat from Reconstruction*, 297; Robert C. Palmer, "The Parameters of Constitutional Reconstruction: *Slaughter-House, Cruikshank,* and the Fourteenth Amendment," *University of Illinois Law Review* (1984): 739–770.

65. *United States* v. *Reese*, 92 U.S. 214 (1876); Gillette, *Retreat from Reconstruction*, 295–298; Fairman, *Reconstruction and Reunion*, 1120.

INDEX